Critical Terrorism Studies since 11 September 2001

Academic studies of 'terrorism' grew exponentially in number after the September 11 attacks. The problem was that much of this work of 'orthodox' terrorism studies was biased, often shoddily researched and was too closely identified with the power centres of Western states. Its denizens were often former and sometimes current officials or officers in the military, intelligence services or the security industry, or were funded by them.

In response the project of Critical Terrorism Studies was intended to give a more rounded account of political violence in the world. It focuses on neglected issues like state terrorism, Western counterinsurgency, propaganda and misinformation.

More than a decade since the founding of the critical project, this book asks what has been learned. It showcases leading examples of critical terrorism studies and presents an agenda for the expansion of an evidence-based approach to political violence and terrorism.

With chapters by leading authorities such as Joseba Zulaika, Michael Stohl, Mary J. Hickman and Richard Jackson, the book evaluates how far the critical project has come and where it is going next.

This book was previously published as a special issue of *Critical Studies on Terrorism*.

David Miller is Professor of Sociology at the University of Bath, UK and an ESRC Global Uncertainties Leadership Fellow (2013–15).

Jessie Blackbourn is a Postdoctoral Fellow at the University of New South Wales.

Rani Dhanda is a Doctoral Candidate at the University of Bath.

Helen Dexter is a Teaching Fellow at the University of Leicester.

Critical Terrorism Studies since 11 September 2001
What Has Been Learned?

Edited by
David Miller, Jessie Blackbourn, Rani Dhanda
and Helen Dexter

LONDON AND NEW YORK

First published 2014
by Routledge
2 Park Square, Milton Park, Abingdon, Oxon, OX14 4RN

Simultaneously published in the USA and Canada
by Routledge
711 Third Avenue, New York, NY 10017

First issued in paperback 2017

Routledge is an imprint of the Taylor & Francis Group, an informa business

© 2014 Taylor & Francis

This book is a reproduction of *Critical Studies on Terrorism*, volume 5, issue 1.

All rights reserved. No part of this book may be reprinted or reproduced or utilised in any form or by any electronic, mechanical, or other means, now known or hereafter invented, including photocopying and recording, or in any information storage or retrieval system, without permission in writing from the publishers.

Trademark notice: Product or corporate names may be trademarks or registered trademarks, and are used only for identification and explanation without intent to infringe.

British Library Cataloguing in Publication Data
A catalogue record for this book is available from the British Library

Typeset in Times New Roman
by Taylor & Francis Books

Publisher's Note
Every effort has been made to contact copyright holders for their permission to reprint material in this book. The Publisher would be grateful to hear from any copyright holder who is not here acknowledged and will undertake to rectify any errors or omissions in future editions of this book. The Publisher accepts responsibility for any inconsistencies that may have arisen in the course of preparing this volume for print. The Publisher requests to those authors who may be citing this book to state, also, the bibliographical details of the special issue on which the book was based.

ISBN 13: 978-1-138-05689-3 (pbk)
ISBN 13: 978-0-415-83852-8 (hbk)

Contents

Citation Information   vii

1. Introduction: Editor's Introduction: A decade on from 11 September 2001: what has critical terrorism studies learned?
   Jessie Blackbourn, Helen Dexter, Rani Dhanda and David Miller   1

2. Unknown knowns: the subjugated knowledge of terrorism studies
   Richard Jackson   11

3. Don't confuse me with the facts: knowledge claims and terrorism
   Michael Stohl   31

4. Drones, witches and other flying objects: the force of fantasy in US counterterrorism
   Joseba Zulaika   51

5. Reinventing prevention or exposing the gap? False positives in UK terrorism governance and the quest for pre-emption
   Charlotte Heath-Kelly   69

6. Social cohesion and the notion of 'suspect communities': a study of the experiences and impacts of being 'suspect' for Irish communities and Muslim communities in Britain
   Mary J. Hickman, Lyn Thomas, Henri C. Nickels and Sara Silvestri   89

7. 'Events dear boy, events': terrorism and security from the perspective of politics
   Andrew W. Neal   107

8. Terrorism and violence: another violence is possible?
   Helen Dexter   121

Index   139

Citation Information

The following chapters were originally published in *Critical Studies on Terrorism*, volume 5, issue 1 (April 2012). When citing this material, please use the original page numbering for each article, as follows:

Chapter 1
Editor's Introduction: A decade on from 11 September 2001: what has critical terrorism studies learned?
Jessie Blackbourn, Helen Dexter, Rani Dhanda and David Miller
Critical Studies on Terrorism, volume 5, issue 1 (April 2012)
pp. 1–10

Chapter 2
Unknown knowns: the subjugated knowledge of terrorism studies
Richard Jackson
Critical Studies on Terrorism, volume 5, issue 1 (April 2012)
pp. 11–30

Chapter 3
Don't confuse me with the facts: knowledge claims and terrorism
Michael Stohl
Critical Studies on Terrorism, volume 5, issue 1 (April 2012)
pp. 31–50

Chapter 4
Drones, witches and other flying objects: the force of fantasy in US counterterrorism
Joseba Zulaika
Critical Studies on Terrorism, volume 5, issue 1 (April 2012)
pp. 51–68

Chapter 5
Reinventing prevention or exposing the gap? False positives in UK terrorism governance and the quest for pre-emption
Charlotte Heath-Kelly

CITATION INFORMATION

Critical Studies on Terrorism, volume 5, issue 1 (April 2012)
pp. 69–88

Chapter 6
Social cohesion and the notion of 'suspect communities': a study of the experiences and impacts of being 'suspect' for Irish communities and Muslim communities in Britain
Mary J. Hickman, Lyn Thomas, Henri C. Nickels and Sara Silvestri
Critical Studies on Terrorism, volume 5, issue 1 (April 2012)
pp. 89–106

Chapter 7
'Events dear boy, events': terrorism and security from the perspective of politics
Andrew W. Neal
Critical Studies on Terrorism, volume 5, issue 1 (April 2012)
pp. 107–120

Chapter 8
Terrorism and violence: another violence is possible?
Helen Dexter
Critical Studies on Terrorism, volume 5, issue 1 (April 2012)
pp. 121–138

Please direct any queries you may have about the citations to clsuk.permissions@cengage.com

INTRODUCTION

Editor's Introduction: A decade on from 11 September 2001: what has critical terrorism studies learned?

Jessie Blackbourn[a], Helen Dexter[b], Rani Dhanda[c] and David Miller[c]

[a]*Law School, University of New South Wales, Sydney, Australia;* [b]*Department of Politics and International Relations, University of Leicester, Leicester, UK;* [c]*Department of Social and Policy Sciences, University of Bath, Bath, UK*

> The articles in this special issue are drawn from papers presented at a conference held to mark the 10th anniversary of the September 11 attacks. The conference, entitled *A Decade of Terrorism and Counter-Terrorism since 9/11: Taking Stock and New Directions in Research and Policy*, was organised by the Critical Studies on Terrorism Working Group of the British International Studies Association and was held at the University of Strathclyde with support from the British Academy from 8 to 11 September 2011. The conference aimed to play a significant role in the reorientation of terrorism studies towards a more empirically informed and theoretically sophisticated practice of studies of political violence through the engagement of scholars in a multidisciplinary dialogue. The articles in this issue reflect those aims.

On the conference

September 11, 2011 marked 10 years since the terrorist attacks on the United States and the start of the global 'war on terrorism'. The extensive changes engendered by these processes in the last decade gave rise to a real need for rigorous and sustained retrospective analysis. In a year that saw a wide range of special commemorative and academic events, this conference sought to assess the widespread impact of terrorism and counterterrorism since 2001 from a distinctly 'critical' perspective. More specifically, the conference foregrounded interdisciplinary approaches and sought to review what we have learnt in a period of unprecedented interest in the study of terrorism and counterterrorism.

After four days of events including a public meeting, plenaries, research workshops and panels including almost 60 speakers from four continents, delegates were asked to remember the almost 3000 dead as a result of the attacks as well as the subsequent deaths of the hundreds of thousands of civilians and combatants on all sides.

At the public meeting on Thursday evening (8 September 2011), panellists reflected on the events of 9/11; the invasions of Iraq and Afghanistan; and more recent events including the Arab Spring, the murders allegedly committed by Anders Breivik in Norway and the riots in England some weeks previously. Panellists included Helen Dexter of Leicester University who challenged those who would dismiss political violence or public disorder, such as the recent riots, as irrational and key note speaker Bob Lambert from Exeter, formerly of the Metropolitan Police Special Branch Muslim Contact Unit. He pursued an argument on the need to work with communities to protect public safety as opposed to treating the Muslim community as a 'suspect community'.

Scotland's leading human rights lawyer, Aamer Anwar, reminded the audience of the false information that was used to justify war in Iraq and the abuse of civil liberties at home as a result. Talking of the case of his client Mohammed Atif Siddique, a young man from Alva, just north of Glasgow, Anwar recalled and read out the words he had spoken on the steps of the High Court on his client's conviction on terrorism charges:

> Today Mohammed Atif Siddique was found guilty of doing what millions of young people do every day, looking for answers on the internet. This verdict is a tragedy for justice and for freedom of speech and undermines the values that separate us from the terrorist, the very values we should be fighting to protect . . . Atif Siddique states that 'he is not a terrorist and is innocent of the charges, that it is not a crime to be a young Muslim angry at global injustice.' The prosecution was driven by the State, with no limit to the money and resources used to secure a conviction in this case, carried out in an atmosphere of hostility after the Glasgow Airport attack and ending on the anniversary of 9/11. In the end Atif Siddique did not receive a fair trial and we will be considering an appeal. (Anwar 2007)

Anwar was himself arraigned for making that statement, although as he noted at the meeting Atif Siddique was later freed on appeal – an acknowledged victim of a miscarriage of justice (Anon 2010).

In papers stretching over four days, the issue of evidence and data in the study of terrorism was returned to again and again with delegates questioning the certainty in much public and policy debate. Papers ranged from heavily empirical to sweepingly theoretical, with much discussion about the merits of contending approaches to the study of terrorism. The UK policy of preventing violent extremism was subject to searching critique in a large number of papers (HM Government 2011).

Plenary speaker Richard Jackson, Professor in International Politics at Aberystwyth University, spoke on 'Unknown knowns: the subjugated knowledge of terrorism studies'. Commenting on the event, Jackson said:

> It is important that we encourage a more critical approach to the issue of terrorism but first, we need to take stock of what has already been achieved over the last 10 years. What we need to do to improve such studies is to bring subjugated knowledge to the field and take into consideration other forms of knowledge, for example peace studies. This will ultimately help us advise governments and key policy makers. (Cited in Miller 2011a)

Other keynote addresses were given by Michael Stohl (California), Joseba Zulaika (Nevada) and Caron Gentry (Texas/St Andrews). Each of their plenary sessions was video recorded and is available online.[1] Jackson, Stohl and Zulaika have their contributions published in this special issue. A separate editorial team is currently pursuing a book contract for a further collection from the conference. Because of their varied disciplinary backgrounds (career in the police, international relations, media studies, anthropology and women's studies), the plenaries were not only inspiring and catalytic (as might be expected) but also provided a quite novel gathering of social scientists focusing on terrorism from a range of complementary disciplinary perspectives.

On 10 years and critical terrorism studies

In the 10 years since 11 September 2001, the enterprise of 'critical terrorism studies' has come a long way. It seems pertinent to reflect on the long 10 years that saw the 2001 attacks, the launch of the 'war on terror' beginning with the attack on Afghanistan and then Iraq, with all the consequences that has had in terms of suffering and death. It was following the invasion of Iraq that critical terrorism studies as a project got off the ground. The first conference in the United Kingdom organised by the Critical Studies on Terrorism Working Group was held in Manchester in 2006. It asked 'Is it Time for a Critical Terrorism Studies?'[2] It is noteworthy that at that stage orthodox terrorism studies, if it registered its critical twin, did little more than curl its lip (Miller 2006). In the five years since we are at least having something of a debate, bad-tempered though it is at times. Without wishing to engage in the debate at this point, it is worth noting the inability of some orthodox commentators to register that 'critical' terrorism studies is not a cohesive project in which we are all signed up to the Frankfurt School, to post-structuralism and to the latest interpretation of Foucault (Jones and Smith 2006, 2009). The lively debate at the conference in September 2011 between the various approaches to the 'critical' study of terrorism is a clear indication of the need for some orthodox scholars to read a little bit further so they can distinguish their Marxists from their Postmodernists or 'critical realists' from devotees of 'deconstruction', 'discursive practice' or the 'argumentative turn'. Perhaps, though we should be grateful that they are at least – finally – engaging with the critique. It remains frightening, though that figures associated with the orthodoxy like M.L.R. Smith are called up as experts by the UK government, an indication, if we needed another, that the phrase 'terrorism expertise' can be an oxymoron (Miller and Mills 2009).

It is certainly clear that there are various currents within critical terrorism studies that overlap with concerns in the orthodox approach. Perhaps most of these currents agree that progress in attaining deeper knowledge is more likely in an atmosphere where debate is valued and fostered. Jones and Smith (2009, p. 302) appear to oppose this, criticising critical terrorism studies for apparently maintaining that 'un-coercive communication must be practiced'. Events at the conference and just after certainly reminded us of the importance of non-coercive communication and of the need for students of terrorism and political violence to be open about their activities as well as to be allowed to conduct research and writing without let or hindrance. To take the latter issue first. Delegates at the conference on the Sunday morning (11 September 2011) heard early news that one of the delegates at the conference – PhD student Rizwaan Sabir – had won £20,000 compensation from Nottinghamshire police and an apology for being stopped and searched. The news was featured in the press a couple of days later (Jones 2011). The case reminds us of the threats to independent research and 'un-coercive communication' posed by the forces of the state. Stop and search is not necessarily conducive to efficient conduct of one's doctoral research.

Another participant at the conference was also in the news shortly afterwards. This was Bob Lambert, the former Inspector in the Metropolitan Police Special Branch Muslim contact Unit, who had spent years combatting Islamophobia in the force and after he retired and took up an academic career. In fact, Lambert had spoken at the very first critical terrorism studies conference in Manchester in October 2006. One of the present authors (Miller 2006) wrote an account of his contribution:

> One of the more interesting speakers at the conference was . . . happy to waive the Chatham House rule. Bob Lambert is at the liberal end of the Special Branch, in its eight person Muslim Contact Unit. He promotes the idea of partnership working with Muslim community organisations. He explicitly counterposes this to repressive policing and attacking the Muslim community in politics, the press such as the assault unleashed by Jack Straw's remarks about the veil or the 'terror experts' who suggest that universities are a hotbed of Muslim 'radicalisation'.
>
> This means he is seen by some in government and the press – including some 'left' journalists such as those supporting the Euston Manifesto – as an appeaser of radical Islam . . .

Lambert's view is that the best way to turn young Muslims away from jihadist tendencies is to work in partnership with the community and in particular with influential community figures. 'The only really effective response to this political propaganda – this is political – are leading community figures', he noted. 'They are the only ones who can do anything about it'. Lambert highlighted the case of al Qaradawi who he sees as a very effective propagandist against al Qaeda. Yet, al Qaradawi and others are subject to 'character assassination' in the press and from government sources as well as being the targets of 'counter terrorism activity' – from Lambert's own colleagues.

In discussion Lambert was also clear that recruiting young Muslims to the anti-war movement and organisations like Respect also resulted in isolating the Jihadis. This, of course, highlights the underlying problem with the whole anti-terror strategy. As Lambert noted – if the political grievances of the Muslim community and the anti-war movement were dealt with there would be 'precious little' basis for the grievances. The grievances of the 7/7 bombers were plain enough – Iraq, Palestine and the war on terror. In Lambert's view there is 'an incredible lack of understanding of Muslim communities' in official circles. Lambert's refreshing approach (when compared with his colleagues) directs our attention to UK foreign policy as perhaps the most important single way to tackle 'terrorism'.

Since then, Lambert has contributed regularly to public debate on the issue earning much opprobrium from neoconservative think-tanks, commentators and blogs (Mills *et al*. 2011). Just after a month after the 2011 conference, however, Lambert was unmasked as an undercover spy who infiltrated a number of environmental and other protest groups on a long-term basis in the 1980s. Whilst it was obviously known that Lambert had been in the Special Branch, the issue raised by this was that his critique of the 'counter subversion' approach to terrorism adopted by the present government appeared to be undermined by his own role in such activities in the 1980s. Lambert was invited both to apologise for his past activities and betrayals and to explain what he now thought of his previous counter-subversion activities (Miller 2011b). Lambert did apologise but did not distance himself from his previous activities (Lambert 2011, Miller and Lubbers 2011). The case, like that of Sabir, does suggest that openness and free communication are not always in abundant supply when it comes to researching and writing about terrorism.

The articles in this special issue

Richard Jackson's article, 'Unknown knowns: the subjugated knowledge of terrorism studies', asks important questions about the types of knowledge that are 'known' or 'unknown' to orthodox terrorism analysts. He considers this a puzzle: 'why and how – that is, by what mechanisms – certain kinds of knowledge remain unacknowledged and excluded from terrorism studies'. The knowledge he refers to here is the vast quantity of research carried out on terrorism by other (non-terrorism studies) disciplines, in particular peace and conflict studies. Using Foucault's concept of subjugated knowledge as a tool to uncover why certain knowledges remain 'simultaneously "known" and "unknown" in the terrorism studies field', Jackson identifies two sets of factors at play: endogenous knowledges and exogenous knowledges. Endogenous knowledges are knowledges that remain unknown in the terrorism studies field, despite their broader acknowledgement in policy and other academic circles. Jackson offers various examples of these knowledges, including that state terrorism is more deadly than sub-state terrorism, that terrorists are unlikely ever to deploy weapons of mass destruction, that terrorism is driven by grievances and that al-Qaeda is not driven by a religious ideology. For Jackson then, these knowledges, derived from non-terrorism studies disciplines and from government and military sources, remain subjugated in terrorism studies as they challenge the dominant assumptions of the field.

Further to these endogenous knowledges, exogenous knowledges are those knowledges that are excluded by the terrorism studies field for being 'naïve, inferior or below the required level of scientificity' because they originate outside the field of terrorism studies. Disciplines such as peace and conflict studies or anthropology are thus excluded from the field of terrorism studies in favour of statistical 'scientific' analyses and broad generalisations based on secondary research. By excluding these knowledges, terrorism studies as a field reifies its own knowledge and subjugates other disciplines of analysis that leads to a bias. This is important, as terrorism research is not constrained to theoretical practices but has real-world applications. The research carried out by the traditional terrorism studies field has found a hegemonic home within government and security circles, to the exclusion of other disciplines that research terrorism. Not only does this have an impact on counterterrorism policy, but within academia it serves to prioritise one set of voices over many others, creating a closed shop of terrorism studies academics at conferences to the exclusion of other scholars. According to Jackson, the critical terrorism studies project must challenge this hegemonic control over the terrorism studies discourse by actively engaging with the traditional terrorism studies field and seeking to 'move beyond solely intellectual forms of struggle and engage in more diverse and creative cultural forms of activism which go beyond academic production'.

Jackson's article, based on his keynote address at the conference, is a clarion call to the critical terrorism studies community to engage in research that seeks to challenge the dominant discourse of the terrorism studies field by de-subjugating its endogenous and exogenous knowledges. This call was taken up by the academic, practitioner and activist presenters at the conference, who came from many different disciplinary backgrounds, including politics, international relations, sociology, anthropology, geography, feminist theory and gender studies, communications studies, peace and conflict studies and area studies including Middle Eastern studies, Irish studies and American and Canadian studies. The call has also been taken up by the contributors to this special issue of the journal, who have challenged some of the prevailing assumptions in the field through rigorous empirical and theoretically informed analyses of terrorism and counterterrorism. Michael Stohl and Joseba Zulaika's articles follow on from Jackson and both address issues of terrorism and counterterrorism knowledge over the past 10 years, whilst Charlotte Heath-Kelly and Mary Hickman et al. examine the practices of counterterrorism in the same period. Andrew W. Neal and Helen Dexter complete the issue by suggesting that we need new paradigms for thinking about the violence of terrorism.

Michael Stohl focuses his article 'Don't confuse me with the facts: knowledge claims and terrorism' on what he argues is an underutilised research technique in terrorism studies, that of testing knowledge claims through the principle of falsifiability. Stohl argues that the numerous studies of 'the state of the discipline' have demonstrated a dearth of theoretically grounded empirical studies and it is this that he claims is responsible for the fact that a lot of what is considered terrorism 'knowledge' is merely based on accumulated 'wisdom'. Stohl, therefore, aims to challenge one of Jackson's endogenous subjugated knowledges through rigorous empirical testing. The knowledge claim chosen is that of the concept of 'new terrorism' as distinctly different from 'old terrorism'. Stohl asks: 'How well do these knowledge claims about the new terrorism fare when they are confronted with the data on insurgent terrorism of the past forty years?' Stohl first assesses the claim that new terrorism is different from old terrorism through a statistical analysis of the communicative aspects of terrorism. According to Stohl, the proponents of the new terrorism thesis claim that it is different to old terrorism on the grounds that new terrorism no longer seeks to communicate a message through violence, but instead uses violence as an end in itself and aims to inflict a maximum number of casualties. This is a reversal of what the old terrorism sought to achieve. Stohl uses statistics from several terrorism databases, including ITERATE, the Global Terrorism Database and the National Terrorism Center Report Series, to test this identified claim. What he finds is that new terrorism is no less communicative and no more lethal than old terrorism. This is a rejection of the new terrorism thesis.

Second, Stohl tests the claim that one of the key characteristics of new terrorism is that it is founded as a 'network' rather than an organisation. Again, he finds no evidence to support this claim and argues that terming it such is not only misleading, but adds to a sense of insecurity by making it difficult to assess counterterrorism successes. Stohl points out the very real implications of a new terrorism thesis not based in fact: 'the damage that the new terrorism thesis caused in the wars and the other measures undertaken to defeat the falsely identified new terrorism have been both devastating and true'. This article demonstrates the very real need to challenge the hegemonic assumptions of the terrorism studies field, assumptions that are not based on empirically grounded research but instead on the perceived 'wisdom' of terrorism studies scholars. Further work of this sort will help in Jackson's project to de-subjugate knowledge and open the field of terrorism studies to internal and external critique.

Joseba Zulaika offers an analysis of counterterrorism and violence often excluded by the terrorism studies field, that from the perspective of anthropology, a field identified by Jackson in his article as key to broader understandings of violence and terrorism. In his article entitled 'Witches, drones and other flying objects: the force of fantasy in US counterterrorism', Zulaika updates his earlier (2009) work on counterterrorism as a self-fulfilling prophecy. He examines the recent use of pilotless drones in Pakistan by the US military to test the question of whether counterterrorism, by act or omission, contributes to terrorism and so acts as a self-fulfilling prophecy. Zulaika highlights the self-fulfilling nature of the counterterrorist use of pilotless drones: 'over 40 countries are developing military robots, with the likelihood that in a not far away future they might fall into the hands of terrorists'. Zulaika asks us to remember the example of Springer anti-aircraft missiles which the CIA provided to Afghan rebels in the 1980s that later fell into the hands of anti-American radical Islamists. He concludes that US counterterrorism became the greatest ally of America's enemies and that the self-fulfilling prophecy of US counterterrorist drones being used by terrorists is not far away. Zulaika uses the anthropological concepts of divination and witchcraft to explain the US counterterrorism policy; he argues that counterterrorism rests on the assumption that the next attack will happen, as he puts it, 'it is not if, but when'. This leads to a fatalistic attitude in which pre-emptive action against events that *will* happen in the future becomes rational; nuclear deterrence, for example. However, Zulaika argues that the Cold War rationale of deterrence has been superseded in this nuclear era in which terrorists *will* one day obtain and use nuclear weapons by a need to act pre-emptively to prevent this from happening. Zulaika explains that: 'The terrorist threat also creates the temporality of waiting. Actual historical temporality becomes subservient to the feared future. If there are no terrorism attacks the counterterrorist can claim success in preventing them; but if the attack does occur, then the counterterrorist can say "I told you so," and argue that he was right in his predictions. At this point terrorism foretold becomes prophecy fulfilled.'

Charlotte Heath-Kelly takes a different approach to the study of counterterrorism in her article, 'Reinventing prevention or exposing the gap? False positives in UK terrorism governance and the quest for pre-emption'. Heath-Kelly offers a post-structuralist interpretation of the concept of prevention in British counterterrorism policy, in order to provide a 'mini-genealogy' of the term through two eras: Northern Ireland under the Prevention of Terrorism Acts and the UK post-9/11. Heath-Kelly argues that the concept of prevention has two different meanings in the two eras. According to Heath-Kelly, prior to September 11, the Prevention of Terrorism Acts' conception of prevention would, if transposed to the contemporary setting, fit into the PURSUE strand of CONTEST rather than the PREVENT strand. Prevention in those Acts, such as exclusion, internment and proscription, was aimed at organisations and represented the Foucauldian concept of sovereign power. Prevention in contemporary counterterrorism policy, however, can be seen through the Foucauldian lens of governance, as it is aimed at individuals within broader communities and focuses on both the risk that individuals face to those wider communities and the potential vulnerability of the communities.

For Heath-Kelly then, this dual constitution of Muslim communities as both 'at risk' and 'risky' is a product of a counterterrorism policy that constitutes communities both as 'suspect' and as 'allies' in the struggle against terrorism. It is the gap between the suspect communities and the terrorist that Heath-Kelly is interested in exploring and she argues that counterterrorist operations within this gap can be characterised by Judith Butler's concept of the 'petty sovereign' who 'perform sovereign power in an era of diffused governmental power – marking a resurgence of sovereign power in the field of governmentality'. Heath-Kelly utilises the examples of 'misfiring' to expose the gap and reveal the activity of the petty sovereign in both the Northern Irish case (Gibraltar and Loughgall) and the contemporary era (the killing of Jean Charles de Menezes). Whilst she identifies experiences of suspect communities and the gap between the suspect and the terrorist subjectivity in both cases, Heath-Kelly argues that the radicalisation discourse in contemporary policy has served to exacerbate the gap by its focus on individuals, rather than organisations. Heath-Kelly is concerned that the gap will mean an increase in the use of petty sovereigns resulting in a further subjugation of terrorism knowledge, which 'could make the performance of counterterrorism more dangerous in the present era'. Heath-Kelly cautions us to 'mind the gap' in terrorism knowledge.

Following on from Heath-Kelly's interrogation of the gap between the concepts of the suspect community and the terrorist, the next article in this issue examines these same two suspect communities (the Irish or Northern Irish and Muslims) through an interpretive research methodology incorporating both public discourse analysis and the use of discussion groups and interviews. In their article, 'Social cohesion and the notion of "suspect communities": a study of the experiences and impacts of being "suspect" for Irish communities and Muslim communities in Britain', Mary J. Hickman, Lyn Thomas, Henri Nickels and Sara Silvestri consider the impacts and consequences on social cohesion of conceptualising certain populations as suspect. The authors find that whilst the vast majority of their participants 'provided evidence of the everyday nature of being "suspect" in both eras of political violence', a small number of participants disputed that there was or is a notion of suspect communities. They argue that this is sufficient to conclude that 'the concept of "suspect community" still has currency as a theoretical and analytical tool'. As such their research highlights important issues about the nature of suspect and bounded communities in relation to contemporary community cohesion policies that have aimed to break down barriers and emphasise the commonalities between communities rather than their divisions.

In particular, the authors found that the 'experiences of being "suspect" include the process whereby forms of belonging that previously were part of a wider set of identifications for an individual can become more important as a result of being "suspect". This is usually accompanied by a motivation to express this enhanced identification in the public realm.' This led to a situation in which 'processes of "suspectification" operate with notions of bounded "communities" and therefore are more likely to divide communities than bring them together'. The research therefore reveals that the very policies aimed at community cohesion can, instead, lead to greater division and perpetuate suspect communities. The authors conclude by arguing that the narrative on terrorism in the United Kingdom that distinguishes between the two eras of political violence needs to be challenged in order to draw clearer lessons from the negative experiences of those in suspect communities.

Andrew W. Neal makes a case in his article '"Events dear boy, events": terrorism and security from the perspective of politics' for expanding studies of counterterrorism from critiques of the executive branch of government to other political actors, namely legislatures and politicians. Neal argues that the focus on security governance to the detriment of what he terms 'security politics' has been a failing of both the traditional and critical security studies field. He claims that this classic security trope assumes that security transcends normal politics because of its existential importance, but that this creates an analytical blind spot in which the study of normal politics in the sphere of security is subjugated to the study of executive action. This is particularly a feature of securitisation theory, which cannot incorporate any analysis of non-executive actions into its assumptions about how normal politics becomes exceptional action. Thus, Neal argues that to understand security fully, it is necessary to understand how politicians view security, as outside of exceptional circumstances; they play a key role in the formulation of policy. This is important because politicians are constrained by different stakes than the executive, stakes relating to the electoral life of a government or their own political career. Neal states that: 'The fear and threat that drives politicians and governments may not be existential but political . . . This is because security events and the way they are handled or mishandled, regardless of whether constructed or not, can make or break a government. In fact this is true of all events.' Shifting the focus to an examination of events that are significant for political, not existential, survival thus reveals that for politicians there is no difference between a terrorist attack, an economic crisis or a political scandal. According to Neal, this lack of distinction between security events and other events problematises the traditional separation of normal politics and security and thus requires a broadening of focus within terrorism studies away from the executive and towards other political actors.

In her article, 'Terrorism and violence: another violence is possible?', Helen Dexter adds an important dimension that has been missing from the definitional debate on terrorism; whether 'the category of "terrorism" improves or impedes our intellectual understanding of violence'. Central to this is the question of what academic adherence to the terrorism label means for non-terrorist violence, which the author describes as a 'research comfort zone' given the lack of academic consensus on how to theorise violence *per se*. Dexter thus seeks to examine 'terrorism' in the context of 'violence' through an analysis of four key features common to definitions of terrorism. The first of these features is that central to definitions of terrorism are statements regarding the innocent and civilian or non-combatant nature of the victims of the violence. Dexter problematises this aspect of definitions of terrorism by asking 'whether "other" violence can be as easily categorised as violence that targets only the guilty – those deserving of violence'. Moreover, Dexter argues that the distinction between civilian and combatant has legitimised Western violence in the war on terror. By contrasting terrorism to war, Dexter draws out the second key feature of definitions of terrorism; that terrorism is violence that intentionally seeks to target civilians. Dexter then questions whether violence that does not specifically target civilians falls into a separate category. However, Dexter critiques the very notion of intentionality by questioning how non-terrorist violence can be considered not to intentionally target civilians when that outcome is entirely predictable and unavoidable. Thus, intentionality in the definition of terrorism is a moral category without which 'all deaths become equivalent and the institution of war itself comes under question. By reinforcing the centrality of intention in determining legitimate killing from illegitimate killing any definition of terrorism prevents this more fundamental critique.'

The third feature of terrorism definitions identified by Dexter is that terrorism is a process of political communication. However, Dexter questions whether any violence can be perceived not to communicate a message, intentionally or otherwise. This is because, as Dexter points out: 'how violence is interpreted is beyond the control of those who carry it out'. There is no difference, therefore, between terrorism and other forms of violence. Finally, Dexter identifies 'exceptionalism' as a key feature of definitions of terrorism; terrorism is an 'exceptionally *bad* form of violence' because it targets civilians, intentionally so, and because it is a communicative form of violence. However, when compared with other exceptional forms of violence, such as the war crime, there is little that distinguishes the effects of terrorism from the effects of non-terrorist violence. Dexter concludes by arguing that the problems inherent in defining terrorism are not unique to terrorism, but exist in defining both other forms of violence, and violence as a concept itself. Dexter therefore argues that what is needed is a broader critique of violence in order to better understand the category of terrorism.

The articles in this issue represent various fields of study and methodological modes of enquiry. Furthermore, they epitomise the future of the critical terrorism studies project; interdisciplinary research, dialogue, inclusion and the recognition that there is no one way to study terrorism.

Acknowledgements

Thanks are due to the authors and anonymous reviewers for turning round these articles so quickly. We also gratefully acknowledge the British Academy for their support for the conference; Glasgow City Council for hosting a reception for the conference and Baillie Catherine McMaster for her address – particularly her tales from Palestine; Jan Bisset for her Stakhanovite efforts in administering the conference; and the organising committee for all their efforts. Lastly, we gratefully acknowledge the social and cultural forces that combined to encourage Richard Jackson to dance at the ceilidh!

Notes

1. Available at: Mancha Productions, http://vimeo.com/user5073253.
2. Available in the Internet Archive: Is it Time for a Critical Terrorism Studies? Politics, Manchester University. http://web.archive.org/web/20061006065742/http://www.socialsciences.manchester.ac.uk/politics/events/cst/default.htm [Page archived on 6 October 2006, accessed 5 January 2012].

Notes on contributors

Jessie Blackbourn is a postdoctoral research fellow on the Australian Research Council Laureate Fellowship, Anti-Terror Laws and the Democratic Challenge, within the Gilbert and Tobin Centre of Public Law at the Faculty of Law, University of New South Wales. Prior to joining the UNSW, Jessie was lecturer in Terrorism and Security at the University of Salford, UK. Jessie's areas of interest are counterterrorism legislation in the United Kingdom and Ireland, the impact of counterterrorism legislation on human rights and the history and politics of contemporary Northern Ireland. She has published her work in *Terrorism and Political Violence*, *Critical Studies on Terrorism* and *Behavioral Sciences of Terrorism and Political Aggression*.

Helen Dexter is a teaching fellow in International Relations at the University of Leicester. Her current research takes an interdisciplinary approach towards a critical understanding of political violence. Two strands of research make up this general research theme. One strand of her research agenda addresses the nature and logic of violence by analysing dominant categories of war and conflict. The second strand explores the structuring discourses that produce violence. In particular, this strand of research investigates the relationship between moral and legal discourses and contemporary warfare.

Rani Kaur Dhanda is a social researcher in critical issues of racism and gender inequalities. She has researched and taught social justice issues in the Centre for Equality and Discrimination and in the Sociology Department at Strathclyde University, Scotland, for a number of years. Rani is currently working on two projects: conducting a research degree investigating the promotion of race relations by local government and also working on a successful Economic and Social Research Council-funded proposal to identify forums for constructive community engagement. She is interested in the learning and teaching of investigative research applications and tools. Rani is the co-ordinator of the University of Strathclyde publication, *Investigative Manual*, for researchers and is also the convenor of the faculty's postgraduate research society which recently launched the peer-reviewed e-journal, *Social Science Perspectives*.

David Miller is professor of Sociology in the Department of Social and Policy Sciences, University of Bath, UK. He is a director of Spinwatch (http://www.spinwatch.org) and editor of Powerbase (http://www.powerbase.info). Recent books include the co-authored *A Century of Spin: How Public Relations Became the Cutting Edge of Corporate Power* (with William Dinan, Pluto Press, 2008) and as co-editor *Neoliberal Scotland* (with Neil Davidson and Patricia McCafferty, Cambridge Scholars, 2010).

References

Anon, 2010. Laws should not criminalise Muslims for thought crime. *The Herald* [online], 9 February. Available from: http://www.heraldscotland.com/news/crime-courts/laws-should-not-criminalise-muslims-for-thought-crime-1.1005031 [Accessed 5 January 2012].
Anwar, A., 2007. Press release from Aamer Anwar and Co. *Scotland Against Criminalising Communities* [online], 17 September. Available from: http://www.sacc.org.uk/index.php?option=content&task=view&id=527&catid=33 [Accessed 5 January 2012].
HM Government, 2011. *Prevent strategy*. London: The Stationery Office.
Jones, S., 2011. Student in al-Qaida raid paid £20,000 by police. *The Guardian* [online], 14 September. Available from: http://www.guardian.co.uk/uk/2011/sep/14/police-pay-student-damages-al-qaida [Accessed 5 January 2012].
Jones, D.M. and Smith, M.L.R., 2006. The commentariat and discourse failure: language and atrocity in Cool Britannia. *International Affairs*, 82 (6), 1077–1100.
Jones, D.M. and Smith, M.L.R., 2009. We're all terrorists now: critical – or hypocritical – studies 'on' terrorism? *Studies in Conflict & Terrorism*, 32 (4), 292–302.
Lambert, B., 2011. Bob Lambert replies to Spinwatch. *Spinwatch* [online], 24 October. Available from: http://www.spinwatch.org/-articles-by-category-mainmenu-8/50-dirty-tricks/5461-bob-lambert-replies-to-spinwatch [Accessed on 5 January 2012].
Miller, D., 2006. Terrorism studies and the war on dissent. *Spinwatch* [online], 7 November. Available from: http://www.spinwatch.org/-articles-by-category-mainmenu-8/74-terror-spin/3625-terrorism-studies-and-the-war-on-dissent [Accessed 5 January 2012].
Miller, D., 2011a. A decade on: new challenges in studying terrorism. *A Decade of Terrorism and Counter-Terrorism Blog* [online]. Available from: http://decadeofterrorismandcounterterrorism.wordpress.com/2011/09/12/99/#more-99 [Accessed 5 January 2012].
Miller, D., 2011b. An open letter to Bob Lambert. *Spinwatch* [online], 20 October. Available from: http://www.spinwatch.org/-articles-by-category-mainmenu-8/50-dirty-tricks/5459-an-open-letter-to-bob-lambert [Accessed on 5 January 2012].
Miller, D. and Lubbers, E., 2011. Statement: Spinwatch stands in solidarity with the infiltrated. *Spinwatch* [online], 2 November. Available from: http://www.spinwatch.org/-articles-by-category-mainmenu-8/50-dirty-tricks/5462-statement-spinwatch-stands-in-solidarity-with-the-infiltrated [Accessed 5 January 2012].
Miller, D. and Mills, T., 2009. The terror experts and the mainstream media: the expert nexus and its dominance in the news media. *Critical Studies on Terrorism*, 2 (3), 414–437.
Mills, T., Griffin, T., and Miller, D., 2011. *The Cold War on British Muslims* [online]. Glasgow: Spinwatch. Available from: http://www.spinwatch.org/images/SpinwatchReport_ColdWar.pdf [Accessed 1 September 2011].
Zulaika, J., 2009. *Terrorism the self-fulfilling prophecy*. Chicago: The University of Chicago Press.

Unknown knowns: the subjugated knowledge of terrorism studies

Richard Jackson

National Centre for Peace and Conflict Studies, University of Otago, Dunedin, New Zealand

> This article employs Foucault's concept of 'subjugated knowledges' to explore forms of knowledge which provide explanations of the nature, causes and solutions to terrorism and political violence, but which have been suppressed and silenced within the terrorism studies field. Subjugated knowledges include historical knowledges that are present within the functional and systemic ensemble of terrorism studies itself, but which have been masked by more dominant forms of knowledge, as well as knowledges outside of the field that have been disqualified and excluded as naïve, inferior or below the required level of scientificity. This article analyses some of the primary mechanisms and processes by which knowledge subjugation takes place in terrorism studies and the consequences of such suppressions and exclusions. It argues that the presence of subjugated knowledge means that the field exists in a highly unstable condition where certain forms of knowledge are simultaneously known and unknown and where eruptions of subjugated knowledge periodically destabilise the dominant discourse. Among others, the rise of critical terrorism studies represents such an eruption in the field. The article concludes by suggesting that one of the key future tasks of critical terrorism studies must be to liberate a range of potentially important subjugated knowledges and that Bourdieu's concept of the 'collective intellectual' provides a potentially important model for undertaking this difficult task.

Introduction

The observation that 'ultimately the use of terror is a form of conflict' (Richmond 2003, p. 298) is both unoriginal and largely uncontested. This is because, as most scholars agree, 'properly understood, terror is a strategy, not a creed' of contentious politics (Tilly 2004, p. 5; see also Schmid 2004, p. 199). In other words, terrorism is just one among several repertoires of political conflict, which also includes war, civil war, genocide, ethnic cleansing, riots, insurgency, assassination, sabotage, civil disobedience and the like. At the same time, the field of peace and conflict studies has long studied the origins, causes, management, resolution and transformation of different forms of conflict (for an excellent overview of this field, see Ramsbotham *et al.* (2005)), including conflicts where terrorism is prominent (see Burton 1979, Sederberg 1995, Zartman 2003, Hastings 2004). Moreover, as a strategy of contentious politics, terrorism has also been studied extensively in cognate disciplines such as history (see English 2003, Pappe 2009), anthropology (see Zulaika 1988, Feldman 1994), sociology (Della Porta 1995, Johnston 2008), area studies (Dalacoura 2006) and many others.

This condition, in which the same conflict strategy – terrorism – has been studied in parallel in different fields, poses something of a well-noted puzzle, namely, why terrorism analysts have 'tended to work surprisingly independently of mainstream conflict analysis' (Ramsbotham et al. 2005, p. 67), and why 'there is currently a division between conflict analysis and formal studies of terrorism, despite the fact that these various phenomena and attempts to theorize them have much in common' (Richmond 2003, p. 289; see also Franks 2009). In other words, how is it that the 'known' knowledge of the causes and resolution of violent political conflict (including conflicts where terrorism was present), which has accumulated from decades of conflict analysis and peace research, among others, remains largely 'unknown'[1] within the terrorism studies field? Why is it that within terrorism studies research continues apace on questions related to terrorism's causes and effective responses without reference to the key scholars and existing studies of peace and conflict studies?

Possible answers to this puzzle include the terrorism field's long-noted failings of rigorous scholarly research practice (see Silke 2004, Ranstorp 2006), which have clearly contributed to a number of 'gaps' in the field, of which the peace and conflict studies 'gap' looms particularly large (Franks 2009). From this perspective, it may be the case that terrorism scholars remain unaware of these other literatures, in part not only due to the nature of the disciplinary divisions within the academy but also because the particular ontology and epistemology of terrorism studies creates a barrier to cross-fertilisation with peace and conflict studies (Richmond 2003, p. 297). Another explanation may lie in how terrorism studies evolved as a separate field of expertise (see Gordon 2010, Stampnitzky forthcoming). A sociological history of the field demonstrates that its core scholars and experts made deliberate efforts to separate the field's focus and domain from insurgency studies and conflict studies (from where it first emerged; see Stampnitzky forthcoming), in order to legitimise and institutionalise it as a separate scholarly field of inquiry, in the process creating an 'invisible college' or 'epistemic community' that then acted to police its boundaries (see Reid 1993, 1997).

In this article, I attempt to add to these useful insights by applying Foucault's (1997, p. 7) concept of 'subjugated knowledges' to an analysis of the field. Specifically, I am interested in exploring how this concept might help us to better understand (1) why and how – that is, by what mechanisms – certain kinds of knowledge remain unacknowledged and excluded from terrorism studies; (2) how the 'known' and 'unknown' knowledges of terrorism[2] coexist and the consequences of this unstable condition within the field; and (3) how different kinds of knowledge might be de-subjugated within terrorism studies – how the 'unknown knowns' might be made 'known'. As such, this article attempts to contribute to the growing body of recent critical research into the ideological functions of the field (see, among others, Miller and Mills 2009, Raphael 2009). In particular, it builds upon deconstructive studies that attempt to examine the nature and consequences of contemporary counterterrorism discourse (see, among others, Zulaika and Douglass 1996, Jackson 2005, Jarvis 2009).

The article is divided into four parts. In the first part, I briefly discuss Foucault's concept of 'subjugated knowledges' and provide a few selected examples of different kinds of subjugated knowledge within and outside of the terrorism studies field. The second part describes some of the main mechanisms and strategies of knowledge subjugation in terrorism studies, while the third part explores some of the main consequences that come from subjugating these particular knowledges in terrorism studies. In the fourth part, I explore potential strategies for de-subjugating knowledge. Finally, in the conclusion, I argue that the present historical juncture provides a 'ripe' moment for a critical intervention to de-subjugate peace and conflict studies in particular, and that as a type of Bourdieuian 'collective intellectual' project, critical terrorism studies (CTS) is in a prime position to lead such an intervention.

Foucault, subjugated knowledge and terrorism studies

Although relatively undeveloped theoretically, Foucault's concept of 'subjugated knowledge' nonetheless provides a useful tool[3] for excavating the reasons why certain knowledges remain simultaneously 'known' and 'unknown' in the terrorism studies field.[4] Foucault (1997, p. 7) described subjugated knowledges in the following terms:

> When I say 'subjugated knowledges' I mean two things. On the one hand, I am referring to historical contents that have been buried or masked in functional coherences or formal systemizations. [. . .] Subjugated knowledges are, then, blocks of historical knowledges that were present in the functional and systematic ensembles, but which were masked, and the critique was able to reveal their existence by using, obviously enough, the tools of scholarship. Second . . . when I say 'subjugated knowledges' I am also referring to a whole series of knowledges that have been disqualified as nonconceptual knowledges, as insufficiently elaborated knowledges: naive knowledges, hierarchically inferior knowledges, knowledges that are below the required level of erudition or scientificity.

In effect, Foucault is describing two kinds of subjugated knowledges, both of which are directly relevant to the exploration of the puzzle under investigation here.

First, what we might call endogenous knowledge that is present within the functional and systemic ensemble of terrorism studies itself – that is, knowledge that is generated by and, in some senses, 'known' within the systematisation and practices of the field itself – but which has been masked or buried by more dominant forms of knowledge. There are numerous examples of such subjugated knowledge within terrorism studies. For example, the knowledge that terrorism is a strategy which can be employed by both state and non-state actors (see Thornton 1964), that state terrorism is far more deadly and serious than that practiced by non-state actors (see Laqueuer 1977, p. 6) and that 'terror' was initially accepted within the US government as an essential tool of counter-insurgency (see McClintock 1992, p. xvii) was widely 'known' in the earliest discussions among terrorism scholars (see Stampnitzky forthcoming). However, this knowledge has since been masked or buried – subjugated – by a more dominant knowledge, which asserts that terrorism is primarily a violent strategy of non-state actors, Western states do not themselves practice terror and non-state terrorism is the proper sole focus for the field.

Similarly, it is known that terrorism is a statistically minor threat to security (see Mueller 2005) and that terrorists are very unlikely to employ weapons of mass destruction (WMD) in their campaigns, either on their own or with support from rogue states (see Jenkins 1998). For example, the Gilmore Commission in 1999 concluded in its final report that 'rogue states would hesitate to entrust such weapons to terrorists because of the likelihood that such a group's actions might be unpredictable even to the point of using the weapon against its sponsor'; in addition, they would be reluctant to use such weapons themselves due to 'the prospect of significant reprisals' (quoted in Hiro 2002, p. 391); and Condoleeza Rice argued that there was no need to panic about rogue states because 'if they do acquire WMD – their weapons will be unusable because any attempt to use them will bring national obliteration' (quoted in Callinicos 2003). Again, however, such knowledge has been subjugated and masked by the widely accepted knowledge that terrorism, including the serious risk of WMD terrorism, today poses the pre-eminent international security threat.

It is also known that terrorism, as a conflict strategy, is driven by grievances and, in the case of anti-American terrorism, by US military intervention overseas. As Eland (1998) of the CATO Institute puts it in the introduction to his study,

> According to the Pentagon's Defense Science Board, a strong correlation exists between U.S. involvement in international situations and an increase in terrorist attacks against the United States. President Clinton has also acknowledged that link. The board, however, has provided no empirical data to support its conclusion. This paper fills that gap by citing many examples of terrorist attacks on the United States in retaliation for U.S. intervention overseas. The numerous incidents cataloged suggest that the United States could reduce the chances of such devastating – and potentially catastrophic – terrorist attacks by adopting a policy of military restraint overseas.

Related to this, it is known that terrorism is not rooted in or caused by religious ideology or individual pathology and hatred. As a Pentagon intelligence team concluded, 'Al-Qaeda [is] not driven by ideology' (quoted in Hellmich 2011, p. 62). Similarly, As Peter Bergen (2001, p. 242), one of the few people to have actually interviewed Osama bin Laden and a now respected terrorism expert, concluded:

> In all the tens of thousands of words that bin Laden has uttered on the public record . . . [H]e does not rail against the pernicious effects of Hollywood movies, or against Madonna's midriff, or against the pornography protected by the US Constitution. . . . What he condemns the United States for is simple: its policies in the Middle East. . . . [T]he continued US military presence in Arabia; US support for Israel; its continued bombing of Iraq; and its support for regimes such as Egypt and Saudi Arabia . . . The hijackers . . . attacked the Pentagon and the World Trade Center, preeminent symbols of the United States' military and economic might.

Instead, it is known that even al-Qaeda's terrorism is driven by political grievance and opposition to oppressive policies (see Pape 2005, Hellmich 2011, p. 87). As before, however, such knowledge has been masked by, among others, the concept of 'new terrorism', which attributes the causes of contemporary terrorism to individual processes of radicalisation, nihilism and religious extremism.

It has also been widely known since the earliest days of the field that reducing and resolving terrorism involves both refraining from repression and military intervention (Eland 1998, Araj 2008) and engaging in reform (Crelinsten 2009, English 2009) and often direct dialogue, as was undertaken in Israel, Northern Ireland and South Africa, among others (Neumann 2007). Once again, however, such knowledge has been buried beneath a more widely accepted and dominant knowledge that coercive and repressive forms of counterterrorism can be both legitimate and effective and that the 'new terrorists' in particular are incorrigible and not amenable to political dialogue and negotiation.

In short, as this small sample suggests, there is a great deal of 'known' knowledges *within* terrorism studies, which remains largely 'unknown' – that is, unacknowledged, unreferenced and not systematically engaged with – in the core terrorism literature today and among its key scholars. A more comprehensive analysis of subjugated knowledge within terrorism studies would include a systematic analysis of the work of notable scholars, such as Ted Gurr, Michael Stohl and Martha Crenshaw, who generated important knowledge in the early days of the field which challenged dominant assumptions but which was subsequently suppressed and became 'unknown' within the wider practices of the field.

A second form of subjugated knowledge described by Foucault is knowledge that is outside of, or exogenous to, the field of terrorism studies. Such forms of knowledge have been disqualified and excluded by terrorism scholars and their practices as naïve, inferior or below the required level of scientificity. They include both the knowledges of other scientific fields and the non-scientific and subjective experiential knowledges of a range of individuals and communities, such as terrorists themselves, some counterterrorism practitioners, peacemakers who work in conflict zones, journalists, novelists, artists and groups who experience the direct effects of counterterrorism policy first hand.

One of the most important exogenous forms of subjugated knowledge is the knowledge within peace and conflict studies, which has systematically studied the nature, effects, causes and resolution of violent political conflict over many decades. In the process, it has produced a large and sophisticated body of knowledge on different types of conflict, the linkages between physical, structural and cultural violence, the nature and causes of intractable social conflict, human needs-based conflict, escalation cycles, enduring rivalries, and the psychology of inter-group violence, as well as different forms of conflict resolution such as negotiation, mediation, conflict prevention, peace education, dialogic conflict transformation, discourse ethics, trust-building, peace-building, reconciliation and truth-telling, and conflict transformation (see Ramsbotham *et al.* 2005).

The important point is that such knowledge is largely unknown in the terrorism studies field, and many of the most important peace studies scholars – including Johan Galtung, John Burton, Chris Mitchell, Kenneth Boulding, Adam Curle, Edward Azar, Ted Robert Gurr and John Paul Lederach – are rarely cited or engaged with in a meaningful way, despite the fact that many of these scholars have both theoretical and practical experience of resolving violent political conflict. Instead, such knowledge is excluded for its naivety and lack of scientificity in favour of terrorism knowledge, which views it as essentially different from all other forms of violent conflict in terms of its non-political, nihilistic and immoral nature (see Stampnitzky forthcoming) and as immune to the normal methods of conflict management and resolution due to the incorrigibility of terrorists as 'total spoilers', who thus require only suppression or extermination.

Other important forms of subjugated knowledge exogenous to the field can be found in anthropology, much of it based on primary fieldwork and a deep understanding of culture and language, which demonstrates the cultural, political and strategic rationality of terrorist violence; the grievances and local conflict structures driving it; the impact of violence on local communities; the dynamics of state terror; and much more. In terrorism studies, this knowledge is largely ignored or subjugated in favour of broad statistical analyses and generalisations based on secondary research, most often by 'experts' who do not speak the language or have familiarity with the cultural context (see Zulaika 1988 for a discussion). Similarly, research within sociology that focuses on the grievance and opportunity structures facing social movements in situations of conflict, and the role of political entrepreneurs and deep cultural grammar in generating terrorist violence, among other things, has remained, with only a few exceptions, unknown. In the terrorism studies literature, this knowledge has been subjugated in favour of individual-oriented radicalisation or pathological explanations of terrorist violence.

Other important scientific knowledges relevant to understanding terrorism as a conflict strategy which also remain largely unknown in the terrorism studies field include feminist studies, criminology, including the state crime literature, area studies, particularly Middle East studies, history, law, philosophy, social psychology and some forms of social and international theory. Historical studies that document the unique evolution of Irish nationalism and the evolution of the armed struggle in tandem with it, for example, are rarely included in the literature on terrorism's causes or solutions, in part because it is excluded through the assertion of the 'new terrorism' thesis.

Finally, we should mention a range of non-scientific knowledges that have been excluded and subjugated from terrorism studies, including journalistic accounts of terrorism (Yallop 1993, Taylor 2011), memoirs from ex-militants (Khaled 1973, Baumann 1977) and collections of terrorist writings (Lawrence 2005). Artistic representations of terrorism often contain important knowledge or 'truths' about terrorism, which have also been subjugated within the field. Examples of important artistic works that express certain 'truths' about terrorism include the works of street artists such as Banksy, political cartoonists (see Dodds 2007), novelists (see Marciano 2003, Khadra 2007), playwrights (see Soans 2005) and film makers. Films such as *The Battle of Algiers* (1966), *The Terrorist* (1998) and *Paradise Now* (2005), for example, depict terrorist rationalities, perceptions, motives and experiences, which challenge some of the field's assertions about the nature of terrorists and the causes of their violence. For the most part, such accounts are dismissed – and thereby subjugated – for lacking in scholarly 'objectivity' or displaying the necessary standards of social science scholarship.

Processes and mechanisms of knowledge subjugation in terrorism studies

An important initial step towards understanding knowledge subjugation within terrorism studies is to consider how the field is constituted and functions as a discourse. That is, every discourse 'allows certain things to be said and impedes or prevents other things from being said' (Purvis and Hunt 1993, p. 485), in large part, because 'discourses, by way of hegemonic closures, fix meanings in particular ways and, thus, exclude all other meaning potentials' (Jorgensen and Phillips 2002, p. 186). From this perspective, the subjugated knowledge described above represents the unsayable within the dominant terrorism discourse; these subjugated knowledges represent those alternative meaning potentials which have been closed off by the closures inherent to the discourse.

More specifically, scientific discourses in particular function to constitute objects of knowledge (and simultaneously, the non-knowledge outside of the constituted knowledge), legitimate fields of knowledge (and simultaneously, the illegitimate fields) and authorised, legitimate (and simultaneously, unauthorised, illegitimate) speakers. That is, discourses

> work to define and enable, and also to silence and to exclude, for example, by limiting and restricting authorities and experts to some group, but not others, endorsing a certain common sense, but making other modes of categorizing and judging meaningless, impractical, inadequate or otherwise disqualified. (Milliken 1999, p. 229)

In other words, it is an internal functional necessity that a discourse and its authorised 'experts' will suppress and exclude knowledge and meaning which would challenge the proper objects, boundaries and authorised speakers of the field.

From a wider perspective, we can also consider the way in which discourses and fields of knowledge compete for dominance or hegemony in society. In this case, the relative dominance of terrorism studies and security studies can be explained by its institutional and discursive closeness to power – it is a form of 'situated knowledge' – and the degree to which it accords with hegemonic commonsense and cultural narratives of political violence, legitimacy and security. From this perspective, the subjugation of peace studies is both an expression of the relative power of terrorism studies in terms of its overlap with the security field and the perennial weakness of peace studies as a form of outsider or counter-hegemonic/countercultural knowledge. The political and media power of security think-tanks compared with peace studies research centres, for example, is illustrative of the relative position each field holds within existing power structures, as are the demonstrable links many of the leading experts and research institutions have to the state through funding sources, institutional positions, interlocking personnel and policy advice channels (see, e.g., Miller and Mills 2009). Some leading scholars at the RAND Corporation, for example, have previously served as senior officials in several US administrations, and their positions within state-linked institutions and their role in providing counterterrorism advice to the government has led some to describe them as 'embedded experts' (Burnett and Whyte 2005) or 'organic intellectuals' due to institutional, financial, political and ideological ties to the state.

It is one of the sad ironies of the functioning of this hegemonic security discourse that peace activist-scholars with direct and often successful experience of ending terrorism and violent political conflict through direct negotiation with terrorists and other peace-making activities are perennially delegitimised as speakers, and their hard-won knowledge is subjugated, often as naïve and unscientific. Meanwhile, many former counterterrorism practitioners who have never met a terrorist and whose actions have consistently failed to prevent further terrorism are frequently held in high esteem as 'experts' legitimised to speak on the subject and provide direct advice to policymakers and practitioners.

Analysis from the perspective of the sociology of knowledge provides another perspective on processes of knowledge subjugation within the field. For example, it has long been noted that terrorism studies exhibit the characteristics of an 'invisible college' – a group of scholars who exchange ideas, share each other's work, present at the same conferences, use the same information channels and maintain informal links (Reid 1997, pp. 92, 97). Related to this, the field's leading scholars can also be described as an 'epistemic community' – a network of 'specialists with a common world view about cause and effect relationships which relate to their domain of expertise, and common political values about the type of policies to which they should be applied' (Stone 1996, p. 86). As it relates to knowledge subjugation, Reid (1993, p. 28) has demonstrated how the research process among these scholars has often been a closed, circular and static system of information and investigation, which tends to accept dominant 'myths' about terrorism without strong empirical investigation for long periods before empirical research disproves them.

However, in addition to these general macro-level subjugating functions and processes of discourse and field maintenance, it is also possible to identify an assemblage of micro-level processes and mechanisms of knowledge subjugation, many of which are specific to the terrorism field itself. For example, knowledge subjugation occurs through those 'knowledgeable practices' (Milliken 1999, p. 229) – such as research and teaching programmes and modes of analysis which scholars routinely treat as unproblematic – which define the object of the field to be forms of non-state violence which are separated from other forms of violent political conflict by virtue of its exceptional nature and which enclose the field of terrorism studies to the exclusion of peace and conflict studies, anthropology, history and other relevant fields. As such, these practices are rooted in the broader 'ontological binaries' of international politics which are maintained between state and non-state, between terrorism and other forms of violence and which function to maintain the divide between terrorism and conflict studies (Richmond 2003, pp. 297–298).

More broadly, specific knowledgeable practices within terrorism studies which function to subjugate knowledge include the institutionalisation of teaching and research training programmes in terrorism studies which exclude relevant peace studies, anthropological and other texts, fields and scholars; the disaggregation of terrorism from other forms of conflict in data sets and empirical analyses; social practices of excluding scholars who do not share the same epistemic and ontological assumptions about the subject from research activities like conferences, journals and projects (Reid 1997, Ilardi 2004); and the failure to try and build upon and replicate studies by peace researchers but instead the design of entirely new empirical studies. One analysis, for example, concluded that terrorism 'experts' who do not maintain a strong pro-Western bias in their work soon become marginalised in the field and are denied access to policymakers and major conferences (Ilardi 2004, p. 222).

Directly related to this, the terrorism studies field is situated in a broader field where legitimacy flows primarily to positivist, empiricist and rationalist methodologies and epistemologies (and their accompanying claims to 'objectivity' and non-partisan scholarship and advice), but which simultaneously downgrades and denigrates other methodologies and epistemologies such as interpretivist and non-empiricist approaches like ethnography and participant action research. Within terrorism studies, there is a clear privileging of large-n-based quantitative research over other kinds of qualitative research such as field research.

As already noted, one of the key processes by which scientific discourses maintain the boundaries of the field is through the operation of codes of legitimation for speakers. In this case, such codes authorise designated terrorism 'experts', former counterterrorism practitioners, foreign policy officials, defence intellectuals and certain international relations scholars to 'speak' about terrorism, while simultaneously delegitimising peace scholars and activists, anthropologists, former terrorists, journalists and others who would 'speak' about terrorism in alternative ways. Examining the published biographies of terrorism 'experts' who address scholarly and policy forums such as the Henry Jackson Society or the Washington Institute for Near East Policy, it is possible to deduce that the terrorism studies' code of authorisation, often amounting to ritual invocation, prominently includes such factors as social scientific credentials, personal military or counterterrorism experience, institutional proximity to power (the defence establishment academic institutions or state-recognised security think-tanks) and evidence of the provision of advice to policymakers.

Closely aligned with the authorisation of speakers and the maintenance of knowledgeable practices is the oft-noted ritual of moral condemnation required by terrorism experts, a ritual enforced since the earliest days of the field and closely connected with the operation of the 'terrorism taboo' (see Zulaika and Douglass 1996). Lisa Stampnitzky (forthcoming), for example, describes several cases in the 1970s in which terrorism scholars were publicly criticised for a 'morally repugnant' 'degree of sympathy' with terrorists and for not only encouraging terrorists, but even providing scientific rationales for their behaviour. Another expression of such taboo-enforcing practices includes Alan Dershowitz's (2002, pp. 24–25, 85) assertion that 'we must commit ourselves never to try to understand or eliminate its alleged root causes, but rather to place it beyond the pale of dialogue and negotiation', because 'the international community responded to terrorism between 1968 and 2001 by consistently rewarding and legitimizing it, rather than punishing and condemning it'.

More recently, a review by Schmid (2009) of the Jackson *et al.* (2009b) CTS volume condemns it for being 'strangely silent about the worldview of those terrorists who have no self-doubts and attack the Red Cross, the United Nations, NGOs and their fellow Muslims with equal lack of scruples' and argues that 'CTS academics should be the first on the barricades against jihadists' (pp. 61–62; see also Jones and Smith 2009). In short, it can be observed from these regular practices that 'to gain official entry into the terrorist debate one must check critical weapons at the door, and join the chorus of [ritual moral] condemnation' (der Derian quoted in Hellmich 2011, p. 10). This particular discursive ritual functions to discipline scholars and maintain the ontological enclosure (or taboo, in anthropological terms) around terrorism as an essentially immoral form of political violence – unlike other forms of political violence like war and insurgency which can be morally justified and require no ritual condemnation from scholars wishing to speak on the subject.

We might also examine the specific processes by which the terrorism field attempts to 'stabilize and fix dominant meanings' (Milliken 1999, p. 230) through forms of 'hegemonic closure'; that is, the means by which the field attempts to 'fix meaning by excluding all other meaning potentials' and thereby suppresses eruptions of alternative knowledge (Jorgensen and Phillips 2002, p. 190). In this way, 'antagonisms are dissolved through hegemony, whereby the . . . discourse conquers the terrain and appears as objective reality . . . [and] alternatives are pushed out of our vision' (Jorgensen and Phillips 2002, p. 190). Lisa Stampnitzky's (forthcoming) analysis of the ways in which the field, from the early 1970s, made observable efforts to redefine terrorists from their former conception as rational insurgents to irrational and immoral fanatics and to depoliticise them as inherently pathological is illustrative of such discourse stabilisation efforts. More recently, the 'new terrorism' thesis which gained currency in the mid-1990s, and which posits that contemporary terrorists are religiously motivated, nihilistic and unconstrained, functions to stabilise and re-enclose the essential meaning of terrorism in the wake of the end of several terrorist campaigns through direct negotiation and social reforms in Israel, Northern Ireland and South Africa.

Unknown knowns and hegemonic discourse

There is no need to reproduce here the main findings of the growing literature which explores the ideological consequences of the dominant terrorism discourse (see, among others, Silberstein 2002, Jackson 2005, 2007, Jarvis 2009). Broadly, processes of knowledge subjugation function to stabilise meanings, discipline boundaries and maintain hierarchical knowledge-power structures within the broader social structure. In turn, such discourse stabilisation allows the field to perform its key legitimising role in maintaining state hegemony, in part through its securitising role. More specifically, it allows the field to be used instrumentally by state elites as a source of legitimacy for a range of political projects, domestic and foreign, such as extending processes of governmentality (Foucault 1991, pp. 87–104) through practices like social surveillance, counter-radicalisation programmes and the suppression of dissent, to regime change, security assistance programmes and other forms of imperialism (see Jackson 2007).

More specific consequences of knowledge suppressions and exclusions for the terrorism field include the maintenance of a particular series of dominant myths about the nature, threat, causes and resolution of terrorism which are reproduced in academic, political and cultural discourse (Jackson 2009), thereby maintaining a shared society-wide commonsense about terrorism; the continuing distortion, ideological bias and restricted focus of the terrorism field's research, including the ever-growing literature on issues such as bio-terrorism, radicalisation and religious terrorism (see Silke 2009), and the continuing neglect of systematic research by the field's scholars on Western state terrorism (see Jackson 2008, Blakeley 2009); and advocacy and support by many terrorism scholars for ineffective and counterproductive counterterrorism policies – what has been described as a 'passion for ignorance' which has actually led in recent years to a counterterrorism 'self-fulfilling prophesy' (Zulaika 2009).

Importantly, knowledge subjugation processes can also become internalised as a kind of self-governance by scholars or, in anthropological terms, the operation of taboo (see Zulaika and Douglass 1996). An interesting example of this self-subjugating effect can be seen in Pape's (2005) widely lauded study on suicide terrorism, where, after affirming how his research clearly demonstrates that suicide terrorism is driven by opposition to 'American military policies' and 'foreign occupation' (pp. 243, 245), he nonetheless suppresses the implications of this knowledge and instead advocates that the US maintains 'permanent readiness to intervene massively and rapidly if necessary, including maintaining the current infrastructure of military bases in the [Middle East]' (p. 248) as a core policy of defeating suicide terrorism. The previously noted admission by most leading terrorism scholars that state terrorism is the most deadly form of terrorism, but the decision to then suppress the implications of such an admission and instead claim that non-state terrorism represents the greatest security threat today, is another example of this self-subjugation effect in practice.

Apart from the discourse and power-knowledge stabilising effects which function to maintain existing hegemonic social structures and practices, knowledge subjugation also results in a condition whereby the field exists in a highly unstable, overflowing and open-ended state in which certain knowledges are simultaneously 'known' and 'unknown'. Within such an ontologically unstable condition, and despite continuous knowledge subjugation attempts, the field is prone to spasmodic and ongoing knowledge contradictions which are nonetheless tolerated. For example, the knowledge that al-Qaeda is a global viral network (and hence immune to decapitation strategies), and simultaneously a hierarchical, geographically bound organisation requiring decapitation of its core leadership in order to defeat (see Hellmich 2011, pp. 158–159), is a current example of an ontological contradiction tolerated by scholars and counterterrorism practitioners.

Similarly, the incident in which former Attorney General Michael Mukasey, former New York Mayor Rudolph Giuliani, former Homeland Security Secretary Tom Ridge and former National Security Advisor Frances Townsend publicly spoke in support of the Mujaheddin-e Khalq (MEK) in Paris in December 2010 is an example of a spasmodic contradiction (see Cody 2010, Cole 2011). Despite the MEK being a designated 'foreign terrorist organization' according to the US State Department, thus making it a federal crime to engage in public advocacy of the group, the knowledge that such actions were supporting terrorism neither prevented them from speaking nor induced the counterterrorism structures, the media or the terrorism studies field to react in the prescribed manner. Instead, the spasmodic contradiction was ignored, suppressed and ultimately tolerated.

More importantly, the unstable condition of unknown knowing can also result in periodic eruptions of subjugated knowledge that destabilises the discourse. This is what Foucault (1997, p. 9) terms 'the insurrection of knowledge', which is 'an insurrection against the centralizing power-effects that are bound up with the institutionalization and workings of any scientific discourse organized in a society such as ours'. Such eruptions or insurrections may come from sudden rupturing events which destabilise established meaning structures, thus providing a brief opening for the articulation of alternative knowledges before meanings are re-sutured and the discourse re-stabilised. The Oslo terrorist attacks by an anti-Muslim right-wing militant in July 2011 is arguably an example of a rupturing event within which scholars such as Lambert (2011) attempted to inject previously subjugated knowledge. For a brief moment, the established discourse of religious/Islamic terrorism driven by pathological processes of radicalisation appeared inadequate and unsatisfactory as an explanatory or prescriptive framework for the events. Arguably, discourse-stabilising efforts which suggested that the perpetrator was psychologically disturbed, a lone actor unconnected to other groups or networks or part of an entirely different species of political violence have since arguably closed down this space.

Alternately, such insurrections may come about through sustained discursive struggle by strategic actors over a long period. In an important sense, the rise of CTS over the past few years represents an insurrection of subjugated knowledge within the field brought about by deliberate discursive struggle (see below), as has the work of various activist networks concerned with human rights, the anti-war, anti-rendition, anti-torture campaigns and the like.

The central importance of this is that despite the metaphorical allusion present in the description, 'eruptions' of subjugated knowledge are not random or impersonal processes; they are not like natural phenomena such as volcanoes or earthquakes in which observers are by necessity passive. Instead, within the play of discourse in fields of knowledge, individuals and groups can choose to act decisively in attempts to de-subjugate knowledge. In this respect, Foucault's description as 'insurrections of knowledge' is of greater pertinence, implying as it does the wilful action of agents against the workings of oppressive power.

CTS and the de-subjugation of knowledge

Guided by its normative and analytical commitments (see Jackson *et al*. 2009a), and taking note of the potentialities present in the current historical juncture (see below), I would argue that there are three kinds of knowledge in particular need of de-subjugation within the broader project of CTS. First, there is a need to try and de-subjugate the suppressed knowledge within terrorism studies itself – the immediate and intimate 'knowns' which remain simultaneously 'unknown'. This includes the suppressed knowledge of the ways in which terrorism closely resembles war as a form of political violence, the limited threat to state survival and personal safety that terrorism poses, the ways in which military intervention and political grievance causes terrorism and how terrorism can be reduced through policy change, dialogue and reform. In a sense, this is potentially the easiest knowledge to de-subjugate, as it originates from within the legitimised field, often from respected, authorised 'experts'.

Second, there is a particular need at this time to try and de-subjugate the suppressed knowledge in fields like peace and conflict studies, criminology, anthropology, history, feminist studies and many others. Peace and conflict studies in particular, by virtue of its hard-won knowledge about conflict resolution and its normative commitment to non-violence, holds out real emancipatory potential, especially given the general disillusionment with the profound failures of the past 10 years of war on terror. It would be something of a missed opportunity if CTS did not play a key role in liberating relevant knowledge from the peace and conflict studies field in the coming years.

Finally, there is a normative and analytical imperative to try and de-subjugate the suppressed knowledge of individual and group subjectivity, including those who commit violence (see Mahmood 1996), those who suffer it, those who seek to control it and those who suffer from the broader effects of counterterrorism policies (see Hillyard 1993). In other words, we need to de-subjugate the human experiences, perceptions and understandings of the human beings we seek to study. Such knowledge, I believe, has genuine normative and analytical potential for informing both theory and counterterrorism practice, but remains largely subjugated in the field today in favour of general quantitative research.

There are a wide array of different modes and strategies for de-subjugating knowledge, many of which unfortunately remain underutilised to date. Most obviously, knowledge de-subjugation can be pursued through established forms of academic struggle, including pursuing analytical re-description and disrupting the construction of categories, such as the widely accepted category of 'religious terrorism' (see Gunning and Jackson 2011); engaging in primary research, especially in terms of field research into the subjectivity of different actors (see Toros 2008); applying rigorous standards of scholarship, particularly in terms of definition, concepts and theory and the use of data; examining questions and subjects which remain under-explored within the field, such as the hidden histories of particular episodes of terrorism; and promoting inter- and multi-disciplinarity in teaching and research, among others. Specifically, knowledge from peace and conflict studies – its key authors and major studies – can be deliberately employed in teaching programmes on terrorism, and as the basis for future research projects, as a mode of knowledge de-subjugation.

Related to this, forms of critical deconstruction can be employed as a means of exposing contingency and hegemony in order to destabilise the discourse and create new openings for alternative forms of knowledge. This can be pursued by, for example, revealing ideological bias where objectivity is claimed (see Raphael 2009); 'unearthing the silences' and 'closures' within authoritative terrorism texts (Fortin 1989, p. 190); testing moral reasoning in relation terrorism and counterterrorism (see Goodin 2006, Brecher 2007); re-problematising political violence in general to reveal similarities rather than differences (see Jabri 1996); giving voice to the subjugated and adopting the viewpoints of the subaltern (Mahmood 1996); exposing contradictions, contingencies and hegemonic practices within accepted narratives (Jarvis 2009); and de-exceptionalising terrorist violence within the broader array of violent politics (Dexter 2011). Practical deconstructive methods for such struggle include forms of critical discourse analysis (CDA), predicate analysis, metaphorical analysis, the juxtapositional method and the genealogical method (see Milliken 1999). In particular, following Foucault (1997, p. 10):

> genealogy is, then, a sort of attempt to desubjugate historical knowledges, to set them free, or in other words to enable them to oppose and struggle against the coercion of a unitary, formal, and scientific theoretical discourse . . . to reactivate local knowledges . . . against the scientific hierarchicalization of knowledge and its intrinsic power-effects.

Other modes and strategies of knowledge de-subjugation include a vast array of cultural, artistic, political, media and activist activities, such as art installations, writing novels or plays, making films or music, comedy, street theatre, media commentary, blogging, using social media, creative protest and activism, practitioner engagement and a great many other forms of knowledge-based activity. The important point is recognising that discursive struggle, and in particular the de-subjugation of knowledge, is not restricted to the hallowed halls of academia, but takes place across different fields, domains and social spaces. From this perspective, CTS has to this point perhaps been too narrowly focused and must begin to widen its focus and activities.

Conclusion: from Foucault to Bourdieu

In this article, I have adopted Foucault's concept of 'subjugated knowledges' to try and explore some of the ways in which different forms of knowledge have been suppressed and excluded from the field of terrorism studies and some of the consequences of dominant subjugating practices. I have argued that as a result of such processes, the terrorism field exists in a highly unstable condition whereby some forms of knowledge are simultaneously 'known' and 'unknown', and in which periodic eruptions of knowledge destabilise the dominant discourse until meaning structures can be re-sutured and re-stabilised. Further, I have suggested that there are analytical and normative reasons to try and de-subjugate certain forms of knowledge and a range of methods and approaches which can be employed to de-subjugate relevant knowledges. In particular, the subjugated knowledge of peace and conflict studies is highly relevant and contains genuine emancipatory potential for the field; it should therefore, in my view, form a major focus of de-subjugation efforts by CTS scholars in the coming years.

Employing Foucault's concept, it can be plausibly argued that the rise of CTS represents a kind of eruption or insurrection of knowledge into the terrorism studies and IR fields. Moreover, it is an eruption that is starting to demonstrate genuine transformative potential, particularly as it is institutionally embedded in scholarly activities, such as the *Critical Studies on Terrorism* journal, the British International Studies Association (BISA) Critical Studies on Terrorism Working Group (CSTWG), the Routledge Critical Terrorism Studies Book Series and regular conferences, seminars and conference panels; and discursively embedded in a range of 'knowledgeable practices', such as doctoral research (see, e.g., Jarvis 2009, Spencer 2010, Toros forthcoming), scholarly debates in academic journals (see Hulsse and Spencer 2008, Joseph 2009, Stump 2009, Heath-Kelly 2010, Herring and Stokes 2011) and teaching (see Jackson *et al.* 2011). The success of CTS as an insurrection of subjugated knowledge can also be measured by the amount of criticism it has generated from both media (see, e.g., Jones and Ungerer 2006, Phillips 2008) and academic sources (see Bendle 2008, Jones and Smith 2009, Schmid 2009, Lutz 2010, Dixit and Stump 2011, Jones and Smith 2011). Such opposition can be interpreted as an indication of the degree to which CTS is perceived as being a genuine challenge to the dominant discourse which requires stringent efforts at suppression and hegemonic closure in order to re-stabilise the field.

This modestly successful knowledge eruption has, in my opinion, been the result of the combination of sustained discursive struggle within the structural context of a growing 'rupturing' of the dominant discourse as political and academic disquiet has set in over the failures and insufficiencies of the war on terror and counterterrorism more generally. In other words, the sense of disillusionment with the war on terror has created a discursive opening for a 'decisive intervention' of the kind provided by CTS. Nevertheless, at the same time, we must also recognise the limitations of the CTS insurrection, including its localisation and its failure to have a significant impact outside of academia. The fact is that it is confined primarily to scholars outside of the United States and Israel (where the greatest concentration of recognised terrorism scholars are), and it has failed, with only a few notable exceptions, to have any noticeable impact on public debate, the network of security think-tanks and scholars who provide advice to policymakers, counterterrorism policy itself and popular culture. Even academically, CTS is still rather marginal: very few orthodox terrorism studies and IR scholars attend CTS panels at either BISA or ISA, and CTS scholars are (with occasional exceptions) rarely invited to participate in the most important meetings of the orthodox field's experts.

It is in this context – in which CTS is attempting to de-subjugate knowledge and provide a critical challenge to the field but with limited success thus far – that we need to move from Foucault's notion of 'subjugated knowledge' to Bourdieu's conception of the 'collective intellectual'.[5] While the former provides a useful diagnosis of the field's condition, the latter provides a helpful practical prescription for liberating subjugated knowledges. In fact, it now seems clear upon reflection that although it was unconscious and unintentional at the time, the CTS project has much in common with Bourdieu's conception and practice and the particular pathway he followed in his efforts to promote critical sociology at the time (see Swartz 2003, Lenoir 2006, Oslender 2007).

For example, similar to Bourdieu's critical sociology, CTS aimed in part to subject the terrorism studies field to systematic critique of its problematics, concepts, procedures, practices and, most importantly, accepted knowledge (Lenoir 2006, p. 38). In particular, it aimed to challenge the binary thinking and dualisms of the field, dissect 'dominating power's unproblematic self-portrayal' (Swartz 2003, p. 797, Oslender 2007, pp. 98, 101) and study relations between the fields of cultural production of terrorism and the political field of counterterrorism (Lenoir 2006, p. 41), among others. This would, CTS scholars believed, help to expose underlying power relations and denaturalise accompanying forms of taken-for-granted knowledge, consequently opening up new possibilities for modifying those relations and generating new forms of knowledge, and perhaps even having a broader normative political effect (Swartz 2003, p. 797).

In an important sense then, the CTS project 'envisaged the production of realistic utopias through bringing collaborative expert research to bear on urgent civic issues and making common cause with others to resist the entrenched dogmas of domination'. In particular, it sought to bridge the gap between 'theoretical knowledge production and the practical, directly interested aims of practical understanding of the interaction of social actors' (Oslender 2007, p. 107). Like Bourdieu, CTS has tried to engage in both a (negative) critique of existing structures and practices and a (positive) construction of new research approaches, questions and knowledge – in part through bringing 'other knowledges' and alternative proposals into the terrorism studies knowledge system (Swartz 2003, p. 814, Oslender 2007, pp. 117–118). Importantly, CTS scholars have also worked hard to build legitimacy for critical research on terrorism at the broadest possible level, beginning with the terrorism studies field and then moving outwards into social and political spaces (Swartz 2003, p. 795). Moreover, similar to Bourdieu's normative orientation, CTS scholars view critical social science as an act of resistance; its choice of research topics, for example, has often been 'guided by moral and political considerations: inequality, suffering, and domination' (Swartz 2003, pp. 798, 808).

In strategic terms, like Bourdieu, there has always been a commitment to constructing CTS as a form of 'collective research', aimed at the creation of a 'community of intellectuals' – and an associated series of 'critical networks' (Oslender 2007, p. 98) – comprising not only experts in terrorism but also experts in related disciplines (Lenoir 2006, pp. 25–26). In addition, CTS has aimed at the creation of permanent 'structures, organizations, institutions and programmes that bring about a radical change in the way we perceive, project and relevantly practice and perform' terrorism-related research (Swartz 2003, p. 812, Oslender 2007, p. 108). Many of these structures and practices are relatively small, but like Bourdieu, it is believed that lots of small contributions can add up to a larger intervention – that a swarm of mosquitoes can eventually bring down the rhinoceros of the terrorism studies field and the powerful 'terrorism industry' (Oslender 2007, p. 114).

Finally, as with Bourdieu's transition from intellectual entrepreneur to public intellectual in his later years (Swartz 2003), some CTS scholars have realised the need to take the CTS project, particularly its normative and political implications, more strongly into the public sphere and have attempted to try and engage in the public debate more effectively. They have also recognised the need to move beyond solely intellectual forms of struggle and engage in more diverse and creative cultural forms of activism that go beyond academic production. In short, conceiving of CTS as a 'collective intellectual' project, and taking on board its lessons, holds out genuine transformative potential, and CTS as a community of scholars would do well to pursue its realisation.

Acknowledgements

An earlier version of this article was presented at the following conference: 'A Decade of Terrorism and Counterterrorism since 9/11: Taking Stock and New Directions in Research and Policy', BISA Critical Studies on Terrorism Working Group (CSTWG) Annual Conference, 8–11 September 2011, University of Strathclyde, Glasgow, UK. The author is very grateful for helpful comments from the conference delegates, the editors of this special issue and two anonymous reviewers. All remaining errors belong to the author.

Notes

1. I employ the term 'unknown' to mean that certain knowledge claims rooted in theoretical or empirical research remain unacknowledged in the scholarship or texts of the field. Such work is neither mentioned nor systematically engaged with, and if it is mentioned, it is dismissed as inappropriate, naïve or irrelevant. By contrast, what is 'known' is acknowledged, engaged with and referenced, and therefore, legitimised. In many cases, it is also acted upon in terms of the formation of public policy.
2. The playful allusion to Donald Rumsfeld's famous aphorism from February 2002 is a deliberate attempt to subvert the knowledge paradigm that he sought to insert into the counterterrorism field.
3. In this article, I employ Foucault's concept in a largely methodological manner as a useful tool for exploring a particular puzzle that currently exists within the terrorism field. It does not necessarily signal the adoption of a broader post-structuralist ontology for the deconstruction of all forms of power and resistance in the world today.
4. Of course, Foucault's concept does apply not only to the terrorism studies field but to science and politics more generally. This article focuses solely on the terrorism studies field while recognising that its knowledge subjugation processes are embedded within, and part of, a much broader set of hegemonic processes inherent to contemporary society.
5. The conceptual move from Foucault to Bourdieu is not intended to elide the ontological differences between them, merely to suggest that Bourdieu's concept of the 'collective intellectual' provides an additional and perhaps more developed and pragmatic strategic framework for knowledge de-subjugation action than Foucault's original genealogical method.

Notes on contributor

Richard Jackson is the deputy director of the National Peace and Conflict Studies Centre, University of Otago, New Zealand. He is the author or editor of several books on terrorism and conflict resolution, including *Contemporary Debates on Terrorism* (Routledge, 2012, co-edited with Samuel Justin Sinclair); *Terrorism: A Critical Introduction* (Palgrave Macmillan, 2011, co-authored with Lee Jarvis, Jeroen Gunning and Marie Breen Smyth); *Critical Terrorism Studies: A New Research Agenda* (Routledge, 2009, co-edited with Jeroen Gunning and Marie Breen Smyth); and *Conflict Resolution in the Twenty-First Century: Principles, Methods and Approaches* (Michigan University Press, 2009, co-authored with Jacob Bercovitch).

References

Araj, B., 2008. Harsh state repression as a cause of suicide bombing: the case of the Palestinian-Israeli conflict. *Studies in Conflict & Terrorism*, 31 (4), 284–303.
Baumann, B., 1977. *How it all began: the personal account of a West German urban guerrilla*. Vancouver, BC: Pulp Press.
Bendle, M., 2008. Universities hijacking terrorism studies. *Quadrant* [online] LII (9). Available from: http://www.quadrant.org.au/magazine/issue/2008/9/hijacking-terrorism-studies [Accessed 7 February 2012].

Bergen, P., 2001. *Holy war inc: inside the secret world of Osama bin Laden*. London: Weidenfeld & Nicolson.
Blakeley, R., 2009. *State terrorism and neoliberalism: the north in the south*. London: Routledge.
Brecher, R., 2007. *Torture and the ticking bomb*. London: Wiley-Blackwell.
Burnett, J. and Whyte, D., 2005. Embedded expertise and the new terrorism. *Journal for Crime, Conflict and the Media*, 1 (4), 1–18.
Burton, J., 1979. *Deviance, terrorism and war*. New York: St Martins Press.
Callinicos, A., 2003. *The new mandarins of American power*. Cambridge: Polity Press.
Cody, E., 2010. GOP leaders criticize Obama's Iran policy in rally for opposition group. *The Washington Post* [online], 23 December. Available from: http://texasiraniansociety.org/files/paris-ridge-juliani-boton122210.pdf [Accessed 8 February 2012].
Cole, D., 2011. Chewing gum for terrorists. *The New York Times* [online], 2 January. Available from: http://www.nytimes.com/2011/01/03/opinion/03cole.html?_r=3&pagewanted=print [Accessed 20 May 2011].
Crelinsten, R., 2009. *Counterterrorism*. Cambridge: Polity.
Dalacoura, K., 2006. Islamist terrorism and the Middle East democratic deficit: political exclusion, repression and the causes of extremism. *Democratization*, 13 (3), 508–525.
Della Porta, D., 1995. *Social movements, political violence, and the state: a comparative analysis of Italy and Germany*. Cambridge: Cambridge University Press.
Dershowitz, A., 2002. *Why terrorism works: understanding the threat, responding to the challenge*. New Haven, CT: Yale University Press.
Dexter, H., 2011. Terrorism and violence. *Paper prepared for the conference, 'A decade of terrorism and counter-terrorism since 9/11: taking stock and new directions in research and policy'*, 8–11 September. University of Strathclyde, Glasgow, UK.
Dixit, P. and Stump, J., 2011. A response to Jones and Smith: it's not as bad as it seems; or, five ways to move critical terrorism studies forward. *Studies in Conflict and Terrorism*, 34 (6), 501–511.
Dodds, K., 2007. Steve Bell's eye: cartoons, geopolitics and the visualization of the 'war on terror'. *Security Dialogue*, 38 (2), 157–177.
Eland, I., 1998. Does U.S. intervention overseas breed terrorism? The historical record. CATO Institute Foreign Policy Briefing, 17 December. Available from: http://www.cato.org/pubs/fpbriefs/fpb-050es.html [Accessed 5 September 2011].
English, R., 2003. *Armed struggle: the history of the IRA*. London: Pan Macmillan.
English, R., 2009. *Terrorism: how to respond*. Oxford: Oxford University Press.
Feldman, A., 1994. *Formations of violence: the narrative of the body and political terror in northern Ireland*. Rev. ed. Chicago, IL: The University of Chicago Press.
Fortin, A., 1989. Notes on a terrorist text: a critical use of Roland Barthes' textual analysis in the interpretation of political meaning. *In*: J. Der Derian and M. Shapiro, eds. *International/intertextual relations: postmodern readings in world politics*. New York: Lexington Books, 189–206.
Foucault, M., 1991. Governmentality. *In*: G. Burchell, C. Gordon, and P. Miller, eds. *The Foucault effect: studies in governmentality*. Trans. R. Braidotti and revised C. Gordon. Chicago, IL: University of Chicago Press, 87–104.
Foucault, M., 1997. *Society must be defended: lectures at the college de France, 1975-76*. Trans. D. Macey. London: Allen Lane.
Franks, J., 2009. Rethinking the roots of terrorism: beyond orthodox terrorism theory – a critical research agenda. *Global Society*, 23 (2), 153–176.
Goodin, R., 2006. *What's wrong with terrorism?* Cambridge: Polity Press.
Gordon, A., 2010. Can terrorism become a scientific discipline? A diagnostic study. *Critical Studies on Terrorism*, 3 (3), 437–458.
Gunning, J. and Jackson, R., 2011. What's so 'religious' about 'religious terrorism'? *Critical Studies on Terrorism*, 4 (3), 369–388.
Hastings, T., 2004. *Nonviolent responses to terrorism*. Jefferson, NC: MacFarland.
Heath-Kelly, C., 2010. Critical terrorism studies, critical theory and the 'naturalistic fallacy'. *Security Dialogue*, 41 (3), 235–254.
Hellmich, H., 2011. *Al-Qaeda: from global network to local franchise*. London: Zed Books.
Herring, E. and Stokes, D., 2011. Critical realism and historical materialism as resources for critical terrorism studies. *Critical Studies on Terrorism*, 4 (1), 5–21.
Hillyard, P., 1993. *Suspect community: people's experience of the prevention of terrorism acts in Britain*. London: Pluto.

Hiro, D., 2002. *War without end: the rise of Islamist terrorism and global response*. London: Routledge.
Hulsse, R. and Spencer, A., 2008. The metaphor of terror: terrorism studies and the constructivist turn. *Security Dialogue*, 39 (6), 571–592.
Ilardi, G., 2004. Redefining the issues: the future of terrorism research and the search for empathy. *In*: A. Silke, ed. *Research on terrorism: trends, achievements and failures*. London: Frank Cass, 214–228.
Jabri, V., 1996. *Discourses on violence: conflict analysis reconsidered*. Manchester: Manchester University Press.
Jackson, R., 2005. *Writing the war on terrorism: language, politics and counterterrorism*. Manchester: Manchester University Press.
Jackson, R., 2007. Playing the politics of fear: writing the terrorist threat in the war on terrorism. *In*: G. Kassimeris, ed. *Playing politics with terrorism: a user's guide*. New York: Columbia University Press, 176–202.
Jackson, R., 2008. The ghosts of state terror: knowledge, politics and terrorism studies. *Critical Studies on Terrorism*, 1 (3), 377–392.
Jackson, R., 2009. Knowledge, power and politics in the study of political terrorism. *In*: R. Jackson, J. Gunning, and M. Breen Smyth, eds. *Critical terrorism studies: a new research agenda*. Abingdon: Routledge, 66–83.
Jackson, R., Breen Smyth, M., and Gunning, J., 2009a. Critical terrorism studies: framing a new research agenda. *In*: R. Jackson, J. Gunning, and M. Breen Smyth, eds. *Critical terrorism studies: a new research agenda*. Abingdon: Routledge, 216–236.
Jackson, R., Gunning, J., and Breen Smyth, M., eds., 2009b. *Critical terrorism studies: a new research agenda*. Abingdon: Routledge.
Jackson, R., et al., 2011. *Terrorism: a critical introduction*. Co-authors L. Jarvis, J. Gunning, and M. Breen Smyth. Basingstoke: Palgrave-Macmillan.
Jarvis, L., 2009. *Times of terror: discourse, temporality and the war on terror*. Basingstoke: Palgrave-Macmillan.
Jenkins, B., 1998. Will terrorists go nuclear? A reappraisal. *In*: H. Kushner, ed. *The future of terrorism: violence in the new millennium*. London: Sage, 225–249.
Johnston, H., 2008. Ritual, strategy and deep culture in the Chechen national movement. *Critical Studies on Terrorism*, 1 (3), 321–342.
Jones, D. and Smith, M., 2009. We are all terrorists now: critical – or hypocritical – studies on terrorism? *Studies in Conflict and Terrorism*, 32 (4), 292–302.
Jones, D. and Ungerer, C., 2006. Delusion reigns in terror studies. *The Australian* [online], 15 September. Available from: http://www.theaustralian.com.au/news/opinion/david-martin-jones-and-carl-ungerer-delusion-reigns-in-terror-s/story-e6frg6zo-1111112213617 [Accessed 7 February 2012].
Jones, M. and Smith, M., 2011. Terrorology and methodology: a reply to Dixit and Stump. *Studies in Conflict and Terrorism*, 34 (6), 512–522.
Jorgensen, M. and Phillips, L., 2002. *Discourse analysis as theory and method*. London: Sage.
Joseph, J., 2009. Critical of what? Terrorism and its study. *International Relations*, 23 (1), 93–98.
Khadra, J., 2007. *The attack*. London: Vintage.
Khaled, L., 1973. *My people shall live: the autobiography of a revolutionary*. London: Hodder and Stoughton.
Lambert, R., 2011. *Countering al-Qaeda in London: police and Muslims in partnership*. London: Hurst.
Laqueuer, W., 1977. *Terrorism*. London: Weidenfeld and Nicolson.
Lawrence, B., ed., 2005. *Messages to the world: the statements of Osama bin Laden*. Trans. J. Howarth. London: Verso.
Lenoir, R., 2006. Scientific habitus: Pierre Bourdieu and the collective intellectual. *Theory, Culture & Society*, 23 (6), 25–43.
Lutz, J., 2010. A critical view of critical terrorism studies. *Perspectives on Terrorism*, 4 (6), 31–40.
Mahmood, C., 1996. *Fighting for faith and nation: dialogues with Sikh militants*. Philadelphia: University of Pennsylvania Press.
Marciano, F., 2003. *Casa Rossa*. London: Vintage.
McClintock, M., 1992. *Instruments of statecraft: US guerrilla warfare, counterinsurgency, and counterterrorism, 1940-1990*. New York: Pantheon Books.

Miller, D. and Mills, T., 2009. The terror experts and the mainstream media: the expert nexus and its dominance in the news media. *Critical Studies on Terrorism*, 2 (3), 414–437.

Milliken, J., 1999. The study of discourse in international relations: a critique of research and methods. *European Journal of International Relations*, 5 (2), 225–254.

Mueller, J., 2005. Six rather unusual propositions about terrorism; and: response. *Terrorism and Political Violence*, 17, 487–505, 523–528.

Neumann, P., 2007. Negotiating with terrorists. *Foreign Affairs*, 86 (1), 128–138.

Oslender, U., 2007. The resurfacing of the public intellectual: towards the proliferation of public spaces of critical intervention. *ACME: An International E-Journal for Critical Geographies*, 6 (1), 98–123.

Pape, R., 2005. *Dying to win: the strategic logic of suicide terrorism*. New York: Random House.

Pappe, I., 2009. De-terrorising the Palestinian national struggle: the roadmap to peace. *Critical Studies on Terrorism*, 2 (2), 127–146.

Paradise Now, 2005. Film. Directed by Hany Abu-Assad. Palestinian Territories: Augustus Films.

Phillips, M., 2008. Terror in academia. *The Spectator* [online], 15 April. Available from: http://www.spectator.co.uk/melaniephillips/612861/terror-in-academia.thtml [Accessed 7 February 2012].

Purvis, T. and Hunt, A., 1993. Discourse, ideology, discourse, ideology, discourse, ideology . . . . *The British Journal of Sociology*, 44 (3), 473–499.

Ramsbotham, O., Woodhouse, T., and Miall, H., 2005. *Contemporary conflict resolution: the prevention, management and transformation of deadly conflicts*. 2nd ed. Cambridge: Polity.

Ranstorp, M., ed., 2006. *Mapping terrorism research: state of the art, gaps and future direction*. London: Routledge.

Raphael, S., 2009. In the service of power: terrorism studies and US intervention in the global south. *In*: R. Jackson, J. Gunning, and M. Breen Smyth, eds. *Critical terrorism studies: a new research agenda*. Abingdon: Routledge, 49–65.

Reid, E., 1993. Terrorism research and the diffusion of ideas. *Knowledge and Policy*, 6 (1), 17–37.

Reid, E., 1997. Evolution of a body of knowledge: an analysis of terrorism research. *Information Processing and Management*, 33 (1), 91–106.

Richmond, O., 2003. Realizing hegemony? Symbolic terrorism and the roots of conflict. *Studies in Conflict & Terrorism*, 26, 289–309.

Schmid, A., 2004. Frameworks for conceptualising terrorism. *Terrorism and Political Violence*, 16 (2), 197–221.

Schmid, A., 2009. Book reviews. *Perspectives on Terrorism*, 3 (4), 61–62. Available from: http://www.terrorismanalysts.com/pt/index.php/pot/article/view/83/170 [Accessed 3 September 2011].

Sederberg, P., 1995. Conciliation as counter-terrorist strategy. *Journal of Peace Research*, 32 (3), 295–312.

Silberstein, S., 2002. *War of words: language, politics and 9/11*. London: Routledge.

Silke, A., ed., 2004. *Research on terrorism: trends, achievements and failures*. London: Frank Cass.

Silke, A., 2009. Contemporary terrorism studies: issues in research. *In*: R. Jackson, J. Gunning, and M. Breen Smyth, eds. *Critical terrorism studies: a new research agenda*. Abingdon: Routledge, 34–48.

Soans, R., 2005. *Talking to terrorists*. First performed at the Royal Theatre, 21 April 2005. London: Oberon books.

Spencer, A., 2010. *The tabloid terrorist: the predicative construction of new terrorism in the media*. Basingstoke: Palgrave Macmillan.

Stampnitzky, L., forthcoming. *Disciplining terror: how experts and others invented terrorism*. Cambridge: Cambridge University Press.

Stone, D., 1996. *Capturing the political imagination: think tanks and the policy process*. London: Frank Cass.

Stump, J., 2009. The artful side of the terrorism discourse: a response to Hulsse and Spencer. *Security Dialogue*, 40 (6), 661–665.

Swartz, D., 2003. From critical sociology to public intellectual: Pierre Bourdieu and politics. *Theory and Society*, 32, 791–823.

Taylor, P., 2011. *Talking to terrorists: a personal journey from the IRA to al Qaeda*. London: Harper Press.

The Battle of Algiers, 1966. Film. Directed by Gillo Pontecorvo. Italy: Igor Film.

The Terrorist, 1998. Film. Directed by Santosh Sivan. India: Moderne Gallerie Motion Picture.

Thornton, T., 1964. Terror as a weapon of political agitation. *In*: H. Eckstein, ed. *Internal war*. New York: Free Press, 71–99.
Tilly, C., 2004. Terror, terrorism, terrorists. *Sociological Theory*, 22 (1), 5–13.
Toros, H., 2008. Terrorists, scholars and ordinary people: confronting terrorism studies with field experiences. *Critical Studies on Terrorism*, 1 (2), 279–292.
Toros, H., forthcoming. *Terrorism, talking and transformation: a critical approach*. Abingdon: Routledge.
Yallop, D., 1993. *To the ends of the earth: the hunt for the jackal*. London: Jonathan Cape.
Zartman, I.W., 2003. Negotiating with terrorists. *International Negotiation*, 8, 443–450.
Zulaika, J., 1988. *Basque violence: metaphor and sacrament*. Reno: University of Nevada Press.
Zulaika, J., 2009. *Terrorism: the self-fulfilling prophesy*. Chicago, IL: University of Chicago Press.
Zulaika, J. and Douglass, W., 1996. *Terror and taboo: the follies, fables, and faces of terrorism*. New York: Routledge.

Don't confuse me with the facts: knowledge claims and terrorism

Michael Stohl

Department of Communication, University of California, Santa Barbara, CA, USA

> It became commonplace after 11 September 2001 to declare that the events changed 'everything' and that the world would never again be as it was before that date. Many spoke of the dividing line of the pre-9/11 and post-9/11 world, and it became commonplace to assert that the events conclusively demonstrated the validity of the thesis that there was a 'new' terrorism, at base religious and apocalyptic, more networked rather than hierarchical and very different from the 'old' terrorism. This article reflects upon and evaluates the development of knowledge claims about insurgent terrorism and measures them against the standard of how well these claims have advanced the formulation of theories of terrorism that can be subjected to observational testing. The article examines changes in the lethality of terrorism, the characterisations, boundaries and control structures of the network claims and differences amongst the old and new terrorists and concludes that claims of a 'new terrorism' are vastly misleading.

Introduction

On 11 September 2001, Michael Nicholson, one of the members of the founding British International Studies Association (BISA) executive committee and after whom BISA's Doctoral Thesis Prize is named, received the first Lewis Fry Richardson Lifetime Achievement Award from the European Consortium for Political Research for his work on conflict. Unfortunately, at the time of the award he was very ill and he died on 4 October 2011. I reference Michael Nicholson's award not only for its stunning association with the 10th anniversary of the events about which we have gathered to reflect, but also because I believe that his work provides important insights into the study of terrorism and our accumulation of knowledge about terrorism. While many international relations scholars are familiar with Nicholson's work on conflict theory and international relations and his work on epistemology, for example, *The Scientific Analysis of Social Behaviour: A Defense of Empiricism in Social Science* (1983), few have attempted to think about terrorism in the context of building the kind of empirical social science for which Nicholson strived.

Nicholson sought to provide a theoretically and methodologically grounded basis for a systematic and scientifically rigorous causal analysis in international relations (IR). The

---

This article was originally presented as a keynote address at the conference, 'A Decade of Terrorism and Counter-Terrorism since 9/11: Taking Stock and New Directions in Research and Policy', University of Strathclyde, UK, 10 September 2011.

central purpose was to justify 'what can loosely be called the empiricist tradition in the social sciences, which has as its ambition the formulation of testable theories of human behaviour in various contexts' (1983, p. 6). In this context, Nicholson argued that:

> Three rather loose principles can be stated as being the requirements of a body of scientific belief. First, it should be possible to form propositions which are empirical in the sense that observations can confirm or refute them. Secondly, these statements should be possible to make with a minimum of ambiguity so a writer and his various readers all understand as closely as is possible the same thing. Thirdly, our belief in the truth of statements should be independent of our ethical beliefs. (1983, p. 6)

Nicholson himself began the attempt with a 1986 essay on 'Conceptual Problems of Studying State Terrorism' in which he sought to demonstrate that 'we can evolve theories of state terrorism that are of the same epistemological status as other theories of human behavior' (1986, p. 28), and he investigated the particular issues and problems attendant in such an endeavour.

In the spirit of Nicholson's work and in the context of the 10th anniversary of the Richardson award and the tragedy of September 11, this article reflects on and evaluates the development of knowledge claims about insurgent terrorism and measures them against the standard of how well these claims have advanced the formulation of theories of terrorism where these theories are sets of logically interrelated statements that can be subjected to observational testing. In this context, 'testing' means the confrontation of propositions with empirical evidence such that we can conceive of what evidence would be relevant for the statements to be true and also false.[1] I will argue further that the key to testing is the principle of falsifiability. Falsifiability requires attention to definition, operationalisation, data collection and hypothesis formulation, and it is my contention that all of these are in rather short supply in the study of terrorism. Hence, the title of the article: 'Don't confuse me with the facts: knowledge claims and the study of terrorism'.[2]

The problem

There have been relatively few who have approached the study of terrorism as Michael Nicholson would have wanted us to do. In what follows, I argue that it is our approach to knowledge about terrorism that is the underlying cause of the continuing inability to accumulate and test knowledge claims.

The vast majority of the scholars who have investigated terrorism have not approached their research with the purpose of developing theoretically grounded empirical studies, and consequently they have not applied positivist research methods to its study. This has been a consistent finding of reviews of the 'state of the art' over the past three decades. Schmid and Jongman (1988) argued that: 'Perhaps as much as 80 percent of the literature is not research-based in any rigorous sense . . . ' (p. 219). As a result, Schmid and Jongman concluded that: 'Much of the writing in the crucial areas of terrorism research . . . is impressionistic, superficial, and at the same time also pretentious, venturing far reaching generalisations on the basis of episodal evidence' (1988, p. 177). Ariel Merari concurred: 'By and large, terrorism literature is composed mainly of studies which rely on relatively weak research methods' (cited in Schmid and Jongman 1988, p. 179). And Ted Gurr (1988) agrees, arguing that: 'With a few clusters of exceptions there is, in fact, a disturbing lack of good empirically-grounded research on terrorism' (p. 2). The consequence, as Merari wrote in 1991, is that terrorism research 'resembles hearsay rather than twentieth century science' (Merari 1991, p. 95); and further, that 'This may well be an understatement' (p. 220).

In 2001, Andrew Silke compared this dearth of quantitative analysis in terrorism research for the period at the end of the 1990s with other social sciences, specifically forensic psychology and criminology. By analysing articles published from 1995 to 2000, Silke found 86% of forensic psychology and 60% of criminology scholarly articles utilised statistics. In contrast, only 20% of the scholarly articles on terrorism attempted a quantitative analysis. He concluded that:

> Ultimately, terrorism research is not in a healthy state. It exists on a diet of fast food research: quick, cheap, ready-to-hand and nutritionally dubious . . . It was found that the problems identified in 1988 [by Schmid and Jongman] remain as serious as ever. (Silke 2001, p. 221)

In 2005, Lum *et al.* (2006) systematically identified 14,006 articles about terrorism published between 1971 and 2002 in all the available library electronic databases. They further identified which of the articles were published in peer-reviewed outlets by generating a list of peer-reviewed journals, resulting in 6041 articles. The articles were then sorted with respect to year of publication, subject matter and the general methodology used for the research study.

There are some noteworthy findings in these sorts. As Figure 1 in their article indicates, among the entire 14,006 works located, approximately 54% were published in 2001 and 2002. The 54% written in 2001 and 2002 represent the enormous outpouring on interest and concern after September 11 and are a remarkable total for just two years. They contribute heavily to the second finding about the nature of the publications. Focusing on the peer-reviewed articles, 96% (5800) were classified by the authors as 'Thought pieces'; that is, 'articles where authors discussed an issue theoretically or offered an opinion'. [I should note parenthetically here that by theoretically they mean without grounding in data.] And 1% (60) were 'case studies'; that is, articles 'which examined a particular situation from a (usually) historical approach'. Finally, only 3% (181) involved 'Empirical analysis'; that is, a study in which 'an analysis (either quantitative or qualitative) had been conducted on terrorism data'. In short, it is easy to concur with a 2004 analysis by Andrew Silke that: 'By and large, terrorism literature is composed mainly of studies which rely on relatively weak research methods' (Silke 2004, p. 11). Thus, I would argue that much of the 'knowledge' of terrorism is based on what might be best described as the accumulated 'wisdom'[3] of a generation of scholars who have studied events, perpetrators, responses and contexts, but not, in general, within the confines of a scientific paradigm of agreed upon data, definitions, concepts, relationships and methods.

There has been little change over the past half-decade since Silke and Lum *et al.* have written. The percentage of studies on terrorism conducted within the 'scientific paradigm' remains at the same levels as in the past decades, and the approach of the 10th anniversary of 9/11 actually produced a bubble of research, which though not as large as that identified by Lum *et al.* following the actual events was similarly composed primarily of what they defined as 'thought' pieces reflecting on the meaning and implications of the events of that day and the responses taken as a consequence. Further, as Martha Crenshaw commented in 1981, in a statement that is unfortunately still accurate today:

> Even the most persuasive of statements about terrorism are not cast in the form of testable propositions, nor are they broadly comparative in origin or intent . . . In general, propositions about terrorism lack logical comparability, specification of the relationships of variables to

each other, a rank ordering of variables in terms of explanatory power. (Cited in Schmid and Jongman 1988, p. 41)

To further reduce the possibilities of the accumulation of knowledge and the production of theoretically grounded work, the vast majority of the literature on terrorism consists of one-offs, that is, work by scholars enraged or energised by a particular act, for example, 9/11, and mobilised to contribute something to the debate – hence the vast outpouring of research discovered by Lum *et al.* after 9/11. The consequence is that it is rare for the majority of contributions to place the study of terrorism either within a historical context of the event itself or within a scholarly context that builds upon the studies which have come before. Rarer still is the placement of these studies in the context of the political conflicts and the contest for power – including trust and legitimacy – that underlies the conflict, violence and choice of terrorism as a strategy or tactic. The net result is far less accumulation of knowledge than might have been expected given all the scholarly time and effort that has been invested in the past four decades.

September 11 and the new terrorism

It became routine after 11 September 2001 to declare that the events changed 'everything' and that the world would never again be as it was before that date. Many spoke of the dividing line of the pre-9/11 and post-9/11 world, and it became commonplace to assert that the events conclusively demonstrated the validity of the thesis that there was a 'new' terrorism, at base religious and apocalyptic, more networked rather than hierarchical and very different from the 'old' terrorism (Tucker 2001, p. 1).[4] How well do these knowledge claims about the new terrorism fare when they are confronted with the data on insurgent terrorism of the past 40 years?

Terrorism as communicatively constituted violence

To answer the question, I begin with an assertion: terrorism is communicatively constituted violence. To justify that assertion I will proffer a definition of terrorism and argue that this definition establishes the boundaries that differentiate terrorism from other acts of violence and why it is important to do so. It is my contention that, whether you accept the nuances of my definition or do not, it is important to keep the distinctions between terrorism and violence clear when evaluating knowledge claims about terrorism. Alex Schmid, who has been cataloguing definitions of terrorism for the past 30 years, recently (2009) recorded more than 200 different definitions of terrorism used in the social science and policy literature. Many of the definitional conflicts are centred on the 'legitimacy' of the perpetrator (state or insurgent, legal or illegal) and the standing of the victim (combatant or non-combatant, innocent or culpable). However, when one sorts through the definitions the keywords that distinguish terrorism from violence in the vast majority of the definitions, despite their variety, are *purposeful, violence, fear, victim* and *audience*. Incorporating these elements, I define terrorism as: 'The purposeful act or threat of the act of violence to create fear and/or compliant behavior in a victim and/or audience of the act or threat' (Stohl 1988, p. 3).

It is intentional that this definition does not distinguish among perpetrators who are in-groups and out-groups, state or non-state actors or legitimate or illegitimate wielders of violence. Rather, the definition focuses upon the act or threat of the act of violence and the victims and audience(s) to whom it is directed. What this definition highlights is that the victims of the violent act must be distinguished from the multiple targets of the act, that is, the audience(s) of that violence. Thus, for an act of violence to be considered as *terrorism* it has to *purposefully communicate* a message. Three points need be emphasised here. First, all acts of violence may be interpreted as sending a message, but not all actions intentionally send a message. When a political murder (assassination) occurs, its 'purpose' may simply be the elimination of the person murdered, no more, no less. The perpetrator has no intention of sending a message to a wider audience and such assassinations (or failed assassinations) should not be considered terrorism. That does not, however, imply that some members of the audience will not, as a result, be fearful. Second, the use of intent is consistent with the definition found in the criminal codes of many nations including, for example, the Australian Criminal Code Act 1995, Australian Terrorist Act; the United Kingdom's Terrorism Act 2000 amended by the Terrorism Act 2006; Canada's 2001 Anti-Terrorism Act; the Uganda Terror Act of 2002; and in both Title 18 (domestic) and Title 22 (international) of the United States Code. Third, the operational definitions contained in both the scholarly and the government databases utilised by almost all analysts of terrorist behaviour employ the concept of intent, premeditation or purpose (see Grabosky and Stohl 2010, p. 40).

It is also important to emphasise the reality of multiple audiences of the message. These audiences consist of those who are targeted for fear; those who approve the targeting of the fearful audience and who might draw satisfaction from the damage or fear of the reprisal; and those who simply acquiesce to the act. When we examine an act of terrorism, we are cognisant that the actions are denoted by three key elements. First, threatened or perpetrated violence is directed at some victim(s). Second, the violent actor intends for violence to induce terror in witnesses (mediated or unmediated) who are generally distinct from the victims – the victims are instrumental. Third, the violent actor (an insurgent group or the state itself) intends or expects that witnesses (the audience) will effectuate a desired outcome, either directly (in which case the witness is the target) or indirectly through pressure on political actors who can effectuate the change (in which case the witnesses and the target are distinct – the witness is also instrumental). What distinguishes terrorism from other acts of violence, in addition to the act of violence carrying a message, that is, its communicative constitution, are its instrumentality and its targets. And regardless of the horror of the violence, whether we are examining insurgent or state terrorism, how the multiple audiences of the terror react is almost always far more important than the act itself and the instrumental victims who are the direct casualties of the act. Clearly then, terrorists are primarily interested in communicating with the audience(s) – not the victims and, to reiterate, that is the core of what distinguishes the terrorist act from the violent act whose purpose is simply the target itself (see Schelling 1966, pp. 16–17).

At the same time, terrorists are also interested in reinforcing or creating the boundaries between and among the groups in the audience and employ their violence and the anticipated reactions of the audience to assist the process of boundary creation and maintenance. This is why the reactions of the audience are the most important part of the process in determining the actual success of both producing fear and creating boundaries, far more important than the original act of violence by the terrorist. The vast majorities who receive that message in the contemporary global environment are not eyewitnesses in the event's locale; they are a member of the audience as a consequence of the global media environment. It is also important to remember that there are now many audiences for the messages that are communicated and that these audiences do not all receive or interpret the 'message' in the same way.

The delivery of such messages primarily has been 'mediated', that is, brought to the global audience through print in the form of newspapers for the past two centuries, radio for the past 100 years and television for the past 60 years. One of the extraordinary changes that we have seen in the past decade is the emergence and ever more widespread distribution of social media, and thus the delivery of this message is now less dependent upon choices made by governments and traditional media about what information and news should be distributed to the public. This may very well have important consequences in future years on how the public reacts to reports of terrorism, because there will be implications for framing the report of events and the choice of whom brings 'the news'.

The 'new' terrorism

In 1995, Bruce Hoffman asserted:

> ... the religious imperative for terrorism is the most important characteristic of terrorist activity today ... and none of the 11 identifiable terrorist groups active in 1968 (the year credited with having marked the advent of modern, international terrorism) could be classified as 'religious.' Today, at least twenty percent of the approximately 50 known terrorist groups active throughout the world can be described as having a dominant religious component or motivation. Admittedly, many contemporary terrorist groups – such as the Provisional Irish Republic Army, their Protestant counterparts in Northern Ireland, the Palestine Liberation Organization, various Armenian terrorist movements, and both the Tamil Tigers and J.V.P. in Sri Lanka – have a strong religious element. But the political aspect is the dominant characteristic of these groups, as evidenced by the pre-eminence of their nationalist or irredentist aims. (Hoffman 1995, p. 272)

In 1998, Hoffman further argued:

> whereas secular terrorists attempt to appeal to a constituency of . . . actual supporters or potential sympathizers . . . religious terrorists are at once activists and constituents engaged in what they regard as a total war. They seek to appeal to no other constituency than themselves. (1998, p. 95)

A little later, Walter Laqueur, another prominent voice for the idea of a new terrorism, asserted:

> the 'new' terrorism has increasingly become indiscriminate in the choice of its victims. Its aim is no longer to conduct propaganda but to effect maximum destruction. [An] important difference between the old terrorism and the new terrorism is the crucial importance of paranoiac elements in the terrorism of far right and extreme left, perhaps most of all in terrorists inspired by religious fanaticism. (2003, p. 9)

Proponents of the new terrorism were thus arguing that terrorism had been transformed. They asserted that no longer was the violence of terrorism communicating what Schelling (1966, pp. 16–17) had identified as the message of pain and the promise of more for coercive bargaining purposes and political ends. The new terrorism was described as a form of violence that not only had lethality as its ultimate goal but also eschewed political goals. As Martha Crenshaw argued:

> Nevertheless, the assumption of the 'new terrorism' school of thought is that rather than choosing among alternative ways of achieving political ends, the new terrorists seek primarily to kill. Lethality is their aim rather than their means. (2008, p. 123)

The declared consequence was that Jenkins' (1975) observation that 'terrorists want a lot of people watching not a lot of people dead' (p. 16) was no longer valid. For example, Bongar (2007, p. 5) argued that 'today it is more accurate to say that terrorists want a lot of people dead – and even more people crippled by fear and grief'. Even Jenkins himself seemed to now question his earlier statement. In 2006, he wrote:

> At one time, I wrote that terrorists wanted a lot of people watching, not a lot of people dead. They were limited not only by access to weapons but by self-constraint. Mayhem as such was seldom an objective. Terrorists had a sense of morality, a self-image, operational codes, and practical concerns – they wanted to maintain group cohesion, avoid alienating perceived constituents, and avoid provoking public outrage, which could lead to crackdowns. But these constraints gave way to large-scale indiscriminate violence as terrorists engaged in protracted, brutal conflicts; as the more squeamish dropped out; as terrorism became commonplace and the need for headlines demanded higher body counts; and as ethnic hatred and religious fanaticism replaced political agendas.
>
> Perhaps the most striking development is that terrorism has become bloodier, in terms of what acts are committed and how many victims are involved. The order of magnitude has increased almost every decade. In the 1970s the bloodiest incidents caused fatalities in the tens. In the 1980s, fatalities from the worst incidents were in the hundreds; by the 1990s, attacks on this scale had become more frequent. On 9/11 there were thousands of fatalities, and there could have been far more. We now contemplate plausible scenarios in which tens of thousands might die. (Jenkins 2006, pp. 118–119)

If the new terrorism thesis was correct, the data should show significantly more deaths beginning with the period in which it was first observed than in previous periods. The lethality curve should be upward (and perhaps dramatically so). In this next section, we will review multiple data claims and evidence from the major data sets that scholars have employed to examine the claim of increasing lethality. To set the stage, we start with data presented by Jenkins (1988, p. 254) in a list titled 'Deaths from major incidents of sabotage and terrorism'. Jenkins identifies the most deadly terrorist incidents since the turn of the twentieth century. The top 10 are given below (Table 1).

Jenkins' data indicate that two of the top 10 events took place in the 1920s, one in 1946, one in 1960, four in the 1970s and two in the 1980s. This is not a progression of major events that one would expect given Jenkins' description of what was occurring over time.

Similarly, Peter Flemming, using the International Terrorism: Attributes of Terrorist Events (ITERATE) data set, compiled the following list from the period 1968 to 1998 (Table 2).

Table 1. Deaths from major incidents of sabotage and terrorism.

1979 – fire in Iran theatre (430 killed)
1985 – bomb aboard Air India flight (329)
1983 – bombing of marine barracks (241)
1978 – bombing of PLO headquarters in Beirut (160)
1925 – bombing of Sofia cathedral (128)
1921 – bombing of palace (100)
1960 – sabotage of ammunition ship (100)
1977 – hijacking and crash of airliner (100)
1946 – bombing of King David hotel (91)
1974 – bomb aboard airliner (88)

Note: PLO, Palestine Liberation Organization.
Source: Jenkins (1988).

Table 2. Flemming's most deadly international terrorist incidents (1968–1998).

1. 1985. The bombing of Air India Flight 182 off the coast of Ireland – 329 dead
2. 1998. The bombing of the American Embassy in Nairobi, Kenya – 291 dead
3. 1988. The bombing of Pan Am 103 over Lockerbie, Scotland – 273 dead
4. 1989. The bombing of UTA Flight 772 over Niger – 171 dead
5. 1978. The bombing of PLO apartment in Beirut, Lebanon – 161 dead
6. 1987. The bombing of KAL Flight 858 over South East Asia – 115 dead
7. 1983. The bombing of an Emirates Boeing 737 near Dubai – 111 dead
8. 1989. The bombing of Avianca Flight 203 over Colombia – 110 dead
9. 1981. The sabotage of a Far Eastern Air transport near Taiwan – 110 dead
10. 1977. The hijacking and crash of a Malaysian Airlines 737 – 100 dead

Note: PLO, Palestine Liberation Organization.

Both Flemming and Jenkins concur that the deadliest recorded incident of international terrorism until 11 September 2001 occurred on 23 June 1985 with the bombing of Air India Flight 182, a Boeing 747 en route from Toronto, Canada, to Bombay, India.

What we can see when we compare the two lists is that the 1980s did indeed have a greater number of deadliest terrorist incidents than the 1970s, but the 1990s did not have a greater number of more deadly incidents than the 1980s. Despite the observations of commentators such as Hoffman and others, there was not a striking increase in terrorist spectaculars in the 1990s. In addition, strikingly, most of these major deaths were as a result of the groups that are considered old terrorists and not new terrorists. At the same time, it is noteworthy that there is a major discrepancy in these lists. Definitional integrity in the ITERATE list keeps the 23 October 1983 bombing of the Marine barracks in Beirut, Lebanon – 241 dead and at least 80 wounded (the same day also saw a similar attack launched against the French military in Lebanon, resulting in the deaths of 58 soldiers and the wounding of at least another 15; see Mickolus *et al.* 1989, p. 451) – off the list, since the targets were Marines, who are not generally considered as non-combatants, which the data set definition of terrorism requires.

John Mueller, in a paper 'Reacting to Terrorism' (2007) presented at the International Studies Association (ISA), argued that the reaction to the threat of terrorism is, as indicated in the book length argument based on this and other data, *Overblown*. The data he presents are from the US Department of State on international terrorist events. If you focus on the line representing global deaths from international terrorist events, you can see that there is no dramatic increase in lethality in the overall series and that 9/11, thankfully, is clearly an absolutely horrendous exception to the data series. There is no clear increasing lethality trend, and in fact, absent 9/11 the trend is in the other direction for many of the years since 1985 and most assuredly during the years that the arguments for the new terrorism were being formulated (Figure 1).

One further piece of evidence on lethality comes from the National Terrorism Center (NTC) Report Series. One of the analyses that the report contains is the distribution of events with 0, 1–2, 2–4, 5–9 and more than 10 fatalities. This data series includes both domestic and international terrorist events. If we look at the 2009 report, we can see that only 234 of 10,999 events or 2% have 10 or more fatalities, while more than 81% have one or no fatalities. Peter Flemming and I examined the international terrorism series for 1968–1994 and found that 93.1% had one or no fatalities (Flemming and Stohl 2001). That 12% difference might appear to be significant, but the NTC data set includes domestic terrorism events, as well as international and also includes the terrorism that occurs in the context of the Iraq and Afghanistan wars. Thus, while there is more lethality in the

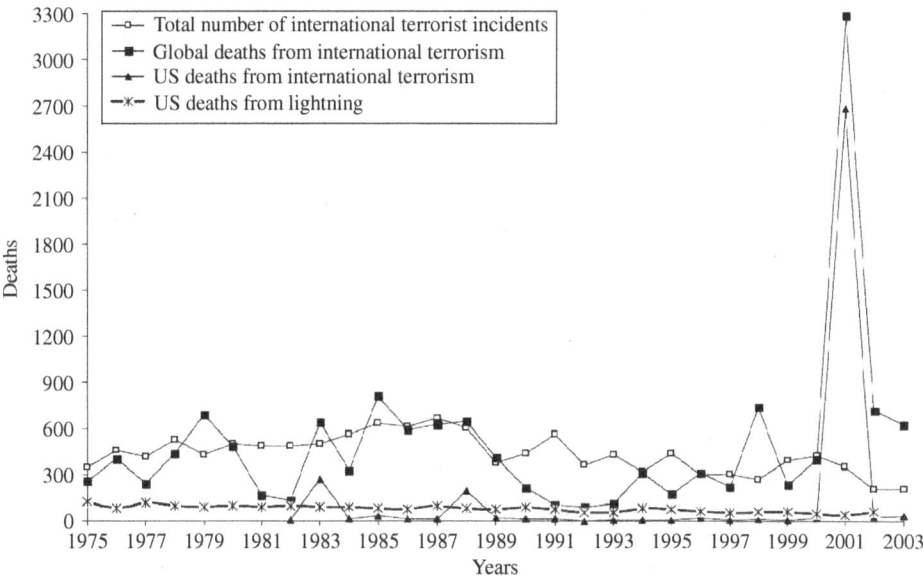

Figure 1. Mueller international terrorism and lightning 1975–2003.
Source: Mueller (2007), 6 February 2007.

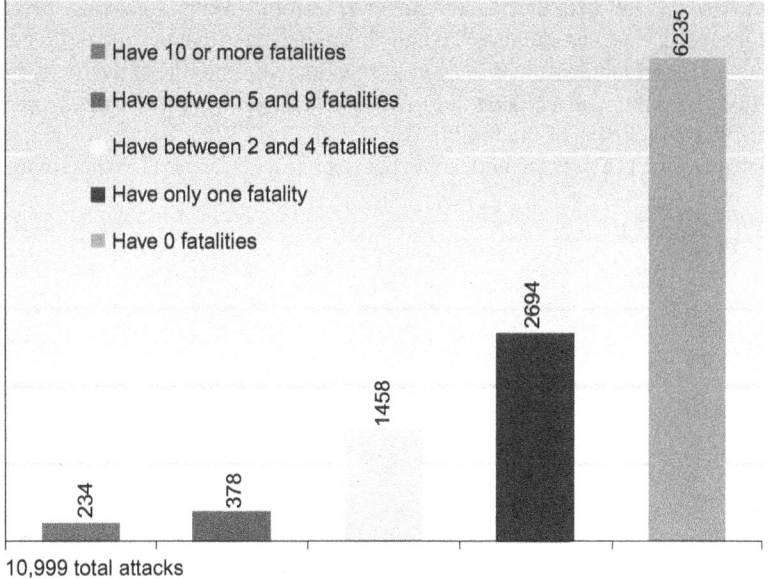

Figure 2. The 2009 NTC report.
Source: NTC Report 2009.

more recent data set, it is most likely that the lethality is due to a focus on the violence of war than it is to a change in terrorist tactics. This interpretation is supported by additional information in the NTC data set which shows that more than 50% of all the terrorist events in 2009 occurred in Iraq and Afghanistan (Figure 2).

In addition to arguing that the increased lethality of events was an indicator of the new terrorism and discarding the idea of violence as communication which distinguished the old terrorism from the new, a subsidiary claim was that the decline in claims of responsibility for acts of terrorism was further indication that the new terrorists had no interest in the communicative aspects of violence. The argument was that they were disinterested in taking credit because their purpose was to kill and destroy, not bargain.

Gary Free, Nancy Morris and Laura Dugan provide evidence from the National Consortium for the Study of Terrorism and Responses to Terrorism (START) Global Terrorism Database which should provide some pause to these claims. Unlike the ITERATE and State Department databases that I have thus far discussed with respect to fatalities, this database has both domestic and international events (Figure 3).

While I question the inclusion of all the events in the database (see Grabosky and Stohl 2010, p. 43), what we can see is that while there are deviations from year to year, the three series of total number of events, attributed events and fatal events all move in tandem throughout the period 1970–2006. That is, while the total number of terrorist events climbed slowly during the 1970s, the series then settled at a higher level for the years 1988–1993 and then turned lower and settled back to the level seen in the 1970s soon thereafter.

At the same time, the relative number of attributed events (based largely on verified claims of responsibility) and the relative number of fatalities per event (which is also the case in the ITERATE and State Department series) have not increased, in statistical terms, at any point in the period or following a particular point in time. Rather, these two series continue to rise and fall with the actual number of terrorist events. Checking the ITERATE data set for reports vis-à-vis claims of responsibility indicates that they do not report claims as such but do report incidents whose agents are unknown. Looking at the decades at issue, we find that the unknown incidents are 39.5% of the total events in the years between 1968 and 1991 and 36.4% of the total in the period 1991–2010. Between 2001 and 2010, the percentage is 41.1. These are noticeable but not particularly great changes which would

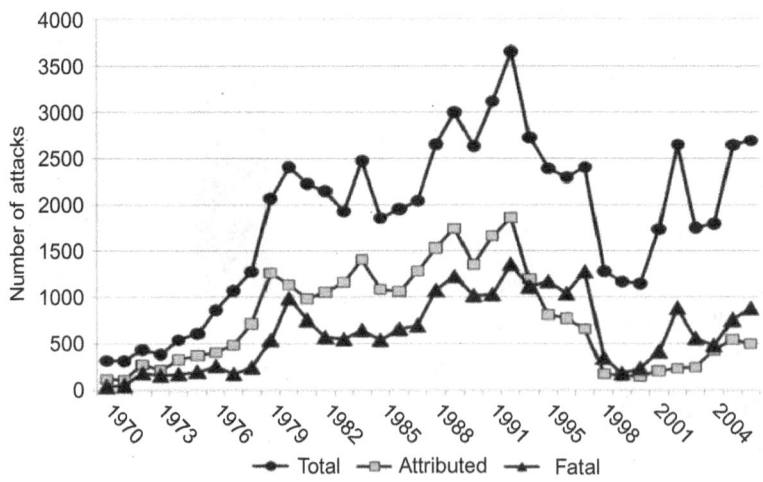

Figure 3. LaFree et al.'s cross-national patterns of terrorism.
Note: Excludes cases from Iraq after 20 March 2003.
Source: LaFree et al. (2010, p. 631).

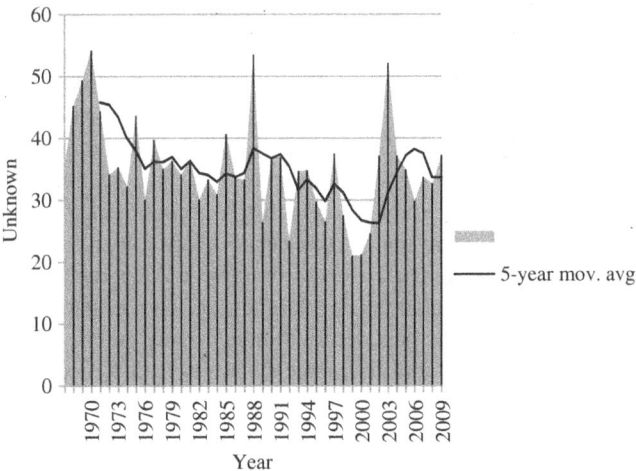

Figure 4. Percentage of unknown perpetrator acts by year with moving average.

signal a dramatic shift in the purpose of the violence. The chief explanation with respect to the ITERATE data set is in the large unknown incidents related to bombings. If we examine the data as a five-year moving average, we can further explore the trend of change over time. This analysis of the data indicates that ITERATE data set actually had higher sustained periods of unknown terrorists in the 1970s than in more recent years. Again, this suggests that there is no evidence for the new terrorism hypothesis that either characterises or predicts changes in the communicative purpose of terrorism through changes in the willingness to make claims of responsibility (Figure 4).

Terrorism and organisations: the boundaries of in and out and the nature of organisational networks

It is clear that since 9/11, and particularly since Mr Bush formulated his response in the form of the war on terror, a major contentious issue has been the nature of the network of terror that the war was intended to defeat. One of the key assumptions stated by the Bush administration was that the new terrorism thesis was correct and that organisations like al-Qaeda and the religious-based organisations with which they were networked were interested only in killing and that no bargaining was intended. Mr Bush posed the justification for our response in the following language on 20 September 2001 in his address to a joint session of Congress:

> They hate what they see right here in this chamber: a democratically elected government. Their leaders are self-appointed. They hate our freedoms: our freedom of religion, our freedom of speech, our freedom to vote and assemble and disagree with each other.
> They want to overthrow existing governments in many Muslim countries such as Egypt, Saudi Arabia and Jordan. They want to drive Israel out of the Middle East. They want to drive Christians and Jews out of vast regions of Asia and Africa.
> These terrorists kill not merely to end lives, but to disrupt and end a way of life. With every atrocity, they hope that America grows fearful, retreating from the world and forsaking our friends. They stand against us because we stand in their way.

However, note that even while expressing the underlying tenet of the new terrorism thesis, namely, their lethality, Mr Bush actually makes reference to the terrorist's use of violence to communicate what the terrorists want, as well as their intention to punish, to coerce and to intimidate '*us*' to get what they want. Much of this latter communicative message was lost in both the media coverage and the subsequent discussion of the war on terror. In his recent *Foreign Affairs* contribution, McCants (2011) makes clear that the al-Qaeda attacks on the United States, beginning with the initial targets in Africa and Yemen and continuing with the attacks of September 11, were undertaken because Bin Laden saw the United States as the main opponent and as supporter of the repressive Arab regimes (e.g. the Saudis and the Gulf States) which prevented the development of Islamic states. This is consistent with arguments put forward in the past decade (among many others, see Sedgwick 2004, Wright 2006, Gerges 2011). McCants also notes the multiple audiences for the attacks. He argues that the communicative message to the United States was one of punishment for its military presence in Saudi Arabia, its support for Israel and its support for the 'apostate' Arab regimes. The attacks were also meant to send a message of inspiration to the masses to revolt.

There has been much discussion about the implications of the war on terror approach both at home and at abroad, but what is less talked about are the implications of the characterisation of the network of terror underlying both the new terrorism thesis and the war on terror counterterrorism response mode. Knowledge and consideration of the number of terrorist attacks, their location, their perpetrators and their devastation are very much related to how the 'enemy' is defined in the global war on terror. At the heart of the problem is the use of the network metaphor by which scholars and the Bush and later Obama administrations have characterised both the 'new terrorism' discussion and al-Qaeda and all those others who are in Mr Bush's words, either 'with us or against us'. The Bush administration never clearly or fully identified what they actually meant by a network of terror and who (beyond Osama Bin Laden and the leaders of al-Qaeda) actually needed to be brought to justice for the 'war' to be won (see Stohl and Stohl 2007).

The failure of both US presidential administrations since 9/11 stems from either a tactical unwillingness or simply the inability to clearly specify what they have actually meant by the global network. In its simplest form, a network refers to the web of social relations that connect individuals, groups and organisations. An analysis of the 'network(s) of terror' should explain how various terrorist groups and other organisations and states are connected, how they are organised and how they operate as a network. Further, it is necessary to specify the meaning of membership in the network and how the various members are linked. How the members are linked provides multiple possibilities as to the meaning of these connections and how important the connections are. Quite simply, not all connections are equal.

The Bush administration argued at various points that al-Qaeda had had links in the past with Syria, Libya, Iraq, Iran and Sudan. They also had to tiptoe around the known connections between the Pakistan Intelligence Services and al-Qaeda, the Taliban and the Harakat-ul-Mujahideen operating in Kashmir against India, as well as the financial connections between the Saudis and Bin Laden. These were links and connections that they wished to ignore in the public realm.

In the fall of 2001, the Bush administration provided estimates of the number of persons who passed through the al-Qaeda training camps which were reported as high as 25,000–30,000 dispersed to cells in more than 60 countries (see Johnston *et al.* 2002). It should be noted that Barack Obama, during his campaign for the presidency, in the context of criticising Mr Bush's approach to combating the al-Qaeda threat, indicated that al-Qaeda was operating in 80 countries (Obama 2008).

Using publicly available data, there is no easy way to determine what the actual size of al-Qaeda was at any one time nor the number and scale of its affiliates and proxies, or who its donors, active supporters and potential sympathisers were and are. Local governments often do not know, deliberately conceal, or may at times exaggerate, the al-Qaeda's presence in their countries. Thus, from the start it was difficult to create a reliable baseline (or even baseline estimate) by which to determine if al-Qaeda or the global network of terror was becoming larger or smaller, before or after a particular point in time. This becomes apparent when one examines the data released by the administration on the size of al-Qaeda and notes the changes regarding the baseline figures.

As the war in Afghanistan commenced, Miller (2001) reported that:

> Intelligence officials say some 5,000 militant Muslims from more than 50 countries have passed through the camps, spending from two weeks to more than six months learning the general and specific skills that modern terrorism requires. In addition to his own training camps, the Taliban and militant Muslim groups affiliated with Al Qaeda have trained thousands more in similar facilities. Some estimates put the total veterans of these camps at more than 50,000 men.

In the aftermath of the first six months of the Afghanistan war the incentive to demonstrate success led to rather more conservative descriptions of organisational size, connections and possibilities. For example, in June 2002, Johnston *et al.* (2002) reported:

> ... senior officials suggest that although sworn members of Al Qaeda were estimated to number no more than 200 to 300 men, officials say that at its peak this broader Qaeda network operated about a dozen Afghan camps that trained as many as 5000 militants, who in turn created cells in as many as 60 countries.

In July 2002, Rebecca Carr, quoting two senior FBI officials, wrote:

> 'Everyone tries to tie everything into 9/11 and al-Qaida', said one of the two officials interviewed Friday on condition of anonymity. 'There was a recent report suggesting that al-Qaida is about 5,000 strong. It is nowhere near 5,000 strong . . .'
>
> While thousands of Islamic extremists and future terrorists have passed through Mr. bin Laden's training camps, it does not mean they are actual al Qaeda operatives, the officials said. The war in Afghanistan has successfully dispersed, killed or captured al-Qaeda leaders, leaving the terror network fractured and diffused . . . (Carr 2002, p. A10)

The size, structure and nature of al-Qaeda as an organisation have been contested for much of the past two decades. Either as a cause or as a consequence of this confusion, the organisational theorists, pundits, journalists, government officials and scholars attempt to create organisational sense for al-Qaeda by describing the organisational in terms of an organising structure with which they are most familiar; most frequently, the corporation, an entity with clear boundaries and structures of membership. As al-Qaeda increasingly frustrated the West, a meta-text converged among these voices.

CNN's Peter Bergen (2001, p. 32) portrayed al-Qaeda as a holding company, bringing different network partners and various combinations of physical and non-physical assets together, to complete various projects. The *New York Times*' Thomas Friedman (2005) argued that: 'The al Qaeda threat has . . . become franchised. It is no longer vertical, something that we can punch in the face. It is now horizontal, flat and widely distributed, operating through the Internet and tiny cells'. Meyer cast al-Qaeda as an organisation 'executing corporate style takeovers of regional Islamic extremist groups' and which 'co-opts affiliates' (Meyer 2007, p. A12). This construction of al-Qaeda as a huge monolithic global corporation trying to take over the world evokes for Western audiences a competitive, winner-take-all, evil organisation that will not stop until it has conquered everything and everyone. Al-Qaeda is thus presented in terms of a global corporation that has established a 'brand name' which has soared in popularity because of its increasingly sophisticated multimedia campaigns in various countries (Meyer 2007, p. A12).

Miles Kahler (2006) noted five years ago:

> As ' . . . Jonathan Raban recently complained,' 'the name al-Qaeda means something different practically every time it's used.' . . . Jason Burke claims that Osama bin Laden and his partners 'never created a coherent terrorist network in the way commonly conceived,' instead adopting a model that was much more like a 'venture capital firm.' Olivier Roy tags it as 'an organization and a trademark.' Marc Sageman portrays al Qaeda as part of a 'global Salafi jihad,' which is 'not a specific organization, but a social movement . . . '[5]

As evidence mounted that there were numerous terrorists and terrorist organisations that while they conducted operations in the name of a global violent jihad had no actual links or visible connections to al-Qaeda or any of its members, al-Qaeda was then designated as an inspiration and as a model. Explorations of al-Qaeda's rationale and reading of the historical record and contemporary political situation provided the background and context for the creation of organisations which acted on al-Qaeda's behalf. Again, a corporate metaphor was employed to provide the conversational organisational framework. Brad McAllister argued that:

> Al Qaeda has gained notoriety as an organization that not only seeks to establish itself in the international *jihad*, but wants to encourage others to do so also. Thus, al Qaeda not only works as a network firm, but as a venture capitalist enterprise, encouraging like-minded entrepreneurs to create start-up organizations in the same field. (McAllister 2004, p. 305)

What was left unstated was the specification of how McAllister's network firm, venture capitalist enterprise and its various franchises were connected. McAllister and others neglected to provide evidence for the lines of authority or to demonstrate how its actions and resources – material and otherwise – were controlled.

Thus, for much of the past decade, the discussion of al-Qaeda as a clandestine organisation created as much confusion as clarity in determining the constitutive nature of the political dimensions of the organisation. With respect to clandestine organisations, it becomes apparent that different voices, within and without the organisation, often have had quite disparate needs in determining the contours and content of what Taylor (2008) refers to as the organisational conversation which establishes the nature and boundaries of the organisation. It is frequently the case, for example, that external observers talk about and assume much greater organisational scale and scope of clandestine organisations than the evidence suggests. Ironically, the magnification of the size and exaggeration of the scope of a clandestine organisation may constitute the organisation and its boundaries in ways that are beneficial for all parties in the short run: for governmental organisations, the larger the clandestine organisation the more justification for measures and actions that might otherwise be unacceptable; for the clandestine organisation, such discussion and actions on the part of the state, press and community increase their appeal to the community at large; and for the media, the larger threat promotes greater interest and readers or viewership. The communicative inflation of an organisation and the threat it poses also benefits the terrorists who threaten states and regimes, because the enlargement creates doubt in the minds of the greater community as to the ability of the regime to prevail. Thus, it served the interests of al-Qaeda to have those claims made as it amplified their potential ability to generate voice and consequent fear in those they were targeting and support and hope among those from whom they were seeking support, both political and material.

Thus, in Taylor's terms (2008, p. 154) there is no consensual co-orientation with al-Qaeda. While we may agree that an organisation we call al-Qaeda engages in terrorism, the actual organisation itself remains very much in dispute. The conditions of secrecy ensure that the constitutive texts, conversation and meta-conversation cannot be primarily rooted in the mutual interaction that Taylor and his colleagues envision, but rather in conversations and political processes that observers conduct external to the organisation. Kahler, for example, notes that:

> Although it may not be typical in every respect, al Qaeda's notoriety has produced more data on its internal operations than can be found for most other clandestine international networks. Unfortunately, that data must be used with great care for two reasons. First, much of the available information derives from unreliable or questionable sources. Given the covert nature of measures taken against al Qaeda and other terrorist groups, available public information is often based on official sources promoting their own agendas and counter-terrorist strategies (of which information manipulation may be a part). (2006, pp. 3–4)

One of the continuing debates within the literature of al-Qaeda (scholarly, journalistically and within the public sector) is the status of the various organisations that have al-Qaeda in their names. Three recent discussions of three of the al-Qaeda 'franchises', al-Qaeda in Iraq (AQI), al-Qaeda in the Arabian Peninsula (AQAP) and al-Qaeda in the Islamic Maghreb (AQIM) illustrate the problem. Porter argues that:

> Despite ideological affinities, AQIM's relations with al-Qa`ida's central leadership are similar to those of al-Qa`ida in Iraq (AQI) and al-Qa`ida in the Arabian Peninsula (AQAP) in that they do not seem to reach the operational level. AQIM appears to carry out its operations without the guidance of al-Qa`ida's central leadership; instead, it pursues al-Qa`ida's modus operandi and target set. (2011, p. 11)

On the other hand, Farrall argues that: 'AQAP is often referred to as an al Qaeda franchise, but it is better described as a branch. It was created by, and continues to operate under, the leadership of core al Qaeda members' (2011, pp. 131–132). And, at the same time, Tawil suggests that: 'In line with al-Qa`ida's franchise model, AQAP has been allowed to pursue its tactics and target set against the Gulf rulers without any public interference from al-Qa`ida's central leadership' (2011, p. 7). With respect to the 'tightness of the organization', Farrall argues:

> Another factor is the closeness of the ties between the subsidiary and the central organization; the tighter the ties, the more likely the request will be honored. AQI has a closer relationship with al Qaeda than AQIM. Still, AQIM has generally cooperated at least with requests to stay on message and present the image of a united and hierarchical organization. (2011, p. 135)

Meanwhile, Tawil contends that: 'Even under Bin Laden's leadership, al-Qa`ida was largely unable to control the actions of AQI's leader, Abu Musab al-Zarqawi' (2011, p. 7).

The result is that even with the death of Bin Laden and the gleaning of the documents he left behind, we are still not close to agreement on the organisational nature or scale of the threat that remains. The impact of 10 years of the assertions that al-Qaeda and its network posed an existential threat and that the network was dispersed in 60 or 80 countries, consisting of either hundreds or tens of thousands of members, reporting to and acting under the direct orders of or simply inspired by Osama bin Laden, and most importantly interested only in killing or pursuing political goals, has resulted in an inability for governments to communicate to the public whether they are more secure now than they were 10 years ago. The Gallup Poll in January 2011 (Saad 2011a) found that the number of Americans worried about being victimised by terrorism still hovered at about 40%, a figure that had not substantially been altered since 2003, and that the range of worry while fluctuating between 28% and 48% during the decade had been very consistent around a mean of 40% throughout the period (Figure 5).

Likewise the percentage of Americans who thought that there would be a terrorist event in the United States in the next several weeks remained over 40% for almost the entire period and was higher in the early months of 2011 than it had been at any time since 2003 (Figure 6).

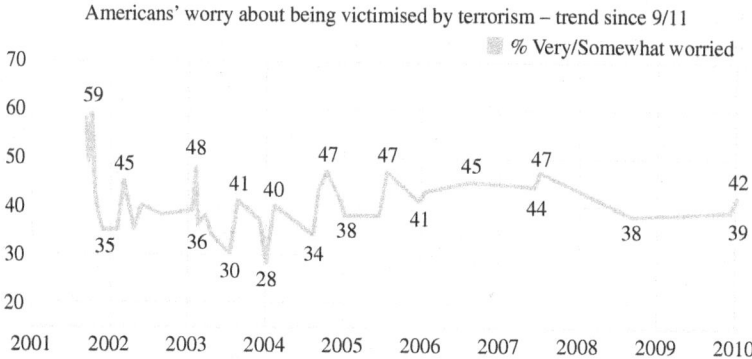

Figure 5. The Gallup Poll: Americans' worry about being victimised by terrorism. Source: Saad (2011a).

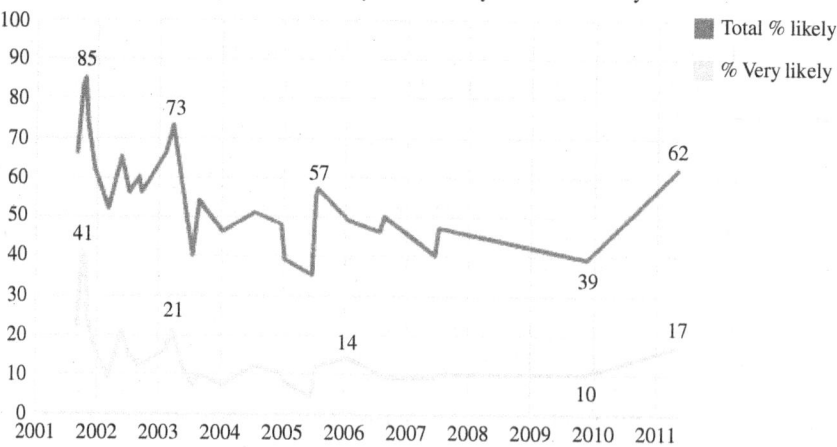

Figure 6. The Gallup Poll: perceived chance of terrorism in the next several weeks. Source: Saad (2011b).

Conclusion

Thus, the data indicate that the enormous investment in counterterrorism and the war on terror, brought about because of the untested (and as we have seen, false) assumptions of the 'new terrorism' argument, has not brought a greater sense of security to the American public. The audience is not persuaded that they are more secure by the endless recounting of statistics of the number of terrorists killed. The American public (and American policymakers), having accepted the new terrorism thesis and the narrative frame provided by the Bush administration after the tragedy of September 11 (and for the most part continued with the Obama administration), are seemingly trapped within the consequences of both the narrative and the wars and devastation that they created. While the new terrorism thesis had no clear evidence to support its claims at the time it was made and the trends that it falsely identified did not move in the directions indicated, the damage that the new terrorism thesis caused in the wars and other measures undertaken to defeat the falsely identified new terrorism has been devastating.

Notes

1. This approach to empirical social science advocated by Nicholson is therefore not at odds with many aspects of a 'critical' approach – the most important of which is the investigation (the critical evaluation) of the context and formulation of knowledge claims, which implies a reflexive emphasis on social context and the derivation and evaluation of knowledge claims. It is at its root a pragmatic epistemology.
2. Rep. Earl Landgrebe, of Indiana's 2nd Congressional District, was one of President Nixon's strongest supporters. On 5 August 1974, Nixon released the documents that showed him issuing orders to his aides to hinder the FBI investigation of the Watergate break-in. Landgrebe was interviewed by the Associated Press on 7 August 1974. He said, 'Don't confuse me with the facts; I've got a closed mind. I will not vote for impeachment'. Nixon resigned two days later (McShane 1994). The title is also cited in Schell (1974, p. 19) and used by White (1998).
3. Here I use the term wisdom in the same sense that John Kenneth Galbraith used in *The Affluent Society*: 'It will be convenient to have a name for the ideas which are esteemed at any time for their acceptability, and it should be a term that emphasizes this predictability. I shall refer to these ideas henceforth as the conventional wisdom' (1956, p. 9).
4. All references to the 'new terrorism' of which I am aware refer only to insurgent terrorism (see, for example, Tucker 2001, Duyvesteyn 2004, Spencer 2006, Mockaitis 2008). While there was increased discussion of rogue states and the axis of evil, as identified by the Bush administration, the discussion did not proceed along the same lines as the 'new terrorism' debate.
5. See also Burke (2004) and the contributors in Greenberg (2005).

Notes on contributor

Michael Stohl is professor of Communication and professor of Political Science at the University of California, Santa Barbara (UCSB), and an international partner investigator for the Australian Research Council-funded Centre of Excellence for Policing and Security, a partnership of the Australian National University and Griffith University. Dr. Stohl's research focuses on political communication and international relations with special reference to political violence, terrorism and human rights. He is the author or co-author of more than 100 scholarly journal articles and book chapters and the author, editor or co-editor of 15 books. His most recent publications on terrorism include with Peter Grabosky, *Crime and Terrorism* (London and Thousand Oaks: Sage, 2010); 'State terror: the theoretical and practical utilities and implications of a contested concept', in Richard Jackson and S. Justin Sinclair (eds.), *Contemporary Debates on Terrorism* (Oxon: Routledge, 2011). His 2007 article with Cynthia Stohl, 'Networks of Terror: Theoretical Assumptions and Pragmatic Consequences', *Communication Theory* (47, 2) was awarded both the International Communication Association best published article of the year award and the National Communication Association best published article in Organizational Communication award.

References

Bergen, P., 2001. *Holy war, inc.: inside the secret world of Osama bin Laden*. London: Weidenfeld and Nicolson.

Bongar, B., 2007. The psychology of terrorism: defining the need, describing the goal. *In*: B. Bongar, et al., eds. *The psychology of terrorism*. Oxford: Oxford University Press, 3–12.

Burke, J., 2004. *Al Qaeda: the true story of radical Islam*. Harmondsworth: Penguin.

Carr, R., 2002. Only 200 hard core members [online]. *Palm Beach Post*, 29 July. Available from: http://www.why-war.com/news/2002/07/29/onlyhard.html [Accessed 1 June 2005].

Crenshaw, M. 1981. The causes of terrorism. *Comparative Politics*, 13, 379–399.

Crenshaw, M., 2008. 'New' vs. 'old' terrorism: a critical appraisal. *In*: R. Coolsaet, ed. *Jihadi terrorism and the radicalisation challenge in Europe*. Aldershot and Burlington, VT: Ashgate Publishing, 25–38.

Duyvesteyn, I., 2004. How new is new terrorism? *Studies in Conflict and Terrorism*, 27 (5), 439–454.

Farrall, L., 2011. How al Qaeda works: what the organization's subsidiaries say about its strength. *Foreign Affairs*, 90 (2), 128–138.

Flemming, P. and Stohl, M., 2001. Myths and realities of cyberterrorism. *In*: A.P. Schmid, ed. *Countering terrorism through international cooperation*. Vienna: ISPAC (International Scientific and Professional Advisory Council of the United Nations Crime Prevention and Criminal Justice Program), 70–105.

Friedman, T., 2005. If it's a Muslim problem, it needs a Muslim solution. *The New York Times*. Available from: http://www.nytimes.com/2005/07/08/opinion/08friedman.html [Accessed 1 July 2011].

Galbraith, J.K., 1956. *The affluent society*. New York: New American Library.

Gerges, F., 2011. *The rise and fall of al Qaeda*. Oxford: Oxford University Press.

Grabosky, P. and Stohl, M., 2010. *Crime and terrorism*. Thousand Oaks, CA: Sage.

Greenberg, K.J., ed., 2005. *Al Qaeda now*. Cambridge: Cambridge University Press.

Gurr, T., 1988. Empirical research on political terrorism: the state of the art and how it might be improved. *In*: R. Slater and M. Stohl, eds. *Current perspectives on political terrorism*. New York: St. Martin's Press, 115–154.

Hoffman, B., 1995. 'Holy terror': the implications of terrorism motivated by a religious imperative. *Studies in Conflict and Terrorism*, 18, 271–284.

Hoffman, B., 1998. *Inside terrorism*. New York: Columbia University Press.

Jenkins, B.M., 1975. International terrorism: a new mode of conflict. *In*: D. Carlton and C. Schaerf, eds. *International terrorism and world security*. London: Croom Helm, 15–31.

Jenkins, B.M., 1988. Future trends in international terrorism. *In*: R. Slater and M. Stohl, eds. *Current perspectives on political terrorism*. New York: St. Martin's Press, 246–266.

Jenkins, B.M., 2006. *The new age of terrorism* [online]. Santa Monica, CA: RAND Corporation. Available from: http://www.rand.org/pubs/reprints/RP1215 [Accessed 1 July 2011].

Johnston, D., Van Natta, D. Jr., and Miller, J., 2002. Qaeda's new links increase threats from far-flung sites. *The New York Times*, 16 June, p. A1.

Kahler, M., 2006. Political networks and collective action. *Paper presented to the annual meeting of the American Political Science Association*, 30 August–3 September 2006, Philadelphia, PA.

LaFree, G., Morris, N.A., and Dugan, L., 2010. Cross-national patterns of terrorism comparing trajectories for total, attributed and fatal attacks, 1970–2006. *British Journal of Criminology*, 50, 622–649.

Laqueur, W., 2003. *No end to war*. New York: Continuum.

Lum, C., Kennedy, L.W., and Sherley, A.J., 2006. The effectiveness of counter-terrorism strategies: a Campbell systematic review. *Journal of Experimental Criminology*, 2 (4), 489–516.

McAllister, B., 2004. Al Qaeda and the innovative firm: demythologizing the network. *Studies in Conflict and Terrorism*, 27, 297–319.

McCants, W., 2011. Al Qaeda's challenge. *Foreign Affairs*, 90 (5), 54–65.

McShane, S., 1994. 'We'll stick with Dick': Earl Landgrebe, Watergate, and the vocal minority. *Traces of Indiana and Midwestern History*, 6 (4), 30–39.

Merari, A., 1991. Academic research and government policy on terrorism. *Terrorism and Political Violence*, 3, 88–102.

Meyer, J., 2007. Al Qaeda grows by adding affiliates. *Los Angeles Times*, 16 September, p. A1, A12.

Mickolus, E.F., Sandler, T., Murdock, J.M., and Flemming, P.A., 1989. *International terrorism: attributes of terrorist events, 1978–1987 (ITERATE 3)*. Dunn Loring, VA: Vinyard Software.

Miller, J., 2001. Pentagon says bombs destroy terror camps [online]. *The New York Times*, 10 October. Available from: http://www.nytimes.com/2001/10/10/world/a-nation-challenged-the-damage-pentagon-says-bombs-destroy-terror-camps.html?ref=alqaeda [Accessed 15 August 2011].

Mockaitis, T.R., 2008. *The new terrorism: myths and reality*. Stanford: Stanford University Press.

Mueller, J., 2007. Reacting to terrorism: probabilities, consequences and the persistence of fear. *In*: *Paper presented at the annual meeting of the International Studies Association*, 26 February–4 March, Chicago, IL.

Nicholson, M., 1983. *The scientific analysis of social behaviour: a defence of empiricism in social science*. London: Frances Pinter.

Nicholson, M., 1986. Conceptual problems of studying state terrorism. *In*: M. Stohl and G. Lopez, eds. *Government volence and repression: an agenda for research*. New York: Greenwood Press, Inc., 27–44.

Obama, B., 2008. Transcript of Barack Obama's acceptance speech. *The New York Times*, 8 July 2005. Available from: http://www.nytimes.com/2008/08/28/us/politics/28text-obama.html [Accessed 1 July 2011].

Porter, G., 2011. The impact of Bin Ladin's death on AQIM in North Africa. *CTC Sentinel*, May, pp. 10–12.

Saad, L., 2011a. *U.S. fear of terrorism steady after foiled Christmas attack* [online]. Available from: http://www.gallup.com/poll/125051/u.s.-fear-terrorism-steady-after-foiled-christmas-attack.asp [Accessed 1 July 2011].

Saad, L., 2011b. *Majority in US say Bin Laden's death makes America safer still, 62% say it is likely that terrorists will act against the US in the next few weeks* [online]. Available from: http://www.gallup.com/poll/147413/majority-say-bin-laden-death-makes-america-safer.aspx [Accessed 1 July 2011].

Schell, J., 1974. Comment [online]. *The New Yorker*, 26 August. Available from: http://www.newyorker.com/archive/1974/08/26/1974_08_26_019_TNY_CARDS_000310568#ixzz1U6Tepbr5 [Accessed 1 August 2011].

Schelling, T., 1966. *Arms and influence*. New Haven: Yale University Press.

Schmid, A., 2009. *Handbook of terrorism research*. London: Routledge.

Schmid, A. and Jongman, A., 1988. *Political terrorism: a new guide to actors, authors, concepts, data bases, theories and literature*. Amsterdam: North Holland.

Sedgwick, M., 2004. Al-Qaeda and the nature of religious terrorism. *Terrorism and Political Violence*, 16 (4), 795–814.

Silke, A. 2001. The devil you know: continuing problems with research on terrorism. *Terrorism and Political Violence*, 13 (4), 1–14.

Silke, A., 2004. An introduction to research on terrorism. *In*: A. Silke, ed. *Research on terrorism: trends, achievements and failures*. London: Frank Cass, 1–29.

Spencer, A., 2006. Questioning the concept of 'new terrorism'. *Peace, Conflict and Development*, 8, 1–33.

Stohl, C. and Stohl, M., 2007. Networks of terror: theoretical assumptions and pragmatic consequences. *Communication Theory*, 17, 93–124.

Stohl, M., ed., 1988. Demystifying terrorism. *In*: *The politics of terrorism*. New York: Marcel Dekker, 1–28.

Tawil, C., 2011. How Bin Ladin's death will affect al-Qa`ida's regional franchises. *CTC Sentinel*, May Special Issue, pp. 6–8.

Taylor, J.R., 2008. Organizing from the bottom up: reflections on the constitution of organization in communication. *In*: A. Nicotera and L. Putnam, eds. *Communication in action: the communicative constitution of organization and its implications for theory, research, and practice*. Mahwah, NJ: Lawrence Erlbaum, 153–186.

Tucker, D., 2001. What is new about the new terrorism and how dangerous is it? *Terrorism and Political Violence*, 13 (3), 1–14.

White, R., 1998. Don't confuse me with the facts: more on the Irish Republican Army and sectarianism. *Terrorism and Political Violence*, 10 (4), 164–169.

Wright, L., 2006. *The looming tower: al-Qaeda and the road to 9/11*. New York: Knopf.

Drones, witches and other flying objects: the force of fantasy in US counterterrorism

Joseba Zulaika

Center for Basque Studies, University of Nevada, Reno, NV, USA

> A key concern for critical terrorism studies is the extent to which counterterrorism contributes to the promotion and perpetuation of terrorism. When dealing with either the events leading to 9/11 or the current anti-Muslim movements in Europe, we owe serious attention to the self-generating process by which terrorism and counterterrorism operate as an edge that simultaneously and constitutively links and separates both aspects of the phenomenon. The 9/11 Commission Report established that the events could probably have been prevented; there were after all 50–60 officers who knew two of the future attackers were living in the United States. What requires analysis are the blind spots in counterterrorist thinking that lead to such failures and ultimately to the self-fulfilling nature of the war on terror. This article will examine the conceptual similarities between witchcraft societies and the counterterrorist thought and policies put in practice by various US administrations – having to do with the perversions of temporality, the logic of taboo, non-hypothetical knowledge, secret information, the passion for 'expert' ignorance, mystical causation and dual sovereignty. The need for an epistemic shift that will take into account the constitutive nature of discourse and the political subjectivities of the actors will be advocated.

At the end of the Cold War, with the armaments race and fears of nuclear holocaust over, the United States emerged as the only superpower with no hint of any military enemy on the horizon. And yet the US Defence budget has almost doubled during the last decade after 9/11; it is now larger than that of all other countries combined. Such costs are justified because, after the Cold War, a new enemy has surfaced: the terrorist. The vast new security bureaucracy created after 9/11 encompasses some 1200 government organisations and 1900 companies. Estimates of the total bill for the war on terror range from $3 trillion to $4 trillion.

But the economy is only one aspect of the political climate forced by terrorism. What is most extraordinary is that the state of exception was imposed on American politics as a result of the war on terror. The evidence is there for anyone to see: Guantánamo, indefinite detention, rendition, torture and extra-judicial killings by drones. These are the daily staple news of current politics, officially sanctioned and normalised and broadly accepted by the general public. And yet, these are borderline realities at the intersection of law and politics, in the past clearly illegal and anathema, now official policy. The state of exception means that lawbreaking can be approved by the highest officials and go unpunished. As Agamben put it, a situation obtains in which 'it is impossible to distinguish transgression of the law from the execution of the law, such that what violates a rule and what conforms to it coincide without any reminder' (1998, p. 7).

What concerns me here is a crisis of knowledge in terrorism studies. Right from its inception, a sign of this crisis has been the difficulties of not only defining the term itself, but the very interpretive frameworks of the events covered by the concept. A critical analysis must inquire into the genealogy of this discourse and world view, beginning with the very naming of the phenomenon; it must examine its conceptual premises and policies and question its politics and ethics. In my latest work, I have been engaged in showing the extent to which counterterrorism, caught in its own spiral of a self-fulfilling prophecy, becomes terrorism's best ally. The events leading to the attack on the twin towers provide evidence for such an argument. It is a fact recognised by the 9/11 Commission Report that the plotters could have been found and the attacks prevented. It is well known that the blind sheik, bin Laden, and his followers had been in the past close associates of US counterintelligence services. After the removal of Saddam Hussein, there was information, based on the CIA's interviews with him, that he had been bluffing as to his possession or attempts to possess weapons of mass destruction (WMD). It is also established that reactions to 9/11, such as the war in Iraq and policies implemented by Paul Bremer after the invasion, added to the problem of terrorism. On the basis of this set of facts, the critical question should be, *ex ante*, did counterterrorism actually contribute, by omission or by action, to making 9/11 happen? *Ex post facto*, what are the premises and blind spots in counterterrorism that not only allowed 9/11, but contributed with reactions to making the problem much worse? It is in response to such questions that I presented the thesis of counterterrorism as a self-fulfilling prophecy (see Zulaika 2009). In the section below, I will add how the latest chapter in counterterrorism – the drone attacks – conforms to the same pattern.

My theoretical ground was borrowed initially from discourse analysis and from the anthropological study of taboo, to which I added in my latest book current psychoanalytical understandings of subjectivity. I did not argue that the intelligence communities were unconcerned about terrorist threats, much less voluntarily negligent. The officers in charge of preventing terrorism are likely to be the most concerned ones and the first in wanting to do a more efficient job. And I am not surprised that over 700 security studies scholars wrote in their 'Open Letter to the American People' after admitting that the war in Iraq was 'the most misguided one since the Vietnam period', the following: 'One result has been a great distortion in terms of public debate on foreign and national security policy – an emphasis on speculation instead of facts' (cited in Horgan and Boyle 2008, p. 54). My contention was that the generally admitted massive failure of counterterrorism in preventing 9/11 is paradigmatic of its blind spots and that we can learn the most from them. My argument was that these are problems that have to do directly with a faulty epistemology – beginning with the placement of the entire phenomenon in a context of taboo and the wilful ignorance of the political subjectivities of the terrorists.

The investigation of the crisis of knowledge in the field of terrorism takes me to examine in this article the force of fantasy in counterterrorism. One has to begin such a study by examining what counts as the standard of evidence and as valuable information in such a context of taboo, what type of experience should be respected and what sort of associative logic links together various kinds of events. My argument is that such faulty epistemology derives critically from the lack of attention paid to the role played by fantasy in the entire terrorism phenomenon. Thus, I am not primarily concerned with the usual criticisms received by the critical current of terrorism studies, namely, whether the liberal state should be included in the analysis, what is understood by 'critical', its 'emancipation' agenda and so on. My contention is rather that, in order to identify the *blind spots* in our knowledge of terrorism, the role of fantasy is a central issue. The cultural and political consequences of such work could not be more urgent.

Flying drones over Pakistan from Las Vegas

Pilotless drones to identify and destroy terrorist targets are the latest in counterterrorism – 'the only game in town', as it is widely referred to, echoing the former CIA director and current defence secretary Leon Panetta. Counterterrorism's basic approach has always consisted in tabooing outlawed terrorists as untouchables with whom no communication of any sort was permitted. The latest in counterterrorism, pilotless drones flying in the sky at 10,000 feet, the only contact between the hunter and the hunted, a Hellfire missile launched from a drone that might be operated by CIA agents 7500 miles away at Nellis Air Force Base near Las Vegas in the Nevada desert, perfects the strategy of contact at a distance. The combat air patrols of the drones at any one time has gone from 21 in 2007 to 38 in 2009 to 54 in 2011 (Sluka 2011, p. 70). The flying robots, we are told, soon will be 'in the position to take the initiative against the enemy on a battlefield' and that 'the pressure to let robots take the shot will be very hard to resist' (Caryl 2011, p. 58). Not only in the air, 'there are already more robots operating on the ground (15,000) than in the air (7000)' (Caryl 2011, p. 55). There are 7000 drones ready to fly in the air and 15,000 on the ground. This is the new technological scenario, a Nintendo war in which subjectless machines will identify and eliminate terrorists. Terrorism's metaphoric hierarchy used to be that a superhuman entity (a country, an army, an organisation) killed a subhuman being (a 'dog', a 'pig' or some other beast); in the new weaponry, 'drones' mimic animals such as hummingbirds and seagulls.

The strength of the emerging robotic weaponry, we are told, consists in 'their ability to see and think' (Caryl 2011, p. 55). The drones can programme a destination and fly by themselves; they can follow a target for days from the invisible altitude, while the faraway operator is never in danger of being killed from below. One thing that is obvious about unmanned machines is that they do not have desires of their own, nor intentions, nor are subjectively responsible for their actions – and they cannot commit war crimes, as the required intent to commit them is missing from machines. The killing itself might perhaps now be done in a subjectless manner by machines finding out who the terrorists are and acting on their own.

The disturbing thing for counterterrorism is that both groups, terrorists and counterterrorists, have desires and subjectivities. Studies have shown (Lindlaw 2008) that the far-removed operators of the drone suffer the same combat stress as the combatants in a war zone. They cannot avoid the fact that innocent civilians are being killed by the Hellfire missiles they fire – including an estimated 168 children. It is hard to know how many people have been killed by drones (between 2000 and 3000), let alone how many of them are civilians. Estimates vary widely. Based on media reports, some Western estimates put the number of militants among the dead at 85%. The Pakistani daily *Dawn* calculated that of the 708 people killed in 2009, only five were known militants; the other major English-speaking daily in Pakistan, *The News*, estimated that of the 701 people killed by drones between January 2006 and April 2009, only 14 were known militants (Ahmad 2011). The area is sealed by Pakistan, the available sources being the CIA and Pakistani secret services.

Of the people killed, the CIA knows the names of 125 people and considers 35 of them as 'high value targets' (Ahmad 2011).

Who are these hundreds of killed people of whom we do not even know their names? Counterterrorists' 'passion for ignorance' is well documented on the grounds of lack of basic knowledge regarding the languages or cultures of the peoples they are engaged with, let alone disinterest in their political goals or subjective motivation. Turning into fatal targets, anonymous people about whom not even their names are known, marks a new bar. But such issues, let alone the objection of why the 35 high-value targets should be subject to extrajudicial killing when the United States is not at war with Pakistan, are superfluous in the counterterrorist mindset. You only need apply the logic of taboo typical of terrorist contamination: when anti-Americanism is at an all-time high of 90% in countries such as Pakistan, due in good part to the drone attacks, can anyone on the ground be completely 'innocent' from actual or potential terrorism? Indeed, 'the agency can target all suspect militants based on "pattern of life" analysis collected from surveillance cameras' (Ahmad 2011). Since most adult males traditionally carry guns, such 'pattern of life' makes them all potential targets. But guns might not be necessary, for, as a CIA officer told Jane Mayer of the *New Yorker*, 'no tall man with a beard is safe anywhere in Southwest Asia' (Ahmad 2011). Why should you want to know their names before you kill them?

It is not surprising therefore that reliable information is extremely hard to get and that American and Pakistani official sources issue wildly divergent claims. The impossibility of even counting whether the dead bodies are militants or civilians, when both countries are allegedly close allies in the war on terror, is one more implication of the *secrecy* surrounding counterterrorism; so secret are the attacks that the CIA denies that the drone programme even exists, let alone the criteria by which it chooses its targets. There is not, however, anything secret about such wilfully upheld secrecy turned into a tool of information control, so that even a body count becomes an act of 'magical realism' (Ahmad 2011), as there are recurrent cases of people 'killed' who rose from the dead several times and were killed in later attacks. The Pakistani government publicly disapproves of the attacks but privately they provide intelligence and support. Pakistani sovereignty is another area shrouded in mystery, as it depends on the secret agreements it has with the Americans.

Are these drone attacks legal? 'Outside the context of armed conflict, the use of drones for targeted killing is almost never likely to be legal,' wrote Philip Alston (cited in Caryl 2011, p. 56). But for the global war on terror, is there anything anywhere that is not 'armed conflict'? Thus, under the guise of combating terrorism, US counterterrorism considers itself legitimised to overrule national sovereignties and flaunt international law; in short, to establish a state of exception by which actions that ordinarily are illegal and immoral are suddenly tolerable because the fight against the terrorist demands it. When in the 1980s, various European countries enacted policies of 'shoot-to-kill' against suspected terrorists, they were met with international outrage (Zulaika and Douglass 1996, pp. 158–160). Extrajudicial killings of hundreds of suspect militants, of whom we even ignore their names, are now perpetrated in the name of the war on terror; they no longer elicit international scandal but are praised as most effective.

Ignoring that we know: the impasses in knowledge

What are the practical results of the drone campaign? The number of terrorist attacks in Pakistan has gone up sharply in a wave of anti-Americanism, for Pakistanis 'overwhelmingly believe that most of those who die in the attacks are civilians' (Caryl 2011, p. 56). Given the fact that drone strikes 'have had a particular affinity for hitting weddings and funerals, and appear to be seriously fuelling the insurgency' (Sluka 2011, p. 72), it is no surprise that Taliban recruits have increased. Air strikes are prominent in motivating suicide attacks, a UN report concluded; surveys show direct links between family members killed and joining or supporting the insurgency (Sluka 2011, p. 72). One concrete instance of such links was provided by Faisal Shahzad, the Pakistani-American known for the failed bomb in Times Square in May 2010, who declared in his trial that 'I'm avenging the attack' for the 'drones [that] kill women, children . . . everybody . . . I am part of the answer' (cited in Hari 2010). Sluka's conclusion is shared by many experts: 'By losing hearts and minds, the UAV [drones] war in Afghanistan and Pakistan is losing the fight against and increasing the threat of terrorism, and making further terror attacks on American more likely, not less' (Sluka 2011, p. 76).

Do counterterrorists ignore these too obvious links? Of course not. David Kilcullen is, among others, an example of a 'counterterrorist guru' aware that drone attacks have a negative effect. He told Congress in April 2009:

Since 2006, we've killed 14 senior Al-Qaeda leaders using drone strikes; in the same period, we've killed 700 Pakistani civilians in the same area. The drone strikes are highly unpopular. They are deeply aggravating to the population. And they've given rise to a feeling of anger that coalesces the population around the extremists and leads to spikes of extremism . . . The current path that we are on is leading us to loss of Pakistani government control over its own population. (Cited in Sluka 2011, p. 73)

The ratio of civilians killed for each militant is 50:1, Kilcullen observed; that is, 98% of drone casualties are civilians – so much for technological surgical 'precision'. That this is self-fulfilling is a given for Kilcullen: 'Every one of these dead non-combatants [creates] an alienated family, a new desire for revenge, and more recruits for a militant movement that has grown exponentially even as drone strikes have increased' (cited in Sluka 2011, p. 73). Kilcullen concluded that the use of such drones is 'immoral'.

Counterterrorists know all of this. Yet why is it that these very drones, which help increase terrorist insurgency 'exponentially', are still 'the only game in town'? In short, counterterrorism knows that its tactics operate clearly along the path of a self-fulfilling feedback, and yet there is nothing else better to do. Such an impasse – if we do nothing, terrorism will flourish; if we do something it will flourish even more – shows dramatically the current crisis in counterterrorist knowledge.

Kilcullen's (2009) recent book, *The Accidental Guerrilla*, dramatically states the changes needed in US counterterrorist thinking while also showing the core deadlocks in which it is trapped. A close associate of General David Petraeus in the successful 'surge' to end the war in Iraq, Kilcullen is a vocal advocate of applying a strategy of protecting the population and, contrary to the usual counterterrorism strategy that saw this as a 'soft approach' (2009, p. 145), negotiating with and of co-opting local leaders. Kilcullen is one of the most vocal exponents of the implications of terrorism's 'asymmetric warfare' – the stark facts that 'the United States is spending in excess of $400 million *per day* in Iraq' and that 'the United States has so far spent $1.4 million *per dollar of AQ [Al Qaeda] investment in the attacks* on the response' (2009, pp. 25, 274). He is also much aware that, in relation to the other countries, 'the U.S. defense budget accounted for 54.5 percent of total global defense spending in 2007', and internally, 'the U.S. Defense Department is about 210 times larger than the U.S. Agency for International Development and the State Department combined' (2009, pp. 22, 298). Faced with these staggering numbers, Kilcullen does not hesitate to state that with bin Laden 'we have turned a mouse into an elephant' and that the war on terror has 'largely played into the hands of this AQ exhaustion strategy'. He makes a strong case for 'a radical rethinking of some key Western policies, strategies, and attitudes' (2009, pp. 38, 263, 264).

Kilcullen, however, does not see in his own proposals anything radical or controversial conceptually, for '[m]uch of the best strategic work by the State Department, defense departments of contributing powers, and NATO planners conforms exactly to these prescriptions' (2009, p. 114). He saw the decision to invade Iraq as 'an extremely serious strategic error' and warned against it, but then he adds, again, so did 'almost every other counterinsurgency professional' (2009, p. 268). So how is it that the military establishment *knew* that the consequences of Iraq would be disastrous, officers being aware that the hubris behind the assumption of the efficacy of American military power was breathtaking and yet we went to war? Much like how is it that, previous to 9/11, 50–60 officers *knew* for many months that two of the future hijackers were in the country and nothing was done about it. Much like how it is that currently counterterrorism *knows* that drones will produce terrorism 'exponentially' and yet this is the much hyped 'only game in town'? These are *known* facts, yet they are made to be *unknown* when concrete policies are to be taken. This 'passion for ignorance' points to the core of the crisis of knowledge in counterterrorism.

Droning, writing, divining: the perversion of temporality

'The self-fulfilling prophecy is, in the beginning,' writes sociologist Robert Merton,

> a false definition of the situation evoking a new behavior which makes the original false conception come true. This specious validity of the self-fulfilling prophecy perpetuates a reign of error. For the prophet will cite the actual course of events as proof that he was right from the very beginning. . . .Such are the perversities of social logic. (1968, p. 477)

It was false that there was al-Qaeda in Iraq before the invasion but then it became true after the invasion. Anti-American radical Islamists could never afford to have antiaircraft missiles, until the CIA provided Stinger missiles to Afghan rebels battling the Soviets in the mid-1980s. Similarly, over 40 countries are currently developing drone technology to be used as military robots, with the likelihood that in a not faraway future they might fall into the hands of terrorists. Such self-fulfilling prophecy of counterterrorist drones being used by terrorists, we are told, 'is not far away' (Caryl 2011, p. 58).

Kilcullen's main concern is with the formation of what he labels 'the accidental guerrilla' – ordinary people caught in the fight between terrorists and counterterrorists, who end up supporting the local fight against the outsiders and who would be impossible to distinguish from the terrorists, 'except by accident'. His thesis is that most of the adversaries encountered by Western powers after 9/11 are the products of such *accident* – 'people who fight us not because they hate the West and seek our overthrow but because *we* have invaded *their* space to deal with a small extremist element' (Caryl 2011, pp. 34, 263). But even if 'accidental' and a 'guerrilla' (and not a 'terrorist'), still Kilcullen remains within the counterterrorist mindset when he immediately proposes that: 'I theorise that the accidental guerrilla emerges from a cyclical process that takes place in four stages: infection, contagion, intervention, and rejection' (2009, p. 35). The 'cyclical process' is thus not ruled by cultural or political circumstances or by the logic of historical repetition and action/reaction linkages, but by the medical analogy of 'a virus or bacterium' – the primary associations of 'infection' and 'contagion' which point to a thinking that is typical of how the logic of witchcraft and taboo operate in ethnographic communities (Zulaika and Douglass 1996).

The failed approach to insurgency in Iraq is characterised by Kilcullen as 'enemy-centric' (2009, p. 129), with the focus on killing the terrorists. But despite his criticisms of the very notion of the war on terror, still he cannot avoid framing counterterrorism as a *war*, his main reference for comparison/contrast being the Cold War. Kilcullen finds it a 'limited analogy', '[y]et in at least one dimension, that of time, the enduring trends that drive the current confrontation may mean that the conflict will indeed resemble the Cold War' (2009, p. 301). I agree that *time* is central to our analysis but not in the sense that 'we are at the beginning of a very long road', rather, in the perversion of temporality implied in such 'waiting for terror'. In such temporality of waiting, one has to start with the non-hypothetical premise that no matter what, *there will be terrorism*. Imagine all the terrorists disappeared tomorrow; still, for Kilcullen, 'All these [terrorism] trends would endure even if AQ and its *takfiri* allies disappeared tomorrow' (2009, p. 294). What is indisputable is that we should look at 'AQ as a harbinger of a new era of conflict' (2009, p. 294). It is not if, but when. The bedrock premise is that there will always be war and now there will *always* be terrorism.

And once terrorism is defined as inevitable, its very logic will tend to make it self-fulfilling by producing a behaviour that will make the original false definition come true. The reality itself is that 'terrorism constantly morphs into new mutations,' Kilcullen tells us, and therefore 'counterterrorism methods ... are almost by definition already obsolete' (2009, p. 294). Yet, the one fact that can never be put into question is that the thing itself *is* terrorism. The assassination of President Kennedy was not a terrorist act at the time; nowadays, by one of those 'mutations' into which it is morphed, it would be *the* terrorist act by excellence. Your own discursive definitions make things be what you want them to be. Kilcullen is very aware that there are other threats as well, such as proliferation of nuclear weapons, climate change, resource conflict, rogue states, actual wars between states and so on; but terrorism will always be a distinct one, non-reducible to those other threats.

'A new lexicon' is Kilcullen's first proposal among his 'tentative conclusions' (2009, p. 300). Again, counterterrorism knows that its vocabulary and discourse *produce* in part the thing itself of terrorism. But what I find most surprising is that, in the study of terrorism, he advocates not international relations (the grand narrative we read about in daily news about the internationalisation of terrorism), but *anthropology* – with its methodology to '[g]et as close as possible (in time and space) to the actual events, ideally by being present when they unfold but, at the very least, by seeking firsthand descriptions from eyewitnesses' (2009, p. 304). As an ethnographer of political violence myself, I find this recommendation extraordinary in its incongruence with counterterrorism's ordinary *modus operandi*.

In fact, as I completed my ethnography of Basque violence (1988), I was faced with the existence of an international committee of terrorism experts to tackle the very problem I had just studied and which issued a report to much media fanfare that left me wondering what claims to 'knowledge' did anthropology, as opposed to counterterrorism, have (Zulaika 1991). The basic recommendation by the terrorism experts was blunt: never see a terrorist (not even on television), never listen to a terrorist (not even on a radio) and never talk to a terrorist. Anthropology was called upon as a discipline that could help bring valuable information to carry out the grand counterterrorist agenda of cleansing the Basque Country from terrorism. The Irish were given a similar advice, lest someone might identify with their cause.

Kilcullen's proposal that counterterrorism should turn into anthropology, I assume on the basis of the experience gained in Iraq's surge, is a radical departure from the former strategy of complete tabooing and distancing from the untouchable terrorists. But this is unrealistic and misses the key issue: counterterrorism has established a political and moral *cordon sanitaire* regarding terrorism, a strict taboo backed with the most stringent laws that *de facto* prohibits conducting an ethnography of terrorism. Even interviewing a terrorist in prison, let alone while active, is out of the question, as proven recently by the Bureau of Prisons' rejection to grant access to a group of scholars proposing to investigate how they got into terrorism (Shane 2011, p. 26). Truman Capote could write a compelling narrative of multiple murder, identifying with the killers; an equivalent identification with terrorists would turn into the anathema of an apology of terrorism (Zulaika 2009, pp. 37–59). Indeed, one could argue that, as the result of *writing*, the same 'murder' becomes a different reality in the hands of a historian, a sociologist, a journalist, a novelist or a counterterrorist. Similarly, you could argue that the Basque political violence of my ethnography at a village level was not the same 'thing' as the Basque terrorism of the international experts (Zulaika and Douglass 1996, pp. 31–63). In short, there is again this impasse in Kilcullen's proposal, by which an anthropological approach might in fact *dissolve* the violence into cultural patterns and political causes, and yet while terrorism remains the undisputable, permanent category and counterterrorism 'the only game in town'.

A central dimension of terrorism, and one that is crucial to show its self-fulfilling quality, has to do with threats and their perception and the reactions they provoke. A threat plays with the sign as representing a future event, while we never know whether the issuer actually means it or not or whether he might change his opinion in the future. The Unabomber brought the traffic in California airports to a halt by simply sending a letter to a newspaper with the threat of bringing down an airliner, while he sent another letter to another newspaper admitting that the threat was a 'prank'. The actual reality of the threat might be nothing but play: a *zero* that can yet have deadly serious consequences. Counterterrorism is a prime example of what Merton labelled 'the Thomas theorem', namely: 'If men define situations as real, they are real in their consequences' (1968, p. 475). Once the situation is defined as one of inevitable terrorism and endless waiting, what could happen weighs as much as what is actually the case; once a threat, whose intention or possibility is unknown to us, is taken seriously, its reality requires that we must act on it. Terrorism is the catalyst for confusing various semantic levels of linguistic, ritual and military actions.

Anthropologists have examined phenomena such as divination, which manipulates the axis of time in a cultural context of magic and witchcraft. They have compared premodern mystical notions of causation and temporality to our own modern standards of rationality. The discussion leads directly to issues of ontology and epistemology: what is the thing itself of magic or taboo or divination? What is the nature of 'reality' and what type of 'knowledge' is involved in such 'beliefs' by the natives of those cultures as well as by the 'interpretations' produced by their analysts?

As we ask what the rationale and the nature of the information supporting counterterrorism's most fateful decisions were, such as those taken by the Bush Administration before going to war with Iraq or by Bremer after the invasion, an anthropologically informed observer is reminded of secret oracle consultations among the Azande, as famously described by Edward Evans-Pritchard, and which were summed up thus by Peter Winch:

> Oracular revelations are not treated as hypotheses and, since their sense derives from the way they are treated in their context, they therefore are not hypotheses. They are not a matter of

intellectual interest but the main way in which Azande decide how they should act. If the oracle reveals that a proposed course of action is fraught with mystical dangers from witchcraft or sorcery, that course of action will not be carried out; and then the question of refutation or confirmation just does not arise. We might say that the revelation has the logical status of an unfulfilled hypothetical. (1977, p. 88)

The need to consult oracles concerning witchcraft responds to the urge to know the causation of unfortunate events. How they happen is perceived by the senses; why they happen is what magical thinking is all about. This is where revelations by oracles become essential to Azande thought. The spirit of consulting an oracle is obviously very unlike a scientist's experiments.

The central premise of counterterrorism thinking is the oft-repeated formula that 'it is not if, but when'. Hypotheticals are premised with the conditional 'if': 'if A, then B'. What characterises basic counterterrorist knowledge about the next impending attack is that it will happen. In a mindset that parallels Azande witchcraft, the counterterrorist axiom of 'not if' rules out mere hypotheses. The revelations are thus 'unfulfilled hypotheticals' that will become real with time. Counterterrorist projections are the equivalent of oracular certainties: the horror will happen no matter what. This leads in pragmatic terms to the fatalistic attitude of disregarding actual knowledge and not taking responsibility for actual decisions: what does it really matter what we decide since it is going to happen anyway and whatever happens is out of our hands? What matters, therefore, is that we sort of *divine* what the course of action will be.

The practical aspect of this temporality of waiting, in which the certainty of the impending evil is beyond any hypothetical ('not if'), is that we need to act pre-emptively now against events that are to happen in the future. The rationale behind nuclear deterrence was that developing armaments now, ready to strike at the push of a button, guaranteed that they would not be used in the future. Many commentators saw in such logic the quintessence of technological madness. But that was not enough. Since future nuclear attacks by terrorists are only a matter of time, we must wage a war now pre-emptively, even in a nuclear context, thus breaking the historic assumption that nuclear arsenals were for deterrence, not for actual usage. What justifies the use of a 'just war' in the nuclear era is the *desire* of terrorists for having the WMD we possess. There is nothing evil or irrational about having or using them, as it is an established fact that terrorists desire them and one day will have them. Thus, the formula of 'not if, but when' becomes a self-fulfilling prophecy. The counterterrorist thinking makes it an imperative that the war must start now – against Saddam Hussein, against al-Qaeda, against Iran and against all potential terrorists. This is how the American public, including the liberal media, accepted the rationale to go to war against Iraq.

It is the play with the axis of time that is most revealing of the manipulations of associative magic, as well as of counterterrorist thinking. The oracle, based on secret knowledge, reveals whether witchcraft has transpired and whether its danger looms ahead. The terrorist threat also creates the temporality of waiting. Actual historical temporality becomes subservient to the feared future. If there are no terrorism attacks, the counterterrorist can claim success in preventing them; but if the attack does occur, then the counterterrorist can say 'I told you so' and argue that he was right in his predictions. At this point, terrorism foretold becomes prophecy fulfilled. Such imperviousness to error in actual historical events points to a time warp that goes to the heart of counterterrorist mythology. Such waiting implies in fact that historical time has surrendered itself to a fateful future.

The result of this passive temporality regarding events we can do nothing to prevent is a fateful mindset in which the terror events are closer to nature than society and politics, and there is hardly any point in looking into the intellectual premises or subjective motivations that guide terrorist actions. The great political victory of the suicide bombers is that they imposed on US politics their own suicidal temporality of waiting and a culture grounded on the oracular knowledge of secret intelligence, which then justified the war on terror.

Secret knowledge and the state of exception

Kilcullen's trenchant, internal criticism of counterterrorism goes to the core of its culture when in his concluding 'new paradigms' he dares question a belief-based intelligence:

> Why, for example, did Western intelligence miss the imminent fall of the Soviet Union in 1992? In part, at least, because we were reading the Soviet leaders' mail – and they themselves failed to understand the depth of grassroots disillusionment with Communism. Why did most countries (including those who opposed the Iraq war) believe in 2002 that Saddam Hussein had WMDs? Because they were intercepting the regime's communications, and many senior Iraqi regime members believed Iraq them . . . [while] their resources were . . . following analytical dead ends. (Kilcullen 2009, p. 293)

The crisis of counterterrorist knowledge begins with the nature and context of the 'intelligence' gathered. We need to inquire as to what is valid information in the counterterrorist situation, what critical information is missing from it and what controls are exerted over such information. Forty percent of the US military budget is secret (Johnson 2007, p. 209), as are the budgets of the intelligence agencies.

The basic political context of counterterrorist intelligence in the Bush-declared war on terror parallels what anthropologists have categorised as 'dual sovereignty'. In many societies, there is an opposition and complementarity between the jural/administrative power of the chiefs and the secretive, mystical authority of priests and sorcerers. A classic case is the Shilluk's divine kingship studied by Edward Evans-Pritchard (1948). The relationship between the open political process and the secret covert action required by the war on terror evokes in our own society a similar dual sovereignty by which legal authority is complemented with a different type of power that finds its legitimacy in the elusive principle of national security. If overt politics is based on the rule of law, covert politics is grounded on secret information that cannot be shared with the public at large.

The secretive power needed to confront 'unseen forces' in societies ruled by dual sovereignty can be related to the concept of the 'state of exception', when, in Agamben's formulation, the sovereign is both inside and outside the law, and execution and transgression of law coincide. Guantánamo can be seen as both civilisation's ultimate bastion against terrorism and the ultimate denial of international law. Who can decide whether the thousands of people killed by drone attacks are the lawful killings required by the war on terror or are illegal murders? The sovereign is paradoxically both inside and outside the law.

What is the meaning of 'information' in such terrorist scenarios of states of exception and in the presence of a community of believers whose basic structure separates those who 'know' the secret information and the rest of us who are to be kept in the dark? Secrecy means that no critical judgment can be exercised, much like in mystical societies where knowledge belongs only to the sacred specialist. Questioning the effectiveness of the information amounts to lack of faith and goes directly against the community of believers.

In the days previous to invading Iraq, the frequent visits by Cheney to the intelligence community are well documented; essentially, the community did not know what it was asked to know regarding Iraq and the war on terror. Thus, knowledge had to be *created* by tying together the bits and pieces of scattered information while adding inferences and guesswork in order to come up with a plausible scenario. A new intelligence unit was formed at the Pentagon. Only a handful of senators read the classified intelligence about Iraq prior to authorising war.

Intelligence becomes ancillary information when belief drives knowledge. Once the decision has been made that the enemy is Hitler, the ordinary standards of factual evidence are supplemented with untested premises grounded on moral and political principles. The main role of information is no longer procuring factual evidence, but helping uncover the secret intentions of the evildoer. And, given the final goal of defeating evil, if information that contradicts the belief system is provided, then it is better to reject it. Thus, the likes of Wolfowitz become 'this know-it-all who won't believe the intelligence community' (Ricks 2006, p. 30). The 'know-it-all' is essentially in possession of a secret type of knowledge, having to do with the realisation that the world is confronting evil – a secrecy that allows the knower to disregard ordinary information. In factual terms, there might be a problem, namely, that '[h]e's deeply misguided, he's impervious to evidence' (Ricks 2006, p. 31) – including the evidence of lack of evidence – but we are by now deeply immersed in a type of knowledge consisting in a world view engaged in transforming the evil reality at hand. The concerns of military men about the lack of preparation to go to war, as well as of the advisers of the previous administration who suspected that evidence was being fabricated, were dismissed by the Bush administration. Once you are a crusader who 'knows' that Saddam Hussein stands for the apocalyptic combination of terrorism and WMD, the ordinary standards of evidence, information and knowledge no longer apply – not even those of your own military and intelligence communities. By then the only moral imperative is creating and manipulating information to defeat the evil enemy. This is no longer ordinary politics, but counterterrorism is by then 'a religiously sanctioned moral duty' (Leach 1977, p. 36).

But, if the reports of Hussein's WMD bluff are true, such a crusading attitude was unable to detect it. The inability to sort out real threat from a feigned one is in a nutshell the problem with counterterrorism. The problem is fundamentally *epistemological*, namely, what type of knowledge is missing if the actuality or the fakery of a threat cannot be assessed? It is the kind of problem an ethnographer faces in an alien culture, a psychoanalyst in the symptoms of a patient, a writer such as Capote when he wants to produce a true account of a multiple murderer or when a detective has to solve a crime. Why should we not demand from a counterterrorist the basic knowledge and skills of current knowledge as we do from these other types of writers? This is also the pragmatic knowledge expected from a good poker player always facing the probability of the opponent's bluff.

The issue does not affect only the counterterrorist official and expert, but the entire political establishment and intellectual culture and media discourse in general. The problem is that not even a Colin Powell, with all his experience and access to the most privileged information, can penetrate what is behind the 'secret knowledge' of counterterrorism – the secret being essentially ignorance regarding the terrorists. And that even the *New York Times* can publish on its front page fabricated reports because it assumes the legitimacy of a 'secret knowledge' forced on the community of believers. The role of critical terrorism studies has to be to remain fiercely sceptical about this new mythology. It is reminiscent of the myth of the wild man and points to a discourse that, at its core, holds on to the dichotomy between *their* 'barbarism' and *our* 'civilisation'. The unrecognised premise is one of tabooing their voices and desires, by categorising their madness, suicides and killings as qualitatively distinct from ours, that is, by denying them a complex subjectivity like ours. The final outcome of such discourse is to justify a war of choice as a 'just war', for the phantom of terrorism has become the only justification in the nuclear era. The latest fantasy scenario is one in which the West's superior drone technology can detect terrorists from 10,000 feet above in the sky and kill them by remote control as if in a video game.

The British historian Hugh Trevor-Roper, having analysed the 'grotesque mental construction' of European witchcraft, concluded that during the Renaissance, there was in fact a regression in superstitious modes of thought from the Middle Ages. He had the following uncanny observation: 'Indeed, the more learned a man was in the traditional scholarship of the time, the more likely he was to support the witch-doctors' (1969, p. 154). Is current counterterrorism knowledge also in the ironic predicament that the more it 'knows' the more fooled it is? As a sample, here is a similar commentary on experts predicting biological terrorism by Milton Leitenberg: 'The less the commentator seems to know about biological warfare the easier he seems to think the task is' (cited in Mueller 2006, p. 22).

Following on from the earlier discussion on the value of 'information' in the counterterrorist episteme, the question is, does having more of it help? Or is not having more of the same thing even more obfuscating? What historians of the CIA have concluded is that its game of deception included fooling itself and thereby becoming incapable of sorting out true information from self-deception. Already in the mid-1950s, an internal report regarding widespread frustration in the agency came to the conclusion that its young officers saw that the intelligence service 'was lying to itself' (Weiner 2007, p. 78). Lying, in fact, becomes an imperative sworn under oath. There was nothing more destructive to the agency's morale than Carter's post-Nixon moral allergy to deceit and its pledge never to lie to the American public, when deceit is the quintessence of a secret intelligence service. Carter's naïve aversion to deception and secret action amounted to a radical dismantling of the 'dual sovereignty' of American politics throughout the Cold War.

The other issue with information being by definition 'secret' is what you do with information that is in the open. Imagine that the name of your next airplane hijacker is in a city's phone book, as was the case, and that 50–60 officers know that the hijacker is in the country: should you take it seriously? When such information is by nature ultra-secret, would paying attention to a phone book not betray in itself ignorance of what you are dealing with? In short, the information was in the system, yet why did the system refuse to read and act on it? Does such oversight not suggest that there is, at some level, unconscious but systemic complicity between terrorists and counterterrorists? Perhaps the complicity springs from sharing a culture of ultra-secrecy in which open information is dismissed as irrelevant and in which the temporality of waiting tends to grant more urgency to what *could* happen than to what is actually the case.

From the one per cent doctrine to poker thinking

It is well known that Vice President Cheney wanted to rule out any chance from the system when he maintained that if Saddam Hussein had a 1% chance of obtaining WMD, the United States had to act to prevent it (Suskind 2006). In order to see the limits and catastrophic consequences of such an inflexible doctrine, one only has to look at the role of change in human action through the lens of the most prevalent American card game – poker. The art of the game of poker consists in minimising the element of luck, yet is based on the knowledge that not only can it never be completely eliminated from the game, but luck becomes the key strategic component to use to one's advantage and prevail.

If detecting bluffs and false threats is central to counterterrorism, then poker might indeed be its best model for systemic knowledge – not chess, where the moves can be predicted in advance, but poker, where the cards are unpredictable and bluffing is an essential tactic to the game. The crucial tactic for poker thinking is: 'cheating and thwarting cheaters, leveraging uncertainty, bluffing and sussing out bluffers, managing risk and reward' (McManus 2009, p. 18). The admission that there are elements of 'luck' or 'chance' or 'bluff' in poker is not a denial of its systemic nature, but only a realisation of its more complex statistics (see Neuman and Morgestern 1944).

Playing with chance is pivotal to the terrorist *modus operandi*. Non-feedback action based on chance, innocence of the victim, ritual sacrifice and suicidal madness are all aspects of a logical space dominated ultimately, even if within a previously delimited field, by random election. The arbitrary election of the victim by chance carries the action to a different realm of possibility and meaning. The terrorist typically engages in a course of behaviour that strategically rules out feedback: once the airplane is hijacked for a suicide mission, there is no way back. It is the study of *purpose* that should be of key concern for terrorism studies: if feedback is required for teleological behaviour, the terrorist's non-feedback action is not only 'purposeful' in its objectives but also deliberately 'purposeless' in its means. The use of purposeless tactics in pursuit of political goals is what makes terrorism strategically so unpredictable. This is a system closer to poker than chess.

There is one ancient concept in military theory that is central to terrorism: stratagem. It includes deception, surprise, ambush, feigned moves, disinformation, betrayal and other ploys. These trickeries have been in use from primitive warfare to nuclear deterrence. They are key to the ritualised action of warfare in traditional societies. The military strategy of the Cold War has been frequently compared with poker, beginning with D-day when Eisenhower employed various bluffing manoeuvres to outfox the Nazis. The second part of the twentieth century has been characterised 'as an age of stratagem, in which theories of deterrence exploit the idea of bluff, intelligence agencies have become masters of deceit, and guerrilla warfare and terrorism consistently employ surprise, psychological tactics, and avoidance of battle' (Wheeler 1991, pp. 24–25). Diplomacy during the nuclear age was well described by the mathematician theorist of poker, Morgenstern, as a 'real-life version of poker' (cited in McManus 2009, p. vii). The most dramatic example of such poker playing was when, on the brink of triggering a nuclear war, John Kennedy called Khrushchev's bluff during the Cuban missile crisis.

Terrorism is the culmination of these tactics of deception at all military and information levels; hence, the need for poker thinking. There is a Basque card game, *mus*, which I used as a model of activism in my work on political violence. I compared the *ekintza* 'action' of the militant with the all-or-nothing *hordago* in the mus game. The hordago point eliminates the point-by-point continuous process and, if accepted, condenses all alternatives in a single bet. Hordago is the final self-corrective point, usually a bluff, when one is losing. The hordago interruption of the gradual process introduces a premise of ritual condensation – an on/off, either/or digitalisation. The hordago is the last recourse of the loser – an almost obligatory bluff – and ritual premises of condensation and discontinuity are intrinsic to the entire phenomenon. Even if counterintuitive, professional gamblers also know that one should use the worst hands when bluffing, since, unlike for checking, one expects to lose if called for bluffing, it does not matter what hands are used. What is critical for counterterrorist thinking is not to be fooled by randomness and bluffing.

The national trauma of 9/11 confronted the United States with the alternative of either not responding to the attack and thus implying defencelessness or replying massively and thus possibly making things worse. In terms of counterterrorist thinking, the alternative was between a regression to a premodern mindset or a jump into a more creative thinking that would avoid its own self-generating repetition. The reaction by the Bush administration happened in terms of mechanical action/reaction responses with a medieval type of thinking, including the use of torture, a crucial component of the entire witchcraft demonology. In political terms, the regression consisted in returning to a 'state of exception' that led to Guantánamo and was visualised in the Abu Ghraib photographs of torture and sexual humiliation committed by the US forces.

A different approach requires a radical departure from this counterterrorist mindset. It must borrow clues from a detective as to how to read the actor's desire; it must have a novelist's capacity for projection into the murderer's subjectivity; it must be able to interpret the politics of the unconscious of the suicide killer's 'death drive'; it must strategise the way a poker play does. The political commentator Bill Schneider called President Bush's decision to go to war 'Texas political poker, the ultimate high-stakes gamble' (McManus 2009, p. 332) – but it was poker premised on Cheney's blind inflexibility of the one per cent doctrine. It has been remarked that, in the nuclear era, the most important skill for a president may be the ability to sort out a genuine threat from a bluff. This requires genuine poker thinking, dominated by probability and making use of various kinds of inference and chance. This is a kind of thinking in which

> players gauge pot odds, randomise bluffs, fold when their hand is a statistical underdog, raise when it's the favourite . . . decoys and stealing are crucial, but patience is just as important . . . players spend most of their time picking up signs, moving into position, and working the count, but once every nine plays or so, on both offence and defense, their skills really have to pay off. Yet more than in most competitions, luck becomes pivotal. (McManus 2009, p. 339)

Such complexity of various types of information, including those of the detective and the novelist and the art of the poker face, is what is missing from counterterrorism.

Buddhist thinkers have argued that technical knowledge is not enough to master an art and that it must become an 'artless art' that grows out of the unconscious. Not surprisingly, good poker players are believed to rely on intuition in order to read the states of mind of their opponents. This is also called 'strategic flexibility', the ability to playfully randomise by a sense of 'feel' and create algorithms that, in the words of the mathematician David Berlinski, 'belong to the world of memory and meaning, desire and design' (cited in McManus 2009, p. 389). As Bill Gates put it:

> In poker, a player collects different pieces of information – who's betting boldly, what cards are showing, what this guy's pattern of betting and bluffing is – and then crunches all that data together to devise a plan for his own hand. I got pretty good at this kind of information processing. (Cited in McManus 2009, p. 397)

Being skilful at poker requires first of all that one learns to view the world from the other's point of view. The poet Katy Lederer even talks of poker's 'dirty' intimacy when you are able to 'read' peoples' thoughts and feelings (cited in McManus 2009, p. 417).

Getting into the other's subjective intimacy nowhere appears as 'dirty' as in terrorism, but if one wants to have the skills of a good poker player, it becomes necessary to project oneself into the other's mind and subjectivity. In the end, this requires that the analyst, as Capote observed of the writer, and as it is standard in ethnography, should look at the terrorist subject through his/her own subjectivity and conclude that they belong to the same field. But this would require as a prerequisite dissolving the essential myth of the terrorist as a human being entirely unlike the rest of us.

Conclusion: the force of fantasy and the real

We began with the statement that terrorism testifies to a crisis in knowledge and as such is a salient condition for thought in the current world. Those of us critical of the uses of terrorism discourse to further military approaches to world problems such as nuclear armaments or world poverty tend to take to heart Giambattista Vico's advice that the first science to be learned should be mythology or the interpretation of fables. A current way of updating Vico's teaching is to say that one must take into account the force of fantasy behind current politics.

A critical perspective on terrorism discourse confronts us at the outset with the ontological ambivalence of what is the *real* of the thing itself. The figure of the terrorist gives ground to a reality, the menace of which requires the almost doubling of the defence budget since the Cold War. The task of a critical approach is to problematise that *real* as necessarily imbued in fantasy. This requires we deploy a valid theory by which fantasy is not equal to the *not-real*, but rather 'it constitutes a dimension of the real' (Butler 1990, p. 108). This is a theory of fantasy removed from the representational realism of the media whose reports on terrorism tend to be oblivious of the 'state of the exception' in which they are gathered and produced (censorship, one-sided sources, information obtained under torture, etc.). In such realism, 'representation becomes a moment of the reproduction and consolidation of the real' (Butler 1990, p. 106). In our view, fantasy interrogates the real, considers it a political postulate and does not have a mimetic relationship to it. A positivist view of the real stabilises itself by the phantasmatic exclusion of all absence as unreal. Terrorism is that disavowed phantasmatic exclusion, included in the system as exception that solidifies and gives ground to the politically real. As this real is shaped by the phantom of terrorism constrained by the state of exception, the exceptional phantasmatic draws the boundaries of the real and 'assumes the status of the real, that is, when the two become compellingly conflated' (Butler 1990, p. 107). Thus, fantasy merges with the mask of the real.

Not surprisingly, the current drone war has been described as 'sheer fantasy, if not literally science fiction' (Sluka 2011, p. 72). It has become part of the huge military–media–entertainment industry. Politicians easily become fascinated with technological novelties and special operations. The fantasy plays into the seductive illusion of virtual war 'as a surgical scalpel and not a bloodstained sword,' wrote Michael Ignatieff, adding: 'We need to stay away from such fables of self-righteous invulnerability' (2000, pp. 214–215). But these 'fables' are now the dominant culture, believed not only by the general public but also by the political class and the media elite. You will not read or hear in the mainstream media reports indignant of the drone killings on grounds that, in Kilcullen's numbers, 98% of the victims are innocent. John Quincy Adams wrote in 1821 that 'America . . . goes not abroad in search of monsters to destroy'; in that case, he added, 'She might become the dictatress of the world: she would be no longer the ruler of her own spirit' (cited in Kilcullen 2009, p. 1). Currently, America is taken by the powerful fantasy of the monster/terrorist. A candidate such as John Kerry, a war hero, may lose the presidency for being perceived as 'soft' on terrorism. For the same reason, President Obama is unable to close Guantánamo.

The phantom of the terrorist is responsible for historically charged events, such as sending the blind sheik, Omar Abdul Rahman, to life in prison after a trial that for the *New York Times* was a sham. He is among Islamists, the maximum spiritual and legal leader, kind of what the Pope is for Catholics, and a blind man who was brought to the United States repeatedly with visas issued by the CIA in order to help recruit mujahidin in the US-led anti-Soviet Afghan war. How much more 'passion for ignorance' can a counterterrorist culture display – including the judicial system, the public opinion and academic silence – than sending such a man to life in prison on the basis of an infiltrated informant working for money, disregarding the effect it was likely to have on his followers, including his closest associates, Osama bin Laden and Ayman al-Zawahiri? The informant, according to the *New York Times*, 'began his testimony by admitting that he had lied to just about everybody he ever met' and whose testimony sounded 'like sheer fantasy' (MacFarquhar 1995, p. A9). For the blind sheik to be condemned, it 'only required [the government] to prove the intention to wage a terror campaign' (Editorial, *New York Times* 1995, p. A14). This is also the informer who turned the alleged fatwa issued by the blind sheik – a charge he could never prove in court – into a self-fulfilling prophecy: once he was imprisoned for life, the blind sheik did issue a fatwa, a supreme command that made 9/11 morally imperative for his followers.

But fantasy, in its semantic excess, also has the potential to interrogate and contest the claims of the real. In an individual's wish-fulfilment, fantasy is both the 'I' who fantasises and the 'I' who is in the fantasised narrative. Fantasy provides the frame and the setting for the individual who is caught in the narrative of images: 'As a result, the subject, although always present in the fantasy, may be so in a desubjectivised form' (Laplanche and Pontalis 1986, p. 27). The terrorist provides that fantasy setting in which the counterterrorist can participate in a desubjectivised manner. This also implies that the very identity of the subject of fantasy is put into question by the multiple identifications available in a fantasy setting; the mastery the subject claims over the fantasy is already undone by the fantasy's own power of fragmentation.

In the final analysis, what is most needed for counterterrorism might be more fantasy and fiction, not less. For anyone who has dealt with real 'terrorists' on the ground, counterterrorism's 'latest game in town' (terrorism resolved by drones shooting from the sky at alleged terrorists, as if in a Nintendo game) will appear as fatal fantasy. Eminent jurists and theologians believed in the seventeenth century that witches flew to the Sabbath, a belief that resulted in many thousands of them being burnt on the bonfire. It is no surprise that in our technology-driven era, counterterrorism officials will expect no less from drones and other flying objects. There is no point in trying to convince people that their fantasy images are unreal. What matters is to realise what kind of existence they do have as constitutive of the real. Here is where *more* fiction, an intensification of the crisis, might be a way out for the ontological problematic of perception and identity provoked by the terrorist phantom.

One way of articulating this solution is the one proposed by Hayden White regarding the myth of the wild man, when he advocated a

> dissolution [of the grounds of the concept] ... that permits us to distinguish between wildness as a myth and as a fiction, as an ontological state and as a historical stage of human development, as a moral condition and as an analytical category of cultural anthropology, and, finally, to recognise in the notion of the Wild Man an instrument of cultural projection that is as anomalous in conception as it is vicious in application. (1978, p. 157)

We need fiction to dissolve the myth of the culture of terror and realise the role of fantasy in constituting the real; Montaigne's irony used the concept of savagery to question the myths of civilisation of his own society. Further, fictionalising the myths of terrorism is one strategy to destabilise its realist representations. Eventually, even the learned theologians, prompted by the detective-like work of inquisitor Salazar (Henningsen 1980), were convinced that witches did not fly and that fantasy must have played a key role in the entire phenomenon. Eventually, even counterterrorists will come to grips with the hard fact that, as sadly proven by drones fired from Las Vegas into the Pakistani mountains being 'the only game in town', it is the force of fantasy that is most *real* in the current culture of terror.

Editor's note

This article was first presented as the Third Annual *Critical Studies on Terrorism* Lecture, an event inaugurated by the journal to celebrate scholars who have made a significant contribution to critical terrorism studies. Professor Zulaika's lecture was presented at 'A Decade of Terrorism and Counter-terrorism since 9/11: Taking Stock and New Directions in Research and Policy', the BISA Critical Studies on Terrorism Working Group (CSTWG) Annual Conference, 8–11 September 2011, University of Strathclyde, Glasgow, UK. The editors are grateful to Professor Zulaika for accepting our invitation and to the conference organisers for including it in the programme.

Notes on contributor

Joseba Zulaika is professor and co-director of the Center for Basque Studies at the University of Nevada, Reno, USA. Among his books are *Basque Violence: Metaphor and Sacrament* (1988), *Terror and Taboo* (with William Douglass 1996) and *Terrorism: The Self-Fulfilling Prophecy* (2010). His main interests are culture and symbolism, the international discourse of terrorism, museums and the revitalisation of cities. He is currently completing an ethnography of Bilbao's urban transformations.

References

Agamben, G., 1998. *Homo sacer: sovereign power and bare life*. Stanford, CA: Stanford University Press.
Ahmad, M., 2011. The magical count of body counts. *Al Jazeera*, 13 June.
Butler, J., 1990. The force of fantasy: feminism, Mapplethorpe, and discursive excess. *Difference: A Journal of Feminist Cultural Studies*, 2 (2), 105–125.
Caryl, C., 2011. Predators and robots at war. *The New York Review of Books*, 29 September, 55–57.
Editorial, 1995. The trial of Omar Abdel Rahman. *New York Times*, 3 October.
Evans-Pritchard, E., 1948. *The divine kingship of the Shilluk of the Nilotic Sudan*. Cambridge: Cambridge University Press.
Hari, J., 2010. Obama's escalating robot war in Pakistan is making a terror attack more likely. *The Huffington Post*, 15 October.
Henningsen, G., 1980. *The witches' advocate: Basque witchcraft and the Spanish Inquisition (1609–1614)*. Reno, NV: University of Nevada Press.
Horgan, J. and Boyle, M., 2008. A case against critical terrorism studies. *Critical Studies on Terrorism*, 1 (1), 51–64.
Ignatieff, M., 2000. *Virtual war: Kosovo and beyond*. Washington, DC: Cato Institute.
Johnson, C., 2007. *Nemesis: the last days of the American Republic*. New York: Macmillan.
Kilcullen, D., 2009. *The accidental guerrilla: fighting small wars in the midst of a big one*. Oxford: Oxford University Press.
Laplanche, J. and Pontalis, J., 1986. *Formations of fantasy*. London: Methuen.
Leach, E., 1977. *Custom, law, and terrorist violence*. Edinburgh: Edinburgh University Press.
Lindlaw, S., 2008. Remote-control warriors suffer war stress. *Associated Press*, 7 August.
MacFarquhar, N., 1995. In bombing, a deluge of details. *New York Times*, 19 March.
McManus, J., 2009. *Cowboys full: the story of poker*. New York: Farrar, Straus and Giroux.
Merton, R., 1968. *Social theory and social structure*. New York: Free Press.
Mueller, J., 2006. *Overblown: how politicians and the terrorism industry inflate national security threats, and why we believe them*. New York: Free Press.
Ricks, T., 2006. *Fiasco: the American military adventure in Iraq*. New York: Penguin.

Shane, S., 2011. Beyond Guantanamo, a web of prisons. *New York Times*, 11 December.
Sluka, J., 2011. Death from above: UAVs and losing hearts and minds. *Military Review*, May–June, 70–76.
Suskind, R., 2006. *The one percent doctrine: deep inside America's pursuit of its enemies since 9/11*. New York: Simon & Schuster.
Trevor-Roper, H.R., 1969. *The European witch-craze of the sixteenth and seventeenth centuries and other essays*. New York: Harper and Row.
von Neuman, J. and Morgestern, O., 1944. *Theory of games and economic behavior*. Princeton, NJ: Princeton University Press.
Weiner, T., 2007. *Legacy of ashes*. New York: Doubleday.
Wheeler, E., 1991. Terrorism and military theory: an historical perspective. *Terrorism and Political Violence*, 3, 6–33.
White, H., 1978. *Tropics of terror: essays in cultural criticism*. Baltimore, MD: John Hopkins University Press.
Winch, P., 1977. Understanding a primitive society. *In*: R. Wilson, ed. *Rationality*. Oxford: Basil Blackwell, 78–111.
Zulaika, J., 1988. *Basque violence: metaphor and sacrament*. Reno, NV: University of Nevada Press.
Zulaika, J., 1991. Terror, totem, and taboo: reporting on a report. *Terrorism and Political Violence*, 3 (1), 34–49.
Zulaika, J., 2009. *Terrorism: the self-fulfilling prophecy*. Chicago, IL: Chicago University Press.
Zulaika, J. and Douglass, W., 1996. *Terror and taboo: the follies, fables, and faces of terrorism*. New York: Routledge.

Reinventing prevention or exposing the gap? False positives in UK terrorism governance and the quest for pre-emption

Charlotte Heath-Kelly

Department of International Politics, Aberystwyth University, Aberystwyth, Wales, UK

> This article considers the developments within UK counterterrorism strategy between the Prevention of Terrorism Acts (PTAs) and the recent (2011) reworking of CONTEST. It argues that the performance of prevention within British counterterrorism *policy* has changed to favour pre-emptive measures, deployed in accordance with knowledge produced about terrorism 'risk'. However, this shift has been accompanied by the continuation of certain *practices* of pre-emption. The article integrates the studies of 'suspect communities' created by counterterrorism practices into its discussion of risk, elucidating how the production of risky subjectivities has enabled the practice of 'preventative' force upon both Provisional Irish Republican Army (PIRA) and contemporary terrorist suspects. The article focuses on these articulations of risky communities, highlighting how they lead to 'false positives' in the identification of terrorists and the use of sovereign force (like the death of Jean Charles de Menezes or the assassination of PIRA suspects in Gibraltar) by painting certain racial characteristics and behaviours as imminently dangerous. The article connects the production of suspect communities to the presence of pre-emptive logics within counterterrorism discourse, logics that have consistently produced a 'gap' between the terrorist event and its pre-emption, between the suspect community and the figure of the terrorist, then. This 'gap' leads to the use of force upon innocent persons – who are temporarily rendered guilty by visualities of 'suspectness'. As such, the apparent novelty of pre-emptive terrorism governance within British *policy* framing does not reflect a similar discontinuity in the *practice* of counterterrorism then – which has consistently deployed suspect communities and produced 'false positives' within a politics of pre-emption.

Introduction

How old is preventative counterterrorism in the United Kingdom? From the large literature that addresses preventative practices within the war on terror (WOT), one might assume that a risk-based pre-emptive approach to governing terrorism is relatively new. And some components of that assumption are correct. However, the status of 'prevention' in the history of British counterterrorism has undergone significant shifts. This article explores the changing conceptions of 'prevention' within UK counterterrorism. While highlighting the equation of prevention with pre-emption in the contemporary era, it also examines the pre-configuration of pre-emptive politics in attempts to suppress Provisional Irish Republican Army (PIRA) militancy. This previous era of British policy utilised the term 'prevention' but was not explicitly framed around the pre-emption of events or the interruption of pre-terrorist processes (like radicalisation) which are understood to produce terrorism. However, while the *policy framings* of counterterrorism in each era are somewhat distinct, both periods have utilised *practices* which speak to a continued preoccupation with pre-emption.

After providing a short genealogy of 'prevention' within UK counterterrorism *policy* (which highlights a recent shift towards a discourse of pre-emption), the article will proceed by examining some similarities in *practice* between different eras of UK counterterrorism – making the argument that (apparent) mistakes in the use of lethal force can reveal much about the performance of preventative security in both eras. The article argues that while policy appears to swerve towards pre-emption, *practices* of pre-emptive counterterrorism – like the production of 'suspect communities' – have continued across both eras. Scholars in criminology and sociology have produced evidence that the practice of counterterrorism has produced both Irish and Muslim 'suspect communities' in the last 40 years. Contemporary counterterrorism fixes Muslim communities in its gaze as risky locales from which threats may emerge and directs large policy responses towards the pre-emptive governance of Muslim communities. However, practices of suspicion were also deployed against Irish communities in a previous era of counterterrorism, despite the lack of any pre-emptive policy framing. The article engages with practices of 'suspecting' communities in both eras to highlight a degree of continuity in a pre-emptive politics of counterterrorism within the United Kingdom.

The concluding argument of the article focuses on the use of counterterrorist violence to conceal 'gaps' in the knowledge produced about terrorism, violence which conceals indeterminacy about the point where suspect subjectivities become dangerous subjectivities. Violence, like that performed upon Jean Charles de Menezes or the PIRA suspects in Gibraltar, seems to conceal the existence of an unknown 'tipping point' where suspect persons become threatening. Counterterrorism discourse, it is argued, needs to conceal gaps in its own knowledge about the production of terrorism. This leads to 'false positives' in the identification of terrorists. The article borrows Judith Butler's conception of the 'petty sovereign' to highlight how counterterrorism practices forcibly locate indeterminate subjects within the frame of 'the terrorist', resolving the 'gap' in terrorism knowledge through violence. The use of force upon 'false positives' speaks to a pre-emptive politics in both the PIRA and WOT eras, where the mistakes of counterterrorist violence (where innocent persons are killed or imprisoned) might actually be understood to function in terms of resolving the unknown. In one sense then, they are not mistakes but functional components of a regime of pre-emptive terrorism governance.

The article concludes by arguing that the explicit focus on pre-emption in the policy of the contemporary era could potentially escalate the numbers of 'false positives' and the practice of making 'mistakes' with violence, because the framing of individuals in terms of pre-terrorist stages within the policy deploys a more substantial regime of knowledge than in previous eras. The more knowledge that is produced about 'pre-terrorist' behaviours and risks, the greater the uncertainty about the 'tipping point' where a suspect subjectivity morphs into the figure of the terrorist. And the greater this 'gap' becomes, the greater the need to suppress and conceal such indeterminacy within counterterrorism discourse. We might see more mistakes, more 'false positives', now that the policy is explicitly concerned with the lives of those 'vulnerable' to extremism, because terrorism knowledge can never encompass the 'tipping point' between the suspect subjectivities it produces and the figure of the terrorist.

Prevention between the Prevention of Terrorism Acts and CONTEST

The first half of this article undertakes a genealogy, or discursive exploration, of the meanings attributed to 'prevention' in British counterterrorism policy. Discourse, as the body of practices and statements which imprints words with their content (Hall 2007), performs a function that is often obscured in the use of language. The content and meaning of words can appear self-evident or fixed but post-structuralist interpretations of Saussure's linguistics have challenged the notion of any fixing of language in an extralinguistic sphere (Doty 1997, pp. 377–378). Instead, the meaning of words is not understood to be fixed in the world, but within constellations of other representations. This severing of a connection between signifiers and the signified has led to the reinvigoration of Nietzsche's genealogical method, where the changing meanings of words are explored across time. Genealogical research notes that these apparent chameleon-esque properties are located not in words, or in the signified, but in the political arrangements that constitute their usage.

This type of research method is appropriate for the consideration of prevention in the UK counterterrorism policy. While 'prevention' currently signifies a swathe of pre-emptive interventions (like the Channel Program or biometric screening) that are deployed in conjunction with conceptions of terrorism risk, it was conceived very differently in pre-2005 legislation. This section will discuss the meaning of prevention in the Prevention of Terrorism Acts (PTAs), before introducing the similarities and differences with the discourse of CONTEST. It will examine the discursive constellation around 'preventing terrorism' in both eras and might be considered a mini-genealogy.

Pre-emptive and preventative logics are of great interest to scholars of the WOT. While those involved in drafting CONTEST frame its structure as a natural response to contemporary threats and the extension of capacities to manage them (Omand 2010, p. 101), critical enquiry has often challenged the supposed 'reactivity' of CONTEST. Instead, scholars have highlighted the ways in which counterterrorism produces the threats it names through anticipatory regimes of knowledge and practice, rather than responding to objective dangers. For example, Marieke de Goede's work is dominant within examinations of 'pursuit' tactics and examines international efforts to 'identify' terrorists through financial legislation and security measures (De Goede 2007), and Nick Vaughan-Williams' work has also generated engagement with the tactics deployed in the 'pursuit' (or framing) of suspected terrorists (Vaughan-Williams 2007). Research into the pre-emptive dimensions of CONTEST has also been undertaken in terms of the PROTECT (Coaffee 2009) and PREPARE (Anderson 2010) workstreams, exploring what it means to pre-emptively govern public space in anticipation of terrorism. Critical enquiry is emerging on PREVENT (Lambert 2008, Kundnani 2009, Githens-Mazer and Lambert 2010) but conceptualisations of the radicalisation discourse as pre-emptive governance are currently absent (however, see Heath-Kelly forthcoming).

Given this recent focus on the anticipatory and pre-emptive logics within CONTEST, and their significance, this article will trace 'prevention' through the history of UK counterterrorism, identifying shifts and continuities in how prevention has been conceived.

The PTA as a criminal justice model?

While the conceptions of prevention displayed within the pre-2005 PTAs bore the moniker of prevention, they do not match the anticipatory logics of CONTEST. Past counterterrorism policy embodied a different understanding of prevention – one which governed terrorism through a criminal justice model rather than through an extensive regime of risk knowledge. However, there are indications that the PTAs prefigured the contemporary regime of pre-emption in a number of ways. Before this investigation begins, a note of caution must be sounded. When we discuss this criminal justice model we must be careful to note that the criminalisation approach to the PIRA and loyalist groups was part of a deliberate campaign by Margaret Thatcher's government to depoliticise the violence. The discussion of the criminal justice model should not obscure the extensive role of the British army in Northern Ireland nor the culmination of the troubles in a peace process (Omand 2010, p. 98). Instead, it is better to consider the criminalisation model within the terms of Thatcher government's attempts to delegitimise threats to the perceived integrity of the United Kingdom and, in Margaret Thatcher's own words, to deprive terrorists of the 'oxygen of publicity' (Hickmann et al. 2011, p. 3).

The first PTA was issued in 1974. The content of the PTAs remained largely stable across the re-enactments and revisions made during the 'state of emergency' – which was invoked after 'direct rule' from London was instituted in 1972 to legitimate exceptional measures in Northern Ireland (like the absence of jury trials for terrorism suspects until 2007 'due to the risk of jury intimidation') (Omand 2010, p. 98). The legal powers engendered by the PTAs built upon previous emergency legislation used to suppress insurrection in Northern Ireland since its creation in 1921. For example, from 1922 to 1973, the Civil Authorities (Special Powers) Act authorised continuous emergency measures regarding interrogation and internment without trial (States of Emergency Database: Queens University Belfast 2011). The PTA (1974) consolidated these measures and additionally granted powers to proscribe specific organisations and to relax the rules of evidence at non-jury Diplock Courts for terrorist suspects. The PTA was amended in 1976 and 1984, then re-enacted in 1989 and 2000.[1]

While the PTA legislation adopts the moniker of prevention, the provisions made for the governance of terrorism through the criminal justice system can be difficult to equate with contemporary conceptions of pre-emption. Instead, the 'prevention' of terrorism was legislated through measures to proscribe organisations, through exclusion orders that enabled the deportation of suspects, and practiced through the outlawing of the broadcast of speeches by legal organisations such as Sinn Fein and the Ulster Defence Association (1988–1994), and the internment of (mostly Catholic) persons suspected of links with terrorist organisations. The conceptions of prevention embodied within these powers resonate with sovereign power, rather than the anticipatory governances of CONTEST.[2] Sovereign power, in Mitchell Dean's popular rendering of Foucauldian governmentality, is contrasted with practices of government. Governmental practices can be understood as those 'productive' techniques that emerged after the sixteenth century and act upon the subject's 'desires, aspirations, interests and beliefs' (Dean 1999, p. 11). They engender the performance of certain conducts and are noted in diverse fields like psychological treatment, social housing provision and military discipline. While governmental power is productive, Dean interprets the Foucauldian understanding of sovereign power as 'deductive' (conceived as an antonym of productive). Sovereign power is evident in practices that remove things from the subject, like wealth, bodily integrity or even life. Roughly conceived, sovereign power is more akin to rule than governance.

The measures deployed to govern terrorism in Northern Ireland can be considered examples of sovereign power. Exclusion orders removed subjects, in the most literal sense, from a territory and cast them elsewhere. Such powers were first used by the British government in Northern Ireland between 1921 and 1923 under the Restoration of Order in Ireland Act, enabling the deportation of convicted criminals *and* anyone 'suspected of acting or having acted or being about to act in a manner prejudicial to the restoration or maintenance of order in Ireland' (Hewitt 2008, pp. 13–14). This is where some preventative dimensions of these sovereign powers can be noted – the mere suspicion that one might act in a rebellious manner could result in the deportation of individuals from the United Kingdom to Ireland. While exclusion orders are also used in the contemporary era, and this regime of counterterrorism prefigures the pre-emptive utilisation of deportation in an important sense, the particular use of exclusion orders speaks to a different understanding of 'prevention'. The function of exclusion orders is currently conceived not only in terms of punishing an offender but also, centrally, in terms of governing of *the rest of the population* through the removal of extremists who might 'glorify terrorist violence or foster hatred which might lead to inter community violence' (Home Office 2011, p. 61). Exclusions are conceived within the terms of the broader project of challenging extremist ideology and governing the beliefs of Muslim citizens, through engagement with community-based organisations (Home Office 2011). While deportations appear to take on a criminal justice framing ('We believe that as a matter of principle foreign nationals who have been engaged in terrorist-related activity here should be deported, where they cannot be convicted or after they have served a sentence' (Home Office 2011, p. 46)), the function of exclusion seems to blur the line between sovereign power and governmentality. Statements are made about the appropriate punishing practices to perform upon suspected sympathisers/members of proscribed organisations, but contemporary counterterrorism policy also suggests that measures of deportation 'are intended to act as a deterrent' (Home Office 2011, p. 47). Exclusion orders are, as such, both punishments and disciplinary measures intended to affect the conduct of others.

In the previous era of the PTAs, there was no blurring between sovereign and governmental power regarding deportation. The role of exclusion orders was not described in terms of preventative governance; rather, they were presented as common sense responses to the presence of those identified as enemies. The PTA (1974) states simply that:

> if the Secretary of State is satisfied that any person . . . is concerned in the commission, preparation or instigation of acts of terrorism . . . the Secretary of State may make an order against that person prohibiting him from being in, or entering, Great Britain. (Home Office 1974, p. 3.3)

There is a shift between the eras, then, with regard to the conception of 'prevention' within deportation efforts.

The other mainstays of the PTAs, the practices of proscribing organisations, the removal of broadcasters' abilities to transmit Sinn Fein and UDA statements and the inflammatory use of internment between 1972 and 1975 also clearly resonate with conceptions of sovereign power. The preventative counterterrorism measures deployed within the PTAs involved the taking away of liberty, freedom of speech and the freedom to organise from suspects.[3] In the criminal justice model used to govern Northern Ireland, preventative policy was characterised by hard measures intended to break the armed organisations. Clearly, these sovereign measures have present-day equivalents in the proscription of organisations, laws that prosecute the possession of 'jihadist' reading material and the voicing of statements seen to support the acts of terrorism, and the detention of suspects (against whom prosecutions cannot be mounted due to lack of evidence) under Control Order schemes and the new Terrorism Prevention and Investigation Measures. These features have been carried over from the model of preventative counterterrorism used against the PIRA. However, while the PTA model prefigures the current regime of preventative counterterrorism, contemporary legislation also frames prevention in terms of pre-emptive governance of *persons*.

Persons were somewhat deductable from the PTAs. Sovereign practices were performed upon suspected militants as a means to disrupting and breaking their organisations. Contrastingly, in the contemporary era where organisations are difficult to discern and the networks that connect militants are understood to be simultaneously local, virtual and global, counterterrorism focuses upon the person – and the dynamics that lead persons to commit violent acts. The difference between the eras and the meanings of prevention are most evident in the contrasting approaches to what might be considered the 'glorification' of terrorism.

The PTAs constituted a terrorism offence from the public display of allegiance to proscribed groups through the wearing of items of dress or the carrying of articles (Home Office 1974, 1989, 2000, p. 13.1). The Acts allocate three or six-month prison terms and monetary fines to the punishment of these offences. In the contemporary era, however, 'glorification' has become a far more salient issue for pre-emptive securitisation. The practices deployed against persons who possess 'articles' – such as the al-Qaeda training manual – have increased. The Crown Prosecution Service details the length of prison sentences given to persons in possession of 'documents likely to be of use to someone committing or preparing an act of terrorism' as between one year (as was applied to Aranachalam Chrishanthakumar) and two years *per document* (as was applied to Houria Chentouf) (Crown Prosecution Service 2009). However, there is an identifiable difference between the eras of punishment for 'possessing articles' in the phrasing of terrorism offences. While the PTAs punished the possession or public display of articles evidencing one's allegiance to a proscribed group, contemporary laws penalise those possession articles 'likely to be of use' to a terrorist and the 'encouragement' of terrorist acts. The framing of terrorism governance in terms of risk now invokes the *government of the potential future*, extending attempts to conduct the conduct of persons beyond organisational allegiances into the realm of pre-emption. The possession of articles is not punished reactively anymore, but rather in terms of pre-empting what is considered 'likely' to occur. British counterterrorism seems to have adapted its existing regime of practices to incorporate a new meaning of 'prevention'.

Furthermore, while British law criminalises the incitement of crime, Tony Blair proposed the criminalisation of the vaguer 'condoning or glorifying terrorism' in September 2005 – damaging a legal connection between speech and a criminal act by attempting to criminalise speech itself. In this area, another interesting comparison between the eras of prevention can be noted. While the performance of counterterrorism in the PIRA era involved the 'broadcasting ban' implemented by MP Douglas Hurd in 1988 (understood by Ed Moloney as 'the most stringent controls imposed on the electronic media since the Second World War' (Moloney 1991, p. 10)), the post 9/11 salience of 'glorification' has focused prevention around pre-emptive efforts at governing political opinions – not the taking away of the 'oxygen of publicity' for organisations, as Thatcher put it. Again, the PIRA era can be seen to prefigure the contemporary regime of preventative practices in significant ways, but to different effects. The focus has shifted from repression of legal political discourse during the 'troubles' as punishment, to the attribution of future terrorist consequences to speech. The focus of prevention has been moved towards the governance of futurity.

Due to legal challenge, Tony Blair's criminalisation of 'glorification' could not take place; however, the terrorism bill of October 2005 did constitute the 'encouragement of terrorism' as an offence – a step beyond the normal prohibition of inciting criminal acts (Saul 2005, pp. 870–871). Such measures display sovereign power, in that they remove liberty from those 'encouraging terrorism', but this deployment of rule is intermixed with biopolitical logics of managing population and the prevention of extremist ideology 'infecting' other persons. This pathologisation of counterterrorism is evident within the wider framing of PREVENT around five anti-contagion objectives, to quote the formulation of PREVENT within CONTEST 2009:

In the next 3 years the workstream has five main objectives:

- to challenge the ideology behind violent extremism and support mainstream voices
- disrupt those who promote violent extremism and support the places where they operate
- support individuals who are vulnerable to recruitment, or have already been recruited by violent extremists
- increase the resilience of communities to violent extremism, and
- to address the grievances which ideologues are exploiting. (Home Office 2009, p. 80)

The centrality of discourses of vulnerability and 'radicalisation' to contemporary counterterrorism points to a reorganisation of policy around risk and pre-emption. Instead of focusing upon the breaking of armed organisations, as in the PIRA era, contemporary policy frames nascent stages of terrorism within Muslim communities and designs interventions to act upon this imaginary process of becoming a terrorist (for critiques of the radicalisation discourse and its use in UK counterterrorism, see Kundnani 2009, Githens-Mazer and Lambert 2010, Richards 2011, Heath-Kelly forthcoming). The role of criminal justice in prevention has been refigured around pre-emption and the neutralising of effects that 'extremists' can have upon wider populations while deploying punishing measures.

However, certain continuities between the eras can also be seen in the bifurcated framing of communities both as origins of terrorists and as assets in the campaigns against them. The production of 'suspect communities' by the UK counterterrorism will now be addressed, with a view to tracing continuities in the practice of 'preventative' security. These practices of producing suspect communities do more than highlight the adjustment of prefigured regimes of preventative counterterrorism; they appear to be directly carried over between eras.

Governing the 'suspect' sea 'they' swim in

During the conflict in Northern Ireland, the criminal justice model was sometimes abandoned in favour of governmental measures. The 'hearts and minds' approach to counterinsurgency was, rather surprisingly, born in Belfast at the pen of General Frank Kitson – a soldier involved in the brutal suppression of the civil rights protests there between 1970 and 1972 (Hewitt 2008, p. 16). In his book, *Low Intensity Operations: Subversion, Insurgency, Peacekeeping*, Kitson stresses the importance of combating insurgency by simultaneously dismantling organisations and attempting to induce co-operation from the 'water they swim in', in an allusion to a statement by Mao (Kitson 1971, p. 50). However, the type of preventative measures he advocated did not centralise the refashioning of individual beliefs and mindsets – like within contemporary counterterrorism. Rather, Kitson encouraged the deployment of 'measures designed to maintain and if possible increase the prosperity of the *country*' (Kitson 1971 – emphasis added).

This focus upon the level of country, and also the economy, was also evident in other governmental strategies directed at Northern Ireland. In the aptly named, *Battling for Peace*, ex-British Secretary of State for Northern Ireland, Richard Needham, described his efforts to construct a glass-fronted shopping centre in Belfast within his attempts to separate the population from organisations like the PIRA (Needham 1998, p. 171). William Neill has noted that the construction of the new Castle Court shopping centre was enacted within a programme to redevelop Belfast city centre in the 1980s and 1990s. He argues that after Richard Needham's statement of 1978 heralded the 'rebirth of Belfast', subsequent urban regeneration projects can be understood as 'an invitation extended to common civic pride with the possibility of the pooling of differencing in a shared identity wrapped up in consumption' (Neill 2010, pp. 307–308). At the level of city and community, then, preventative counterterrorism practices were utilised by the British government which contrasted with the 'criminal justice' provisions of the PTAs. The conduct of the population of Belfast was targeted with governmental measures intended to distance them from the armed struggle.

From this brief description, we might understand the production of two subjectivities in Belfast. 'Criminal' terrorist gangs were identified, and practices were performed upon suspects to try and break those organisations, but the population was also separately identified as 'less-than-radical Others', to borrow Lene Hansen's turn of phrase (Hansen 2006, p. 213). Through normalisation policies and equality agendas (Neill 2010), the rest of Belfast was contrastingly produced as potentially malleable to economic governance and other measures. A distinction was thus made between the criminal terrorist and the 'sea' that insurgents swam in. These kinds of distinction have also been made in contemporary counterterrorism between subjects who are relevant to PURSUE's activities and those who are governed as 'vulnerable' subjects through PREVENT. The literature on 'suspect communities' has addressed the types of experience that both Muslim and Irish communities in Britain have shared when framed as 'seas that insurgents swim in'. This section will address how communities were produced in contrast to terrorists in both eras but were also simultaneously framed as suspect.

In his study of the experiences of the PTA by Irish people living in Britain, Paddy Hillyard found that the practice of counterterrorism constituted the Irish as suspect. He examined how they often experienced practices of detention and police searches not because their behaviour indicated the commission of an illegal act, but because their identities were construed as suspect (Hillyard 1993). Indeed, once inside a police station this differentiation between their subjectivity and that of others was made clear in the documentary labelling of persons as 'Irish suspects' (Hillyard 1993, p. 7). Christina Pantazis and Simon Pemberton describe how the use of police powers granted under the PTAs led to the frequent arrest and questioning of Irish persons, producing a suspect community – a category that can also be applied to the treatment of British Muslims by the police in the post-9/11 era (Pantazis and Pemberton 2009). They argue that the discretionary powers engendered within the Terrorism Act of (2000) fixed Muslim communities, rather than individual suspects, in the gaze of counterterrorist policing – specifically stop-and-search powers that remove the need for police suspicion of terrorist offences. Examining the Home Office Figures for stop-and-search procedures in the year 2006/2007, they conclude that 'Black and Asian people were more than three times as likely as their "White" counterparts to be stopped and searched under police s. 44 counter-terrorism powers' (Pantazis and Pemberton 2009, p. 657).

Alongside the production of a suspect community in each era through the sovereign powers awarded to police officers (and through framings evident in media representations), Hickmann et al. (2011) have also argued that Irish and Muslim communities have simultaneously been framed as 'allies in the struggle against terrorism' – leaving them 'situated in an ambiguous position' (Hickmann et al. 2011, p. 14). This dual constitution is apparent in the discriminatory approach to Irish suspects displayed by the police and the contrasting efforts of government policy to induce the population of Belfast towards an identity 'wrapped up in consumption' through economic and urban renovation (Neill 2010, pp. 307–308). They were framed not only as suspicious but also as a malleable tool in the fight against the armed organisations. Similarly, in the contemporary era, people of Asian appearance experience a far higher rate of stop-and-search than Whites, as Pantazis and Pemberton have shown, but the focus on pre-emptive governance of terrorism has also highlighted a paradoxical constitution of this suspect community as an asset. Muslim communities are also subjected to 'community engagement' interventions aimed at fostering their abilities to challenge extremist narratives (Lambert 2008, Briggs 2010). While heralded as partners in the campaign against violent extremism, they are simultaneously marked as the suspicious sea in which terrorists swim.

This dual constitution can be seen in the competing governances directed at Muslim communities. The initial funding for 'community-based approaches' to counter radicalisation came through the Preventing Violent Extremism Pathfinder Fund, which the Department for Communities and Local Government distributed to those 70 local authorities in England which have Muslims as 5% or more of their population. CONTEST depicts the necessity for, and unique qualifications of, communities to challenge extremists in their midst, stating that:

> the Government and the Devolved Administrations cannot deliver the Prevent agenda on its own. This programme depends on collaborative work alongside the vast majority of people across all communities in this country who reject violent extremism and are determined to challenge it. (Home Office 2009, p. 84)

However, the Department for Communities and Local Government frames British Muslim communities as both assets in the fight against extremism *and* as risky locales from which terrorism emerges:

> It is important that funds are focused on those areas of highest priority . . . The fund will therefore be focused on local authorities with sizeable Muslim communities. As a starting point, authorities with populations of 5% or more should be considered for funding. We are aware, however, that there are areas . . . with significant Muslim communities concentrated in a few wards that fall below the threshold that should [also] be considered. (DCLG 2007, p. 6)

As such, the governance of Muslim communities – including increased stop-and-search rates, community engagement programmes and the funding of mainstream Islamic narratives – frames Muslim communities both as assets in countering extremist narratives and as risky. The simultaneous 'suspectness' of these communities who 'harbour' terrorists and their status as assets in counterterrorism is well evidenced in Rachel Briggs' statement that:

> It is true that the terrorist threat comes from a tiny and marginal minority, but these individuals are integrated within their communities and not, on the whole, loners working on their own. This is why communities need to play a central role in many different areas of the counterterrorism strategy, a principle that is now implicit within government policy. (Briggs 2010, p. 972)

So it seems that the combined formulation of Muslim communities as protagonists in the WOT and as the suspect 'seas that insurgents swim in' has led to insinuations of partial responsibility for terrorism through a failure to appropriately govern themselves. This framing fits the logic of governmentality, where power functions by engendering the capacity for self-governance within populations. Counterterrorism is thus framed in terms of an absence of appropriate self-governance in certain communities that can be rectified through the deployment of intensified governmental technologies – like PREVENT.

PREVENT explicitly produces the British Muslim population as both 'risky' and 'at risk' as part of this intervention. British Muslim communities are classified by PREVENT as 'at risk' – necessitating interventions under a biopolitical duty of care to 'increase the resilience of communities' (in one of many allusions to a risk of contagion), 'tackling the under-achievement of Pakistani boys' and training 'local Muslim women how to access local services' (Home Office 2009, p. 83, DCLG 2008, pp. 21–22). The centrality of categories of vulnerability to the deployment of governmental counterterrorism has even reached the extent to which counterterrorism intelligence officers are even involved in the development of a 'local vulnerability index' (Bettison 2009, p. 136). However, this framing of Muslim communities as collectively 'at risk' or vulnerable to extremism has the paradoxical effect of also *securitising* them concerning what they *might* produce.[4] 'At-risk' populations can thus simultaneously be produced as 'risky' through the actions of risk management and security technologies – blurring the actions of disciplinary and securitising governance and turning vulnerability into potential dangerousness. Indeed, it has been argued that the 'broad brush' identification of terrorism with 'at-risk' Muslim communities within PREVENT communicates this 'riskiness' (Thomas 2010, p. 446), securitising their occupants *in the name of others*, as a locale from which future threats might emerge, while simultaneously disciplining them for *their own good*.

We have seen, then, arguments which suggest that 'suspect communities' were produced in both eras of UK counterterrorism.[5] While this has involved the constitution of 'risky subjectivities' through sovereign practices and media narratives, Irish and Muslim communities have also simultaneously been framed as assets in the contestation of extremist narratives/organisations. The following section examines the function of 'suspect communities' for counterterrorism in both eras and the function of these ambiguous framings. It argues that the dual constitution of communities as simultaneously risky and vulnerable points to further shared features between the emergency in Northern Ireland and contemporary counterterrorism – like the production of 'false positives' – despite divergences in their respective policy performances of 'prevention'.

Petty sovereigns and false positives

The dual constitution of community has been evident in both eras of counterterrorism, and it might be able to tell us more about the way we are governed through preventative counterterrorism logics than has been interrogated so far. This section will examine misfirings, mistrials and detention practices in the light of the dual constitution of communities that has been noted. It will argue that the governance of terrorism through both sovereign logics, that produce suspected persons (while acting upon them), and the governmental logics that produce 'vulnerable' or 'economically malleable' subjects is never truly united. Contrastingly, a lacuna has existed between the different strands of preventative politics in both eras of counterterrorism. The section will argue that the indistinction between frames of 'at risk' and 'risky', or between community and terrorist, is hidden by the actions of 'petty sovereigns', who conceal the 'gap' in counterterrorism knowledge by employing 'decisioning' to allocate persons into subjectivities (through sovereign means).

This kind of gap has been hinted at by David Omand in his reflections upon CONTEST. He details how PREVENT originally engendered counterterrorism practices that utilised 'focused diplomacy' and 'military intervention overseas' before the 'winning back of the hearts and minds of young British Muslims' became centralised within the pre-emptive approach to terrorism (Omand 2010, p. 101). On reflecting upon the difficulties of getting the balance right in this domestic focus, he invokes the indistinction between communities who hold anti-secular views and those who commit terrorist offences within the discourses of 'radicalisation' and PREVENT. The uncertainty of the tipping point between those who are 'at risk' of becoming terrorists and those who are already 'risky' is framed in terms of the unknown:

> Holding radical views, providing that they are promoted in non-violent ways, is not in-itself normally regarded as incompatible with membership of a democratic free society . . . For government to seek to divert extremists from violence into such non-violent but nonetheless highly extreme groups might be thought to serve the ends of counter-terrorism in the short term, but is liable to undermine majority trust in the actions of government. *Nor is there any certainty over whether and when a holder of extreme Islamist views might, if the circumstances arose, tip over into violent action.* (Omand 2010, pp. 101–102; emphasis added)

Where is the tipping point? The 'preventative' governance of terrorism produces a gap between suspect and terrorist subjectivities. Despite the different policy formulations of preventative counterterrorism between the eras of the PTAs and CONTEST, this 'gap' is evident in both the contemporary regime and its prefiguration. It can be seen in the predominance of mistrials and misfirings in both. There are striking commonalities in the production of 'false positives' in both eras, where persons are exposed to the force of sovereign power – and yet later proven innocent. These 'false positives', born of 'gaps', are best understood as the meeting place between governmental regimes and sovereign power. They are the work of 'petty sovereigns' and indicate a 'gap' in both eras of British counterterrorism between the subjectivities of 'suspect' and the 'figure of the terrorist'.

Judith Butler's conception of the 'petty sovereign', a subjectivity consisting of bureaucrats and mid-level officials who are authorised to make security decisions about detention and asset freezing (De Goede 2008, p. 176), can be useful for exploring 'false positives'. 'Petty sovereigns' perform sovereign power in an era of diffused governmental power – marking a resurgence of sovereign power in the field of governmentality (Butler 2004, p. 56). Naming them 'petty sovereigns', Butler evokes the position of these 'decisioners' within large bureaucracies – they are essentially powerless (not controlling the inaugurating forms of power that they deploy) while wielding the power to render unilateral decisions. This is sovereign power performing itself through governmentality, 'ruling' through the application of rules (Butler 2004, pp. 56–65). Marieke de Goede has identified the petty sovereign in the discretionary powers awarded to immigration officials, banking counter staff and financial middle managers in the WOT (De Goede 2007, p. 146), while Amoore and de Goede have scrutinised the US VISIT programme for the function of sovereignty within governmentality (Amoore and de Goede 2005). Similarly, Halit Mustafa Tagma has invoked the petty sovereign in his examination of detention camps in the WOT (Tagma 2009, p. 416).

This section will interrogate the deployment of sovereign power upon Muslim and Irish suspects during the eras of the PTAs and CONTEST, using the conception of the petty sovereign to show how preventative terrorism knowledge leaves a gap between 'at-risk' and 'risky' subjectivities which must be filled. The petty sovereign uses his/her powers of unilateral decisioning to conceal this gap by allocating subjects to categories and potentially unleashing sovereign force upon them. The article will conclude by detailing how the pre-emptive policy interpretation of 'prevention' in CONTEST has made this function, and the gap it conceals, more evident through its deployment of a linear narrative about transitions to terrorism (the radicalisation discourse), but that the production of false positives also speaks to a continuity of pre-emptive politics in both eras.

There are multiple examples of 'false positives' in both eras of counterterrorism, but I will begin by discussing the execution-style killing of Jean Charles de Menezes by metropolitan police officers on 22 July 2005. Senior police officers and assorted military and non-military experts had met with Home Office officials shortly after 9/11 to discuss responses to the risk of suicide bombing. The events of 9/11 were interpreted to require preparedness for suicide bombings, and the resultant policy was named Kratos – which invokes sovereign power, as it is Greek for strength, might and power (Kennison and Loumansky 2007, p. 153). In a nominated Kratos operation, firearms officers become authorised to engender the 'flaccid incapacitation of the brain stem by shooting the suspect suicide bomber . . . in the head a number of times thereby preventing activation of the explosive device' (Kennison and Loumansky 2007, p. 154). Kratos deploys a proactive regime of surveillance practices to pre-emptively disrupt terrorist plots, as were used on Jean Charles de Menezes on the morning of his death. Intelligence is fed up the chain of command to a designated senior officer (DSO) who appropriates the power of decision from officers on the ground. This remote control of operations is meant to increase a more level-headed approach to the situation, divorcing decisions from the affective dimensions of being present on the scene (Kennison and Loumansky 2007, p. 155). The risk that the suspect poses is managed by the DSO, who makes tactical decisions from a control room. On 22 July 2005, such a petty sovereign took the decision that Jean Charles de Menezes posed a terrible risk to passengers on the London Underground and activated the firearms officers following him.

The language of Kratos ('flaccid incapacitation of the brain stem . . . ') and the efforts to locate decisioning power at a highpoint in the chain of command speak to a technologisation of the powers of death. Indeed, the system of alerts and surveillance seems poised to activate by itself and to produce death, almost without the need for human decision – as is shown by the reaction of the DSO to De Menezes' proximity to Stockwell Tube Station, rather than a self-initiated decisioning process. The conception of the petty sovereign is interesting here as it speaks to the embedding of the sovereign power of death within governmental technologies, even to the extent that decisioners themselves are no longer needed. Even the petty immigration official of De Goede and Amoore's works is somewhat removed, as the technologies of prevention select targets and begin operating upon them.

De Menezes, a Brazilian electrician, had been mistaken for Hussein Osman – a failed suicide bomber from the previous day – even through their racial profiles were different. Surveillance officers had also reported that their quarry was an IC1 male (police code for a White man) while tracking him, so it remains unclear how De Menezes was identified both as Hussein Osman and as a White man, and why team members did not challenge him along the journey but continued to track him into Stockwell Station (Vaughan-Williams 2007, p. 180). This again speaks to the automation of technologies of death; no one stopped De Menezes and no one questioned the identification of this man as risky by security technologies. Indeed, Joseph Pugliese has made the argument that there was nothing physiological in the surveillance gaze which tracked Jean Charles on that day, rather 'the physiology of seeing was mediated at every level by a *racialised regime of visuality* that proceeded to resignify virtually every aspect of de Menezes' person' (Pugliese 2006). He was inscribed with risk and framed within a suspect subjectivity upon every move he made that morning. Having somehow caught the attention of the risk technologies primed to disrupt terrorist attacks, Jean Charles embodied the gap between logics of prevention and pursuit – where knowledge about transitions to terrorism cannot tell us about the moment when Omand's 'tipping point' is reached – and his suspect raciality left him stranded between governmental and sovereign logics. Is he merely suspect or he is imminently dangerous? Upon entering the underground system, he was 'decisioned' into the frame of Kratos.

The power of these risk frames can also be noted *after* the deployment of sovereign power. This is evident in the misinformation which followed De Menezes' killing and the killing of others who have been made suspect. A residue of the inscription of riskiness, a risk imprint, lingers upon the person of the suspect in the days after their deaths. Nick Vaughan-Williams and Joseph Pugliese have noted the variations between eye witness testimonies and CCTV footage in the days after the killing of Jean Charles. Eye witnesses were reported in the media as describing De Menezes as looking like a 'cornered rabbit' as he 'burst into the carriage' (Button quoted in Pugliese 2006) and as wearing a 'heavy winter coat with wires protruding from it' (Whitby quoted in Vaughan-Williams 2007) – yet he wore a lightweight denim jacket. Furthermore, the media reports that De Menezes ran onto the carriage have been shown to be false by Kennison and Loumansky (2007, p. 161). Rather, what seems to have happened is that De Menezes was forced into a frame of risky 'south Asian' suspect by security visualities, just as he had been in the previous weeks when repeatedly 'stopped and searched' on the underground according to his close friend Gesio de Avila (Pugliese 2006). The risky subjectivities attributed to persons blur racial profiles through deploying visualities of risk, just as the reporting of the killing confused the events of the day with *expected behaviours* of suicide bombers. Furthermore, it has been reported that in the days after the killing that the following script appeared on a London Underground notice board at Notting Hill station, warning travellers who 'look a bit foreign' and who carry rucksacks not to run on the station for their own safety.

Just as their characteristics might not only suddenly fall prey to the discursive visualities policed by petty sovereigns but also not attract the attention of PURSUIT's risk apparatuses, I am not able to determine the reality or falsity of this image – reportedly a photograph taken at Notting Hill station four days after the killing of De Menezes (see Figure 1).

These functions of the petty sovereign and the lingering risk imprint are also evident in the era of the PTAs. Kennison and Loumansky have noted echoes between the shooting of Jean Charles de Menezes and the pre-emptive killing of three PIRA suspects in Gibraltar by the SAS in 1988. Information had been received that the group was planning to detonate a bomb during the changing of the guard of the Royal Anglian Regiment on the island and when the suspects were seen parking their car next to the parade ground an SAS operation swung into action. On the afternoon of Sunday 6 March 1988, the Ministry of Defence confirmed that a bomb had been found on Gibraltar and three suspects had been shot. The following morning it was reported that 'a large bomb had been defused' and that a shootout had occurred. However, Sir Geoffrey Howe was later to announce to Parliament that there was no bomb and the suspects had actually been unarmed (Kennison and Loumansky 2007, pp. 161–162). The authors ask questions about the use of force in this situation and also in the killing of eight IRA members at Loughall on 8 May 1987. Why, they ask, was it not possible to take any of them alive? And why was Jean Charles de Menezes not approached by security services prior to boarding a bus and then entering a tube station? Who is practicing security when decisions are made about pre-empting terrorist attacks?

Brian Massumi's arguments about 'lightning flashes' of sovereign power can be used to connect these 'false positives' to logics of pre-emption. By the time you see a lightning strike it has already gone, just like the flash of sovereign power that sidesteps the present, or the need for judicial processes, in favour of a perceived need to act on the future without

Figure 1. '26 July 2005: Notice to all passengers: Please do not run on the platforms or concourses. Especially if you are carrying a rucksack, wearing a big coat or look a bit foreign. This notice is for your own safety. Thank you.'
Source: http://gallery.hd.org/_c/bizarre/_more2005/_more07/blunt-but-wise-advice-at-Notting-Hill-Tube-station-London-England-after-innocent-man-mistaken-and-shot-as-potential-bomber-some-days-earlier-after-running-from-police-into-Stockwell-Tube-station-ANON.jpg.html.

delay (Massumi 2005). These flashes of sovereign power and the petty sovereigns which invoke them are situated in extensive diffused regimes of governmental power though, as Butler argues. As we have seen from the statements of De Menezes' close friend, he was often questioned about his presence on the underground network by police officers. The production of suspect communities deploys visualities which displace the physiological and inscribe potential risk, and they function as such to 'mind the gap' between 'suspect' and 'terrorist' frames. The production of the suspect visuality enables the function of the petty sovereign, who can conceal the lacuna within counterterrorism with lightning flash 'decisioning'. Indeed, the persistence of misfiring within counterterrorism throughout both eras of British counterterrorism suggests some kind of function.

These misfirings do not just involve the shooting of suspects, although we should also note the shooting of Mohammed Abdulkahar when counterterrorism police entered his home in Forest Gate on 2 June 2006 but also the detention of persons later found to be innocent. In their studies of 'suspect communities', Hickmann et al. (2011) note the imprisonment of the Maguire Seven in 1976. Somehow, these

> seven family members including two children were tried and convicted for a crime that not only had none of them committed but also had not been committed in the first place: participation in running an alleged IRA bomb factory in their west London home. For this non-crime the family were sentenced between them to 73 years in prison. (Hickmann et al. 2011, p. 10)

It beggars belief, before one frames the event within understanding of the discursive visualities deployed by security and the decisioning functions they engender. Furthermore, the internment of 1981 persons in Belfast between 1971 and 1975 (95% of them Catholic) (Hewitt 2008, pp. 17–18) according to the needs of disrupting terrorist plots might also be considered as a sudden irruption of sovereign power through the knowledge gaps in preventative politics between the suspect community and the subjectivity of the terrorist. Indeed, the slippages between subjectivities of suspectness and imminent riskiness are too numerous to note here, but readers may want to examine Hewitt's chronology of the British WOT (Hewitt 2008, pp. xiii–xxiv) to identify multiple contemporary instances where young Muslims have been detained at gunpoint and the disruption of plots hailed, before the quiet release of almost all without charge.

Why are there so many mistakes made and why do so many innocent people end up detained? This article argues that the deployment of counterterrorism through preventative logics leads to slippery trigger fingers, due to the separate subjectivities produced when framing the stages of pre-terrorism and terrorism in a linear narrative. As we noted earlier, the suspect communities of the PTAs and CONTEST are not only separated from the figure of the terrorist but also implicated in the production of terrorism. They are both 'at risk' and 'risky', but security knowledge can never explain where the transition is made between potentiality and actuality. This indistinction leads to the performance of sovereign power through petty sovereigns, the middle managers of security who sit in bureaucracies but deploy decisions to deduct freedom, bodily integrity or even life. Petty sovereigns deploy 'lightning flash decisioning' to reconstitute subjects within frames of imminent threat and authorise the use of reactive counterterrorism logics upon them, but the repeated use of lethal force on innocent persons speaks to a 'gap' in knowledge about terrorism – specifically the moment between subjectivities of suspectness and danger.

The following section connects the types of prevention within each era of counterterrorism to the 'gap' between suspectedness and danger, arguing that the contemporary use of the 'radicalisation discourse' has exacerbated the salience of the indistinct space between securitised subjectivities.

The contemporary salience of the gap

Despite the different policy understandings of prevention between the PTA era and that of CONTEST, the PTA regime prefigured the contemporary preventative politics in important ways. While preventative counterterrorism in the PTAs was practiced through the criminal justice system, the use of exclusion orders and the stop-and-search of suspects' subjectivities have continued over into the present regime of practices – even if their interpretation in policy is sometimes more governmentally conceived. In terms of a direct continuity between the eras, however, this article has highlighted the production of 'false positives', arguing that this speaks to the dual constitution of communities as suspect and risky.

The 'gap' between these subjectivities has contributed to the function of petty sovereigns, who unleash 'shoot-to-kill' and other sovereign methods upon PIRA and contemporary suspects. However, this article will conclude by arguing that the policy reformulation evident in contemporary British preventative politics might make the function of the petty sovereign *more* dangerous. The policies of the contemporary era, by investing in an understanding of prevention as explicitly pre-emptive, have made the lacuna between anticipatory and reactive logics more evident. A more evident 'gap' could mean an increased function of the petty sovereign. By investing so heavily in the radicalisation discourse, CONTEST has deployed a linear narrative about transitions to terrorism that focuses upon the individual. As was noted earlier, community engagement interventions have been deployed within PREVENT to identify the marginalised individuals who are 'vulnerable' to extremist ideology and who are beginning to show signs of 'riskiness' – including 'expressions of political ideology such as support for the Islamic political system', 'a focus on scripture as an exclusive moral source', 'a conspiratorial mindset' and 'seeing the West as a source of evil' (Kundnani 2009, p. 33, Quilliam Foundation 2008). In this narrative about transitions to terrorism, a subjectivity of young people who need to be protected from becoming risky[6] (DCSF 2008, p. 13) is deployed by government, engendering a series of practices that have included the Channel Program interventions upon Muslim youth and training sessions for Muslim women about how to access local services.

However, this focus on individual vulnerability, described in policy as the result 'of family or peer pressure, the absence of positive mentors and role models, a crisis of identity, links to criminality including other forms of violence, exposure to traumatic events (here or overseas), or changing circumstances (eg a new environment following migration and asylum)' (Home Office 2009, p. 29), has served to make the 'gap' between suspect and terrorist subjectivities more noticeable. If the petty sovereign functions to conceal gaps in terrorism knowledge, then the task at hand is considerably larger – which could point to the multiple 'terrorist scares' where threats are averted at the last second, only for the following weeks to reveal that nothing was planned and the accused were victims of the 'false-positive' effect. Again, readers may want to examine Hewitt's chronology of the British WOT (Home Office 2009, pp. xiii–xxiv) to identify multiple contemporary instances where young Muslims have been detained at gunpoint and the disruption of plots hailed, before the quiet release of almost all without charge.

Conclusions

So, how old is preventative counterterrorism in the United Kingdom? This article has examined the changing meaning of prevention in counterterrorism over two eras of policy, highlighting the ways in which the eras differ but have also stayed the same. The PTA era contained many practices that have prefigured the contemporary regime, but the use of pre-emptive risk technologies within contemporary preventative counterterrorism has resulted in the novel creation of the radicalisation discourse. This discourse provides a narrative about the 'vulnerabilities' that certain people experience to extremist ideology, simultaneously framing persons within 'at-risk' and 'risky' subjectivities. To a certain extent, this double constitution was also evident in Irish suspect communities during the PTA era but the focus on the individual within CONTEST has highlighted the 'gap' within counterterrorism knowledge. These 'gaps' contribute to 'misfirings' of sovereign power upon suspect subjectivities, which have been shown to have occurred in both eras. The article argued that such 'mistakes' speak to the function of petty sovereigns in concealing the 'gap' within preventative politics through lightning flashes of decisioning, but the increased governmental 'knowledge' about individual 'radicalisation' has served to highlight the incomplete governance of terrorism in the contemporary era. This could make the performance of counterterrorism more dangerous in the present era, as the tools of 'prevention' are sharper and more precise than the lumbering internment techniques of old. Prevention has not been reinvented then, but rather refigured – exposing the gap within its own knowledge of the production of terrorism.

To conclude, the performance of preventative counterterrorism appears to have consistently failed to grasp the complexity of population in the history of British counterterrorism. Instead, its flashes of sovereign power betray the reliance of security upon visualities of the suspect and reveal the ways in which we are governed, and viewed, through technologies of prevention. These technologies appear to function almost autonomously in their selection of suspects from prefigured frames, as was seen in the case of De Menezes. We might all do well to 'mind the gap' then, not just in terms of where we put our feet but also in the ways that the Notting Hill display board advises.

Acknowledgements

I thank the two anonymous reviewers who greatly improved this article with their insightful critiques. This would be a much poorer article if they had not contributed their thoughts.

Notes

1. Although similar to the PTAs in content, the 2000 legislation dropped the moniker of 'prevention' and was named the 'Terrorism Act 2000'. I am treating the Terrorism Act as a continuation of the PTAs due to the similarities in content between them.
2. I am going to trouble this distinction between anticipatory governance and sovereign power later in the article. However, for now, I am utilising Mitchell Dean's distinction to contrast the heavy-handed criminal justice approach to the Northern Irish 'troubles' with the re-educational community-based approach to contemporary 'radicalisation'.
3. The interpretation of 'reasonable force' leading to the taking away of life is not addressed here, but will be noted in the Section 'Petty sovereigns and false positives.'
4. Claudia Aradau has written on the dynamic interaction of discourses of risk and pity in the context of trafficked persons (see Aradau 2004).
5. For a dissenting opinion on the analytic utility of the term 'suspect community', see Greer (2010).
6. The phrase used relates to protecting young people from 'harm or from causing harm'.

Notes on contributor

Charlotte Heath-Kelly is a teaching fellow at the Department of International Politics, Aberystwyth University. She has recently completed her PhD and has published articles in *Security Dialogue*, *The British Journal of Politics and International Relations* (forthcoming) and the *Journal of International Relations Research* (forthcoming).

References

Amoore, L. and de Goede, M., 2005. Governance, risk and dataveillance in the war on terror. *Crime, Law and Social Change*, 43 (2), 149–173.

Anderson, B., 2010. Preemption, precaution, preparedness: anticipatory action and future geographies. *Progress in Human Geography*, 34 (6), 777–798.

Aradau, C., 2004. The perverse politics of four-letter words: risk and pity in the securitisation of human trafficking. *Millennium Journal of International Studies*, 33 (2), 251–277.

Bettison, N., 2009. Preventing violent extremism – a police response. *Policing*, 3 (2), 129–138.

Briggs, R., 2010. Community engagement for counterterrorism: lessons from the United Kingdom. *International Affairs*, 86 (4), 971–981.

Butler, J., 2004. *Precarious life: the powers of mourning and violence*. London: Verso.

Coaffee, J., 2009. Protecting the urban: the dangers of planning for terrorism. *Theory, Culture, Society*, 26 (7), 343–355.

Crown Prosecution Service, 2009. *The counter-terrorism division of the Crown Prosecution Service (CPS) – cases concluded in 2009* [online]. Available from: http://www.cps.gov.uk/publications/prosecution/ctd_2009.html [Accessed 27 August 2011].

De Goede, M., 2007. Underground money. *Cultural Critique*, 65 (1), 140–163.

De Goede, M., 2008. The politics of preemption and the war on terror in Europe. *European Journal of International Relations*, 14 (1), 161–185.

Dean, M., 1999. *Governmentality: power and rule in modern society*. London: Sage.

Department for Children, Schools and Families (DCSF), October 2008. *Learning together to be safe: a toolkit to help schools contribute to the prevention of extremism*. Runcorn: Department for Children, Schools and Families.

Department for Communities and Local Government (DCLG), February 2007. *Preventing violent extremism pathfinder fund: guidance note for government offices and local authorities in England*. London: Department for Communities and Local Government.

Department for Communities and Local Government (DCLG), December 2008. *Preventing violent extremism pathfinder fund: mapping of project activities 2007/2008*. London: Department for Communities and Local Government.

Doty, R., 1997. Aporia: a critical exploration of the agent-structure problematique in international relations theory. *European Journal of International Relations*, 3 (3), 365–392.

Githens-Mazer, J. and Lambert, R., 2010. Why conventional wisdom on radicalization fails: the persistence of a failed discourse. *International Affairs*, 86 (4), 889–901.

Greer, S., 2010. Anti-terrorist laws and the United Kingdom's 'suspect Muslim community': a reply to Pantazis and Pemberton. *British Journal of Criminology*, 50 (6), 1171–1190.

Hall, S., 2007. The west and the rest: discourse and power. *In*: T. Das Gupta, *et al.*, eds. *Race and racialization: essential readings*. Toronto, ON: Canadian Scholars Press, 56–60.

Hansen, L., 2006. *Security as practice: discourse analysis and the Bosnian war*. Abingdon: Routledge.

Heath-Kelly, C., forthcoming. Counter-terrorism and the counterfactual: producing the 'radicalisation' discourse and the UK PREVENT strategy. *British Journal of Politics and International Relations*.

Hewitt, S., 2008. *The British war on terror: terrorism and counter-terrorism on the home front since 9/11*. London: Continuum.

Hickmann, M., *et al.*, 2011. *'Suspect communities'? Counter-terrorism policy, the press, and the impact on Irish and Muslim communities in Britain*. London: London Metropolitan University.

Hillyard, P., 1993. *Suspect community: people's experience of the Prevention of Terrorism Acts in Britain*. London: Pluto.

Home Office, 1974. *Prevention of Terrorism (temporary provisions) Act 1974*. London: HM Government.

Home Office, 1989. *Prevention of Terrorism (temporary provisions) Act 1989*. London: HM Government.

Home Office, 2000. *Terrorism Act 2000*. London: HM Government.

Home Office, 2009. *Pursue prevent protect prepare: the United Kingdom's strategy for countering international terrorism*. London: HM Government.

Home Office, 2011. *CONTEST: the United Kingdom's strategy for countering terrorism*. London: HM Government.

Kennison, P. and Loumansky, A., 2007. Shoot to kill – understanding police use of force in combating suicide terrorism. *Crime, Law and Social Change*, 47 (3), 151–168.

Kitson, F., 1971. *Low intensity operations: subversion, insurgency, peacekeeping*. London: Faber & Faber.

Kundnani, A., 2009. *Spooked: how not to prevent violent extremism*. London: Institute of Race Relations.

Lambert, R., 2008. Muslim communities, counter-terrorism and counter-radicalisation: a critically reflective approach to engagement. *International Journal of Law, Crime and Justice*, 36 (4), 257–270.

Massumi, B., 2005. The future birth of the affective fact. *In: Conference Proceedings Genealogies of Biopolitics* [online]. Available from: http://browse.reticular.info/text/collected/massumi.pdf [Accessed 29 August 2011].

Moloney, E., 1991. Closing down the airwaves: the story of the broadcasting ban. *In*: B. Rolston, ed. *The media and Northern Ireland: covering the troubles*. Basingstoke: Macmillan, 8–51.

Needham, R., 1998. *Battling for peace*. Belfast: Blackstaff.

Neill, W., 2010. Rebranding the Renaissance city: from 'the Troubles' to the Titanic quarter. *In*: J. Punter, ed. *Urban design and the British urban renaissance*. Abingdon: Routledge, 305–322.

Omand, D., 2010. *Securing the state*. London: Hurst.

Pantazis, C. and Pemberton, S., 2009. From the 'old' to the 'new' suspect community: examining the impacts of recent UK counter-terrorism legislation. *British Journal of Criminology*, 49 (5), 646–666.

Pugliese, J., 2006. Asymmetries of terror: visual regimes of racial profiling and the shooting of Jean Charles de Menezes in the context of the war in Iraq. *Borderlands*, 5, 1.

Quilliam Foundation, 8 October 2008. *Quilliam Foundation Advice for Teachers* [online]. Available from: http://www.teachernet.gov.uk/wholeschool/violentextremism/quilliam [Accessed 01 November 2010].

Richards, A., 2011. The problem with 'radicalization': the remit of 'prevent' and the need to refocus on terrorism in the UK. *International Affairs*, 87 (1), 143–152.

Saul, B., 2005. Speaking of terror: criminalising incitement to violence. *University of New South Wales Law Journal*, 28 (3), 868–886.

States of Emergency Database, 2011. *States of Emergency Database: Northern Ireland, Introduction* [online]. Belfast, School of Law, Queens University Belfast. Available from: http://www.qub.ac.uk/schools/SchoolofLaw/Research/HumanRightsCentre/Resources/html/Filetoupload,53157,en.htm [Accessed 26 August 2011].

Tagma, H., 2009. Homo Sacer vs. Homo Soccer Mum: reading Agamben and Foucault in the war on terror. *Alternatives: Global, Local, Political*, 34 (4), 407–435.

Thomas, P., 2010. Failed and friendless: the UK's 'Preventing Violent Extremism' programme. *British Journal of Politics and International Relations*, 12 (3), 442–458.

Vaughan-Williams, N., 2007. The shooting of Jean Charles de Menezes: new border politics? *Alternatives: Global, Local, Political*, 32 (2), 177–195.

Social cohesion and the notion of 'suspect communities': a study of the experiences and impacts of being 'suspect' for Irish communities and Muslim communities in Britain

Mary J. Hickman[a], Lyn Thomas[a], Henri C. Nickels[b] and Sara Silvestri[c]

[a]*Institute for the Study of European Transformations, London Metropolitan University, London, UK;* [b]*European Union Agency for Fundamental Rights, Vienna, Austria;* [c]*Department of International Politics, City University London, London, UK*

> In this article, we consider how the practice of conceiving of groups within civil society as 'communities' meshes with conceptualisations of certain populations as 'suspect' and consider some of the impacts and consequences of this for particular populations and for social cohesion. We examine how Irish and Muslim people in Britain have become aware of and have experienced themselves to be members of 'suspect communities' in relation to political violence and counterterrorism policies from 1974 to 2007 and investigate the impacts of these experiences on their everyday lives. The study focuses on two eras of political violence. The first coincides with the Irish Republican Army's (IRA) bombing campaigns in England between 1973 and 1996, when the perpetrators were perceived as 'Irish terrorists'; and the second since 2001, when, in Britain and elsewhere, the main threat of political violence has been portrayed as stemming from people who are assumed to be motivated by extreme interpretations of Islam and are often labelled as 'Islamic terrorists'. We outline why the concept of 'suspect communities' continues to be analytically useful for examining: the impact of 'bounded communities' on community cohesion policies; the development of traumatogenic environments and their ramifications; and for examining how lessons might be learnt from one era of political violence to another, especially as regards the negative impacts of practices of suspectification on Irish communities and Muslim communities. The research methods included discussion groups involving Irish and Muslim people. These demonstrated that with the removal of discourses of suspicion the common ground of Britain's urban multiculture was a sufficient basis for sympathetic exchanges.

In this article, we consider how the practice of conceiving of groups within civil society as 'communities' meshes with conceptualisations of certain populations as 'suspect' and consider some of the impacts and consequences of this for particular populations and for social cohesion. We examine how Irish and Muslim people in Britain have become aware of and have experienced themselves to be members of a 'suspect community' between 1974 and 2007 and investigate the impacts of these experiences on their everyday lives. The article is empirically grounded in the findings of a recent comparative research project focused on the construction of 'suspect communities' in relation to counterterrorism practices and the impact of these representations on Irish communities and Muslim communities in Britain. The study focuses on two eras of political violence. The first coincides with the Irish Republican Army's (IRA) bombing campaigns in England between 1973 and 1996, when the perpetrators were perceived as 'Irish terrorists'; and the second since 2001, when, in Britain and elsewhere, the main threat of political violence has been portrayed as stemming from people who are assumed to be motivated by extreme interpretations of Islam and are often labelled as 'Islamic terrorists'. The project was historically constituted, bookended by the Birmingham pub bombings in November 1974 and the arrests in Birmingham in January 2007 of people suspected of involvement in a suspected plot to kidnap and behead a Muslim member of the armed forces.

There has been no previous systematic research exploring the parallels and differences between these two eras of political violence in terms of the experiences of these communities. In this article, therefore, we explore the implications for social cohesion of the outcomes of processes of 'suspectification' on the everyday lives of Irish communities and Muslim communities and on the possibilities for the expression of a multiplicity of belongings. First, we consider the basis for the comparison between these two eras, noting similarities, whereas much public discourse sees the two eras as clearly delineated. Second, we examine contemporary usages of the term 'community' in relation to problematised populations and the provenance of the concept 'suspect communities' in the context of analysing counterterrorism strategies. Third, we describe how we conducted the research project from which we draw the data analysed in this article. In the next three sections of this article, we present these data organised into sections on awareness of being 'suspect', impacts of being 'suspect' and similarities and differences between the two eras. Finally, we discuss our findings and draw some conclusions.

Two eras of political violence: the basis for comparison

The dominant political narrative about terrorism in circulation in contemporary Britain delineates the two eras of political violence as distinct. In the past decade, the argument has been made that there is a big difference between Irish Republican violence and violence perceived as relating to extreme interpretations of Islam (Blair 2005). This is because the IRA bombing campaigns are in hindsight being described as always in pursuit of political or strategic aims (Malik 2005). This retrospective characterisation of the IRA's strategies as ultimately about explicable and justifiable goals ostensibly marks the major difference between the period of 'The Troubles' and the contemporary terror threat in British political discourses. The current threat is perceived as 'more ideological', that is, more ideologically opposed to 'the West', as having a global reach, and is therefore constituted as a greater threat than the IRA. According to Berman (2003), Islamism, the radical political movement, is an example of a new kind of totalitarianism, an anti-liberal rebellion like fascism, Nazism or Communism.

Differences in the strategies and methods of the IRA compared with 'suicide bombers' are cited as a further reason to characterise the two eras of political violence in Britain very differently. The recent, supposedly more ideologically based, terror threat, it is argued, has less inhibition about using indiscriminate mass violence (e.g. Wilkinson 2006, Greer 2008, although the former describes the Birmingham pub bombings as an act of indiscriminate violence). The emergence of this threat is also seen as coinciding with a historical moment when a political solution was agreed for Northern Ireland. Consequently, in many people's minds, the 'Irish threat' ceased to exist after the signing of the Good Friday Agreement in

1998. This is cited in political discourses as further evidence for distinguishing between the two eras, as it is assumed that al-Qaeda and similar groupings lack concrete demands that are negotiable. This discursive shift has led to the establishment of a clear line between the two eras in much public discourse and amounts to a strategic re-legitimisation of Irish republicanism.

Instead of following the narrative of the dominant political discourse, we consider some similarities. The discursive shift described above has been utilised to paint the current threat as irrational and fanatical. However, as McGovern (2010) demonstrates, irrational and fanatical is exactly how the IRA was portrayed in the earlier period of political violence (see also Schlesinger 1991). The main counterterrorism measures employed today in Britain stem directly from the measures developed during the period of IRA violence (Clutterbuck 2006). In addition, experiences of counterterrorism methods for many Irish people living in Britain in the 1970s–1990s and many Muslims in the 2000s are similar (see Hillyard 1993, Hickman and Walter 1997, Runnymede Commission on British Muslims and Islamophobia 1997, Uniting Britain Trust 2004). A further similarity is that during both eras of political violence, there has been media coverage speculating on the identities and 'nature' of people who would carry out bombings, such as the Birmingham pub bombings in 1974 and the tube and bus bombings in London in 2005. In the latter case, the disturbingly 'new' aspect was said to be that the alleged perpetrators were 'home grown'. But throughout the period of the Northern Ireland 'Troubles', people born in the United Kingdom (including England) who identified as 'British', as well as those who identified as 'Irish', were involved in political violence.

There is a fifth similarity, namely, the positioning of Irish communities and Muslim communities in multi-ethnic Britain. Both these populations are largely the result of post-war migrations into Britain in the 1950s and 1960s, plus their children and grandchildren, and of subsequent significant immigrations since the 1980s of both Irish and Muslims. This common history of immigration is a contextualising similarity. Both Muslims and Irish people form part of the complex and vibrant multiculture that characterises Britain's urban spaces and the complex intermingling that this ensures (Gilroy 2005, Hickman *et al.* 2008). The multi-ethnicity of Britain is accepted sufficiently that people who look different and/or sound different are constituted as a regular part of public space; everyday cosmopolitanism is rendered ordinary. A similarity exists, therefore, in the extent of their integration into Britain; members of both Irish communities and Muslim communities live and work as *normal* Britons (Sharma and Sharma 2003). This, it is arguable, is their most disturbing aspect, whereby the more others who are 'suspect' are indistinguishable from the rest of the population, the more of a threat they constitute. As Hardt and Negri note, cultural racism 'is hatred born in proximity and elaborated through degrees of difference' (2000, p. 194; see also Blok 1998).

Community cohesion and the notion of 'suspect communities'

The use of the term 'community' has widened in recent years and it now embraces both a dominant notion of sociation, such that we are all defined as members of communities based on places, relationships and identities, and acts as a catch-all term for writing about problematised populations (see Clarke and Newman 1997). What is generally defined as a cause for concern within problematised communities are the forms of sociation they entail. Furthermore, the structures of interaction between communities can also come to be perceived as problematic (McGhee 2005). During 13 years of New Labour government, cosmopolitan Britain was portrayed as consisting of a 'mosaic pluralism, fixed communities and a multi-culturalism that is no longer working' (Wetherell 2008, p. 306). This backlash against multiculturalism in Britain was cemented in the government's adoption of a policy of community cohesion (Cantle 2001). 'Community' came to be seen not as a source of social integration, but rather as a set of inward-looking bonding processes. Thus, communities (especially those associated with minority ethnic or religious groups) were depicted as enclaves with little bridging to other groups in society (Blunket 2004, Cantle 2008).

We use the term 'communities' ourselves both because of its wide currency beyond the policy and academic arenas and because we subscribe to a more fluid definition of 'community': that is, 'community' as the experience of communicative belonging in an insecure world. This is 'community' as a sense of belonging peculiar to the circumstances of modern life and the fragmentation of society that is experienced (Delanty 2003). This definition of community recognises that for most people, a variety of cultural repertoires form the basis of their multiple attachments. Simultaneously, we recognise that community identity is constructed as much by the state as by individuals (Alexander 2007). The various community cohesion programmes that have been developed in the past 10 years do a particular type of 'identity work' in and through social capital. They aim to take what are perceived as narrow identities reinforced by bonding social capital and de-antagonise and broaden them out by encouraging bridging social capital. This trajectory of public policy is about achieving the conditions for the eradication of difference (and the isolation or removal of those who resist) and the suppression of conflict.

Within this field of governmentality, there exists a notion of 'suspect communities', and here we consider one manifestation of this: that which operates in respect of political violence. Our understanding of the term 'suspect communities' derives from Hillyard's (1993) study of the impact of the Prevention of Terrorism Act (PTA) on Irish communities in Britain. He explained the concept of 'suspect community' as the process of identification of a threat and of a sign of abnormality and that it worked in the following sense:

> a person who is drawn into the criminal justice system under the PTA is not a suspect in the normal sense of the word. In other words, they are not believed to be involved in or guilty of some illegal act . . . people are suspect primarily because they are Irish and once they are in the police station they are often labelled an Irish suspect, presumably as part of some classification system. In practice, they are being held because they belong to a suspect community. (Hillyard 1993, p. 7)

An example of this process was the arrest and subsequent imprisonment in 1976 of the Maguire Seven. The seven family members, including two children, were tried and convicted for a crime that not only had none of them committed but also had not been committed in the first place: participation in running an alleged IRA bomb factory in their west London home. For this non-crime, the family was sentenced to 73 years in prison between them (A. Maguire 1994, P. Maguire 2009).

There is a debate about the notion of suspect communities currently being waged in the *British Journal of Criminology*. Pantazis and Pemberton (2009) argue that Muslims have replaced the Irish as the main focus of the government's security agenda and argue that the categorisation of Muslims as suspect may be serving to undermine national security rather than enhance it. They demonstrate how the fixing of Muslim communities rather than individual suspects within the gaze of counterterrorist policing is underpinned by the discretionary nature of the powers contained in the Terrorism Act 2000 and has been reinforced by subsequent legislation. This is challenged by Steven Greer who states that while there is evidence that certain individual Muslims, and certain Muslim organisations, networks and neighbourhoods, are, and have been, under official suspicion, there is no evidence that this is systematically based on Islamophobia or that being a Muslim is in and of itself sufficient to arouse official suspicion or that the majority of Muslims in the United Kingdom are under official suspicion (Greer 2010, p. 1186).

This debate primarily focuses on policing and 'official suspicion'. Our concern is not so directly with policing. Rather, it is with the full range of everyday encounters in which an individual might become aware of being 'suspected', although obviously this can involve policing measures. With this focus across two eras of political violence, we are exploring whether being either Muslim or Irish was in and of itself sufficient to be the subject of practices of suspectification in everyday life. Our contention is that some of the most pernicious impacts of the counterterrorism climate result from the general circulation of discourses of suspicion, sustained and encouraged by other social structures and processes in particular the media (Pantazis and Pemberton 2009, p. 4). In our research, we incorporate Hillyard's concept of 'suspect communities' but not, however, his approach – in that we were interested primarily in people who were not detained or arrested. Our aim was to explore the implications for social cohesion of the impact of representations and discourses of 'suspectness' on the everyday lives of Irish communities and Muslim communities. It is important to investigate how 'suspectification' works. While initiated by the authorities, the process of detecting 'suspect' individuals and behaviours can gradually expand and be reproduced by a range of people and social groups, including the media, the general public and members of the communities under suspicion.

Research methods

The research was structured across two dimensions. The first was an analysis of public discourses from 1974 to 2007. It consisted of a media study (see Nickels *et al.* forthcoming-a, forthcoming-b) and a policy analysis (the subject of separate articles in preparation). The second dimension was a study of the impacts, experiences and interpretations of members of Irish and Muslim communities and other key informants. This involved discussion groups and interviews. We report here on this second dimension of the project based in London and Birmingham. The two cities were chosen because they are areas with significant Irish and Muslim populations, and they are places where bombings and/or arrests have taken place in both eras of political violence. In interviewing key informants, we were selectively sampling specialised knowledge of journalistic coverage of the eras, elected politicians at local and national level, legal knowledge of the system of justice across the two eras, religious leaders and local organisations that address the welfare needs and cultural activities of Irish communities and Muslim communities. The criteria for selection of the 42 key informants were that they be strategically positioned in one or more of these arenas and, where possible, have some knowledge or memory of both eras of political violence.

Our aim in holding discussion groups was to bring Irish and Muslim people together to hold a conversation about their comparative experiences and views about the representation of communities as 'suspect' in Britain, in part to see if the participants thought this was a useful exchange. The seven discussion groups took place in London (four) and Birmingham (three), and each involved between four and eight participants. We recruited through existing contacts in both cities; a wide variety of mailing lists; through local community centres; and in London, through a large, private sector employer. Our aim was to include non-hegemonic voices, rather than community leaders or political activists, and this was achieved. It is possible that individuals who had been subject to abuse were more likely to respond to our search for participants. In our search, however, we stressed that the main criterion, other than identifying as Irish or Muslim, was to have lived in either city during one or both eras of political violence. We did not seek people who had been arrested; rather, we sought people whose first response was often 'nothing has happened to me personally'.

The total sample consisted of 19 Muslim participants (10 men and 9 women) and 19 Irish participants (9 men and 10 women). The Muslim participants, a majority of whom were migrants or second generation, came from a variety of ethnic backgrounds including Somali, Moroccan, Yemeni, white British convert, Pakistani, Eritrean and Mauritian. The Irish participants were either migrants from Ireland or Northern Ireland, or of Irish descent. The participants ranged from early twenties to late seventies; so an intergenerational, as well as inter-ethnic and inter-religious dynamic was a significant feature of the groups. Despite differences of generation and experience, the strong empathy between Muslim and Irish participants was a striking feature of the discussion groups. Each group had its own specific dynamic, but without exception, attempts were made to understand the experience of others and to build bridges. A level of trust was established in some groups such that it allowed people to recount quite disturbing experiences. There was a consensus in all the groups that the comparison had been useful and beneficial.

The findings reported here are therefore based on the qualitative part of the project rather than the quantitative research we engaged in for the media and policy studies. We aimed in this part of the research to provide a map of the experiences and impacts in everyday life reported by key informants and in discussion groups. We cannot verify definitively that the catalogue of experiences and impacts of being 'suspect' described in these interviews and discussion groups are likely to be common ones for a sizeable proportion of Irish and Muslim populations. But the combination of key informant interviews, sampling specialised knowledge, with discussion groups, which brought together self-identified members of both sets of communities in mutually engaged exchanges is suggestive that they may well be, particularly in the two cities concerned.

Awareness of being 'suspect'

This section draws on data from the discussion groups in Birmingham and London supplemented by evidence from the key informant interviews.

Everyday encounters and experiences

We begin with two examples of participants in the discussion groups relating how in their everyday lives they became aware of being suspect. It was striking that in both eras, some of the worst abuse took place in workplaces. As this Muslim man's account in one of the Birmingham discussion groups illustrates:

> And like myself, about five, six years ago I was working somewhere where it was, I was the only Asian person there, and at the time it was, the Iraq war was about to start and there was some discussion going on, it was about cricket or something and it was about Pakistan losing. I wasn't from Pakistan anyway, I was trying to tell them I wasn't from there. I am an Arab. But to them, because of the ignorance as you were speaking about, they never even know what the difference was between an Arab and a Pakistani. So basically anyway the discussion went to Iraq and then a person made the comment that, 'When this war starts we're going to get you and hang you.' That's what they said to me. And I said, 'You're going to hang me?' And they

said, 'We're going to hang you'. And I said, 'You and who?', you know, because I was upset at the time that he could make a statement like that and I thought that growing up in this area, in this community, why is it, suddenly it can just turn like that, the whole thing again. So I can see the similarities between us to be honest.

At work people mix and communicate more than in other public spaces outside the home and neighbourhood. It is therefore not surprising that this exchange took place in the work context. This man, who was distinguishable as 'the only Asian person there', was assumed to be Pakistani and by one person at least associated directly with the representations of Iraq at the time as a place with weapons of mass destruction trained on 'the West' and with the 'war on terror'. This is an example of the deployment in an everyday encounter of one of the most important aspects of the dominant narrative of terror, namely that 'Islamic terrorism' poses a massive threat to the security of 'the West'. Here, it is operationalised by pinning responsibility on an assumed Pakistani, indicating how suspicion in the popular imagination attached to both Pakistanis in particular, all assumed to be Muslims and a racialised Asian Other in general.

The ways in which friends, neighbours or acquaintances might communicate to an individual that they were being perceived as a member of a 'suspect community' were not always as directly threatening as in the above example, but could nevertheless be intimidatory and induce fear. For example, one Irish woman described leaving her flat in London one morning in the 1980s:

> I remember going to work one day and one of the tenants downstairs she called me coming out. What have I done wrong, you know. She said, 'Put your arms out' and she was kind of going like searching. Then I realised what it was all about, you know, the devastation, it affects you kind of, you know. Lots of underlying remarks and just ignore them.

This woman early in the discussion group described the experience of living in London at the time as not difficult and that it involved her going to work as usual and living her normal life. But as the discussion progressed, she revealed more and more things that happened to her that she found both upsetting and exclusionary because she realised that people associated the fact that she was Irish with possible connection with or agreement with the IRA. She had rarely discussed these incidents with anyone. In this case, a woman who will have known that her neighbour was Irish half-jokingly but with serious intent communicated her suspicions about Irish people. These fears were fed in part by regular police injunctions to watch out for Irish accents and tell them about Irish neighbours or workmates (Hillyard 1993, pp. 258–259).

We selected these two examples, but there were many others in both eras of verbal intimidation and physical attacks. Both Irish and Muslim discussion group participants described having suffered verbal and physical abuse in everyday encounters. Abuse could be at the hands of both people known to the person attacked and by strangers. These attacks occurred primarily either at work (especially in the Irish case) or on the street (especially in the Muslim case). There were similarities in the type of verbal abuse or intimidation experienced, which included being confronted with media reports of bombings, being asked to account for Islam or Ireland, being called names in the street or even being directly accused of terrorism. For example, one second-generation Irish man said:

> . . . quite often during the working week, and when you were out with your friends socially, you might be defending yourself and your heritage and your background and your people and your country and your religion from their perceptions of what it was all about and what it meant and what they thought was my involvement or support for it.

Key informants that we interviewed elaborated on this process, whereby in the aftermath of violent incidents, it was whole communities who were held responsible. This example is drawn from the era in which it was the Irish community:

> I was on a news desk of the Daily Mirror on the Saturday when the Birmingham bombs had taken place the night before and the vilification towards Irish people that came in from normal members of the public who were ringing in expressing their disgust. And there were other episodes such as the assassination of Lord Mountbatten . . . I was approached in tears by a secretary who prodded me in the chest when the funeral was on TV and accused me, my lot, of having carried out this terrible murder.

Another way in which people became aware in everyday encounters that they were viewed as 'suspect' was by being shunned. Muslim participants recounted being stared at and shunned in the street or on public transport. Irish participants talked about being ignored or shunned at work. This went on for months in Birmingham after the pub bombings in 1974. The other places participants described being ignored or shunned were shops and banks. One woman described how she was 'sidestepped' in the street by people who knew her for months. Public space was therefore the site of potential attack and abuse or of being ignored and shunned.

Being ignored or shunned was described by one key informant, the chair of a Roman Catholic charitable organisation, as one of the practical consequences of 'being a suspect community' in that

> . . . part of the notion of being suspect is if someone sees you on the street and if you belong to a community that they think might be attacking them, they will want to walk away or go in another direction or not encounter you or whatever and you maybe more friendly than everyone else on the street.

He went beyond the comparison being made here and pointed out that there were some similarities with the harassment from the police and other authorities that, in his view, young African Caribbean men experienced. He added:

> we for instance work now with second and third-generation black and Asian young people and we are trying to build their self-confidence and self-respect. Partly because we feel society has undermined their self-confidence and self-respect to a degree by slightly branding them a suspect group.

The negative responses in public space recounted by Muslim respondents were based primarily on appearance, whereas the contexts in which Irish respondents were treated negatively involved speech, and thus the revelation of assumed Irishness through voice or through name recognition (a frequent way in which the second-generation Irish were identified). In these ways, in both eras of political violence, the public realm became problematic to participate in and negotiate. Different locations were problematic with, for example, Irish people experiencing fewer problems on the street than Muslims (except from the police in Irish areas) but more in places like pubs (where they were expected to be and Muslims were not).

A number of participants in Birmingham, both Irish and Muslim, wondered and exchanged views about how people who they had grown up with or lived and worked with in the same 'community' had become suspicious of them seemingly 'overnight'. This was often deeply upsetting and of lasting impact and was recognised as a similarity of experience. This might prompt us to consider the process by which the familiar is made remarkable and then familiar again and how this is a fertile site for the mobilisation of political anxiety (Burman 2010). As Jenny Burman suggests in a discussion of similar processes in Canada, a process of affective recircuitry can occur whereby a crisis-based realignment of vectors of trust and suspicion result in transformations of resident's 'psychogeographic mappings' – nourished by political and media fear-mongering (2010, p. 204). So in periods of crisis, at once manufactured and genuinely 'felt' people are called upon to police each other, which inevitably triggers anxiety in potential suspects and fears amongst those doing the suspecting.

Policing as part of everyday experiences

Part of the account of everyday experiences involved a discussion of policing. Although there were some positive comments on the role of the police, a predominantly negative experience of policing was shared in the discussion groups. A range of similar actions across both eras of political violence were described – stop and search, house raids, being stopped while travelling, being arrested – all of which left individuals in no doubt that Irish and Muslim people were perceived as potentially 'suspect' by the police. The two most discussed aspects – experiences while travelling and surveillance practices – are discussed below.

The experience of discrimination while travelling internationally is common to both groups and both key informants (with personal experience of what they were describing), and discussion group participants felt they were subjected to extra or intrusive checks, particularly at ports in the past for the Irish and airports for Muslims. One second-generation Irish key informant described the regularity of the experience:

> I can remember being pulled in and given an extra form of questioning by immigration staff at Dover as to who am I, where had I been, who had I seen etc – and that happened to me quite a lot – Irish passports during those years in those queues were always singled out for greater attention – you just got used to be held for that extra 10–15 minutes if they chose to, to question you.

Similarly, a young Muslim key informant, a community organiser, described his shock and disgust when one of his Mosque teachers was pulled aside on a plane to Saudi Arabia because he was wearing the salwar kameez, as is traditional for Pakistanis, had a beard because he was an Imam and because he had a hat on. This utilisation of combined markers of ethno-national origins and of religion made him and others, he argued, aware of how widespread the net might be and induced the general fear 'that anybody can get picked up at any time and nobody can do anything about it'.

This young man's concerns were echoed and given flesh by another key informant, an Irish man who was a community leader for many years and frequently visited police stations trying to establish what happened to people who had been picked up under the PTA. He describes his own and others experiences of harassment from the police:

> I had a little situation myself: I was working in a particular place at the time, and a Category A prisoner had asked for me to be added to the visitors . . . and I get on quite well with Special Branch and I got to know a lot of the persons, we saw that each of us had a job to do etc etc – but the Special Branch went to my place of work and they were waiting for me to leave and only realised this later I went out on business and then they went into the office to ask for me. They already knew that I had gone out. And the person they were speaking to, it was in

a small borough but he was the town clerk in a very, very small area. And they told him that I had applied for permission to become a visitor to a Category A prisoner. Now, I mean, that was quite deliberately to make things difficult for me. And as it happened I had told him [the town clerk] that I was going to visit a prisoner regularly. Now if they did that in my case, then what did they say to the neighbours of the person who had been picked up. Were they saying we suspect him of being involved in a bombing plot, whatever.

Fears of being 'picked up' can stem from incidents people hear of happening to others and also from direct experiences of police harassment.

One other category of policing that frequently came up was that of 'being watched': the perpetual gaze of the authorities was cited as a pernicious aspect of being 'suspect'. In the discussion groups, there was a strong sense that Irish areas or likely places of public congregation in the past and Muslim areas or buildings currently were under surveillance (these principally involved pubs and mosques, respectively). A perception of being perpetually watched was therefore very strong and is obviously not illusionary, as the example of Project Champion in Birmingham demonstrates. Project Champion was a secret police operation to place Muslims living in parts of Birmingham under permanent surveillance and implemented with virtually no consultation, oversight or regard for the law (see Lewis 2010).

Impacts of constructing communities as 'suspect'

At some length, discussion group participants and key informants discussed immediate and long-term after-effects that constituted the impacts of being 'suspect'. Broadly, these impacts can be classified as low profile/silencing, alienation and psychological impacts, internal divisions and resistance. A low profile was described as being either an enforced or an adopted response. It was seen as an enforced response when it resulted from the existence of such a skewed public debate that to speak up at variance with the predominant narrative of terror was often sufficient to render someone 'suspect'. This could happen anywhere outside of the home, for example, at work or meeting friends, and was described as part of how people experienced constraints in public space. In this way, individuals felt silenced. Maintaining a low profile as an adopted strategy was largely attributed to a collective siege mentality or, and this was the commonest impact reported, to fear. This included restricting the places they frequented for shopping, meeting friends and family and being very careful about whom they spoke to. In the Muslim case, this involved not discussing politics (e.g. at work), avoiding certain areas of the city, being careful on the telephone and Internet and taking care not to mention al-Qaeda or terrorism, even in jokes. Irish participants frequently described keeping quiet so that their accents would not be noticed and being reluctant to discuss Northern Ireland.

Another widespread longer term after-effect of being 'suspect' was alienation. This resulted in particular from policing practices, from having their loyalty questioned and from pervasive discourses of 'us and them', as this Muslim key informant explains:

> ... the experience is very alienating. And I think, is alienating and creating, is promoting the concept of 'us and them' and dividing communities. And you know, the irony is that sometimes this is done in the name of cohesion ... there is huge problems with the psychological impact of all this demonisation which it has never been measured and I think that needs to be measured, what psychological impact it has got and how that is going to affect the whole community – people have got a lot of psychosis that is connected to police and security and so forth.

For some young Muslims, apart from disaffection, alienation was said to lead to a variety of responses, including an increased inclination to assert a Muslim identity, sometimes to join gangs and in a tiny minority of cases, to develop politically radical views (not to be confused with what are referred to as extremist views, see Spalek and Imtoual 2007).

A further long-term impact was the creation of internal divisions either within communities or within families. The suspicion of a fifth column could cause divisions in families which were sometimes expressed along generational lines. These divisions were seen as a direct result of anti-terror measures, which encourage internal community surveillance and an emphasis on this as a responsibility of individual citizens (for discussion of this process in the contemporary period, see Mythen and Walklate 2006, Spalek and Lambert 2008). Finally, the participants in the discussion groups and interviewees discussed patterns of resistance to being 'suspect'. These practices were generated by the anger felt at being perceived as 'suspect'. Irish and Muslim individuals described deciding to challenge what was being said or done to them in public spaces: on the street, in shops and at work (see also Hickman and Walter 1997, Silvestri and Charti 2007). It is these everyday encounters with 'the public' that have some of the most long-term impacts on their lives, including psychological impacts.

Similarities and differences between the two eras

Key informants were specifically asked to compare the contemporary period with the period when the Irish were 'suspect'. Reinforcing what emerged from the discussion groups, the similarity mentioned more than any other was that both Irish communities and Muslim communities were associated with terrorism and similar measures had been implemented in both eras. One second-generation Irish man working in a community organisation in Birmingham stated:

> Well, it's a bit I suppose the same as the Muslims are suffering now. Erm, all of the Irish people then were treated as terrorists and bombers and that . . . Muslims, yeah. In general conversation, they say, 'oh, these Muslims, you know, they are all at it, they are all making bombs and that'. Same as the Irish. I mean, the Guildford Four. Look at how long they suffered.

A number of Irish key informants responded along similar lines. A young Muslim woman working in a community organisation in London commented on the similarities in another way:

> I would have been very young sadly to remember too much about the Irish experience. But I do remember the bombing of the Conservative Party conference. I remember the notion of it being a threat as great as you now hear in terms of the terrorist threat you now hear from Muslim extremists identified . . . I think there were resonances of what Muslims are now experiencing in terms of questions to whether or not they endorsed parliamentary democracy, whether or not they showed allegiance to the Queen.

In this response, the similarity is drawn in terms of the marginalisation of Irish and Muslims as perceived endorsers of political violence and as potential traitors. Implicitly, both were positioned outside of or in ambivalent relation to Britishness, and the values British citizens are expected to share. Both these key informants are making connections between the two eras and commenting on the process by which whole communities are rendered as 'risk repositories by virtue of sharing some or other of the characteristics of the "typical" terrorist' (Mythen and Walklate 2006, p. 390).

The main differences discussed by significant numbers of the key informants related to their assessments of the relative vulnerability of Irish communities and Muslim communities as immigrants to discrimination and harassment and of their comparative public profiles. Many interviewees thought that Muslims were more straightforwardly identifiable and therefore could not hide and were more easily harassed. A civil liberties activist in London argued:

> I am not saying there wasn't a racist element in the 1970s but you know, but you are more markedly different. I mean, what I am saying is in the 1970s you could probably lower your voice or not speak, which is not great for any human being but you can probably do that and be smart and get out of trouble and you can't, you know, lower your skin tone, that is an added dimension, I think, you know, that sometimes people forget.

A young Muslim professional in Birmingham viewed things to some extent differently:

> ... in terms of differences yes, I think the Irish people probably had it hard because we haven't seen that but when you look at our side maybe they had it more harder than us because they were very much involved with the English community, with the British people, whereas the Muslim community are kind of a Muslim community itself. The only time they probably face our non-Muslim colleagues is probably at work or if we go out of the area where we live. So we probably get it easier to a certain extent ... So I think the Irish probably had it harder some points but then if you look at the other points maybe not as hard because we don't just get attacked because of the religion that we follow, it's also because of the colour and the racism issue comes into it.

His perception of the positioning of Irish people in relation to the English/British results in empathetic comments on how things may have been harder for them in the past. He is implying that their degree of contact with the majority ethnic population and possibly their expectations may have led to a worse backlash. However, his description of Muslims being afforded protection from backlash through their place-based communities also implied the defensiveness against backlash that this can constitute as decisions have to be made about 'if we go outside of the area where we live'. He ends by echoing the point of the previous quotation that visible difference makes Muslims more susceptible to harassment than the Irish.

His analysis of the complexity was borne out in these comments by an Irish woman in Birmingham with long experience in local Irish organisations:

> See the sad part about the Irish as well is that in some cases erm, the older people now as well if they could ... Because of the, how they felt and how they were discriminated against or how they felt not as valued as sort of like a, one of the host country, they felt like they were foreigners and that, if they could get away with being classed as English, they thought that was a great kind of achievement really.

Here, she is expressing a view about the responses of many Irish people in the 1970s, and 'now as well', and their perception of not being valued (see also Hickman and Walter 1997). Her comments are similar to accounts of the 'confidence inside the Muslim community' being 'at an all-time low' and that many feel like 'conditional Britons' (Bari 2011). Another Muslim key informant stated:

> ... definitely being a suspect community has got a psychological sort of cost to it and that has never been measured – people's confidence has been affected so much that they see themselves as a second-class citizen and actually want to conform into that sort of second-class citizenship sort of basis.

A final extract further illustrates the complexity of accounting for differences between the two eras and is taken from an interview with a worker in an Irish voluntary organisation in Birmingham:

> ... in '74 it was fair game in factories and schools and services to racially abuse people ... there was no legislation to protect people. But latterly there has been and that is a, I guess, a slight change in the two communities. Because, I mean I am sure that Muslim people are verbally abused but there was no legislation to protect people in the workplace and in schools etc. But nothing for the Irish in the early seventies. There was no kind of recourse ... You know, an employee couldn't be disciplined for calling somebody an Irish whatever, murderer, murdering bastard in 1974. But latterly if that would have happened and you would hope that procedures would be followed.

A number of key informants, both Irish and Muslim, held the view that the Irish had had no protection in the past, and that by comparison, due to a number of legislative changes, Muslims had more rights in the 2000s. This latter positioning, it was stressed, did not, however, deter being constructed as 'suspect'.

The contrast was also drawn between the more assertive public profile of some Muslims now compared with the lower public profile of the Irish in the previous era. Although the better legislative protection afforded for human rights and against discrimination was seen as underpinning this difference, the explanation was also seen to lie with the response of many of the younger generations of Muslims to being 'suspect'. One common response has been a reassertion of Muslim identifications amongst younger people, with many being proud to express this publicly. Their more confident public response was partly attributed to the second-generation Muslims being older now than the equivalent Irish second generation were in the 1970s. Second-generation and third-generation Muslims are seen as claiming their place as British citizens. In contrast, a majority of other Muslims, usually of the migrant generation, are characterised as keeping their 'heads down' in a similar manner to the response of many Irish in the 1970s.

In summary, the evidence of the discussion group participants and the key informants not only confirms that it has been sufficient to be identified as, or assumed to be, Irish or Muslim in order to be perceived as or treated as 'suspect', but it also details how for most people this is the result of everyday encounters and experiences. It is in their encounters with neighbours, workmates or strangers in shops or on the streets that our research participants have described becoming aware of being suspect. This does not happen all the time, but the fear of it occurring can be ever present as a backdrop to daily life. A state of fearfulness was described by Muslims as existing in the present period and by Irish people in relation to the past, and in both cases, 'lying low' and 'keeping your head down' were common responses. The state of fearfulness and suspicion was said to lead at times to divisions within communities. However, anger and alienation were also felt, and both Irish and Muslim respondents made connections between being treated as 'suspect' and practices of resistance.

Discussion and conclusion

A large majority of our key informants and discussion group participants provided evidence of the everyday nature of being 'suspect' in both eras of political violence. But a small number of our key informants (3 out of 42) and discussion group participants (one group in London made up solely of young people) disputed that in general there either was or is in circulation a notion of 'suspect communities'. The three key informants who disputed the idea are all members of the political or legal establishment. One high-ranking legal office holder and member of the House of Lords said the following:

> I think suspect communities is a dreadful over-simplification. There are certainly communities from whose number, within whose number there may be suspects. I mean, if you were to ask a member of the public who reads the Daily Mail, for example, where would you expect to find terrorists, they might say to you, in Leicester or in Bradford. Which defines the community from which they emerge. However, I think to hold the whole of the Muslim communities, using that deliberate plural, as suspect communities is just too broad a brush . . .
> I don't think it's realistic to suggest that the Irish were a suspect community. It was known that certain Irish people were terrorists but I don't think that the public ever damned the whole of every Irish person, man or woman you've met, with the soubriquet suspect or terrorist. Even though unlike al-Qaeda the Irish terrorists included men and women . . . I don't think the public at large look at a Muslim and say, if they know that he or she is a Muslim they are terrorist.

He went on to say that he thought 'there were elements in the police that had a mindset about suspect communities up to or maybe in the beginning of the Nineties', but that since the McPherson Report had been published, he thought this had receded. What is interesting about the above statement is the strong, and no doubt understandable, wish not to believe suspect communities have been created as a result of policymaking in either era. At the same time, he acknowledges both the possible role of the press influencing readers to conceive of 'communities' and 'places' from which terrorists are likely to come and the possibility that the police did operate with a notion of 'suspect communities'. The young people in London who queried the use of the term 'suspect communities' did so more because of its negative connotations and they did not want to be viewed as 'suspect'.

There is no doubt that the term 'suspect communities' is freighted with negative connotations, and it was not liked by those participants who thought the notion was in wide circulation. Our findings, however, offer evidence that individuals have been responded to and treated as members of 'suspect communities', in relation to political violence, across four decades in Britain and that the concept of 'suspect community' still has currency as a theoretical and analytical tool. In both eras, these notions of 'suspectness' were attached to 'communities' formed predominantly from immigrations to Britain and this has involved consequences for social cohesion to which we now turn.

The experiences of 'being suspected' that our key informants and discussion group participants relate may be, as has been noted, produced by fear on the part of those being abusive or threatening or who actively shun their neighbours or workmates. Communities are being constructed as 'suspect' in a traumatogenic environment (Hollander and Gutwill 2006). Layton (2008), discussing the United States, argues government has retreated from providing functions that might contain anxiety and trauma (while enforcing 'strong legislative measures' which further contribute to engendering fear and alarm) and, in concert with the media, has kept people frightened. As Lianos and Douglas (2000, p. 268) explain, 'presumed dangerousness is the major postindustrial criterion for distinguishing between those who should be avoided and those who we can approach'. The possibility of a terror attack lies in the background everyday reinforced every time someone walks through detecting gates.

This is the backdrop to community cohesion policymaking throughout the 2000s that called for the need to: 'have a common vision and a sense of belonging for all communities' (Local Government Association 2002); 'emphasise what binds communities together rather than what divides them' (Commission on Integration and Cohesion 2007); and 'bring down the barriers that divide people in our country today' (Cameron 2011). This research has generated substantiation across two eras of political violence that processes of 'suspectification' operate with notions of bounded 'communities' and therefore are more likely to divide communities than bring them together. It was enough to be identified as, or assumed to be, Irish or Muslim in order to be treated as 'suspect' and although this did not occur each day, the fear that it could be enduring. 'Bounded community', both as an experience of belonging and as a social practice, may be reinforced both for those who are perceived as 'suspect' and for their neighbours, friends and workmates who now view them differently. Identifying members of 'suspect communities' by generalised characteristics of ethnicity, religion, colour or accent is inimical to social cohesion, due to its potentially polarising effects on the population as a whole and its unjust consequences for Irish communities and Muslim communities. In fact, one of the ironies of the community cohesion agenda is that it creates the idea of minority ethnic and religious communities and fixes identities within these community boundaries while demanding they move outside them (Alexander 2007).

Imposed boundedness as a 'suspect community' limits experiences of belonging by inducing a range of feelings and responses – anger, alienation, resignation, fear, resistance – all of which are potentially exclusionary in impact and undermine feelings of acceptance. The evidence is that the impacts of these experiences of being 'suspect' include the process whereby forms of belonging that previously were part of a wider set of identifications for an individual can become more important as a result of being 'suspect'. This is usually accompanied by a motivation to express this enhanced identification in the public realm (some young Muslim women in the discussion groups described how they now choose to wear the headscarf, whereas previously they would not have done so). In other cases, the impact of being 'suspect' is, due to fear or another constraint, to adopt as low a profile as possible, to stay 'with one's own' and retreat from the public realm (two Irish participants expressed nervousness about attending a discussion group because of their still resonant memories of being part of a 'suspect' community in the past).

Nevertheless, the reinforcement of boundedness by the construction of 'suspect communities' is, we found, in tension with the cosmopolitanism that characterises places like London and Birmingham. Both Irish communities and Muslim communities are part of immigrations that are strongly culturally marked, as well as deeply connected to those around them (Hall 2002). The empathetic connections established between participants in the discussion groups, where discourses of suspicion were not in operation, indicate the limitations and flaws of the community cohesion agenda with its identification of 'communities' as the site of the problem of political violence and as the site of interventionist strategies of cohesion.

One last argument about 'communities' and counterterrorism is worth considering in the light of this research. There have been calls to engage community involvement more positively in a fight against extremism (Jackson 2008, Spalek and Lambert 2008, Bari 2011). Our research suggests that any positive representations of and engagement with Muslims in the current context would be beneficial. But our conclusion is different. Our focus has not been on extremism and we would agree with Michael (2008) that extremists are part of these 'suspect communities' as a result of the boundaries that have been drawn by public authorities and the media. The latter constantly speak of 'moderate Muslims' and 'extremist Muslims' (see Nickels *et al.* forthcoming-b). We have been concerned to chart the impact of being 'suspected' on the everyday lives of Muslims in general. It is necessary to change the negative impacts of the process of constructing communities as 'suspect'. This requires a change in the practice of conceiving of certain communities within civil society as problematic for social cohesion and of conflating this with conceptualising certain populations as 'suspect' where political violence is concerned.

The current government has stated that it seeks to separate the community cohesion agenda from the counterterrorism agenda. This is useful but their location of the problem of political violence and the focus of counterterrorism remains fixed on Muslim communities and a strategy for rooting out extreme ideas (Home Office 2011). This is a classic counter-insurgency strategy of the type that was unsuccessful in Northern Ireland. We have outlined here that there are many more continuities between the two eras of political violence, particularly in counterterrorism policies, than politicians and policymakers readily admit. A dominant aspect of the narrative on terrorism in Britain, that there is a divorce between these two eras of political violence, needs challenging. This idea has led to insufficient lessons being learned, from one era to another, especially as regards the negative impacts of practices of suspectification on Irish communities and Muslim communities. This, possibly, unintended consequence of counterterrorism strategies has also had negative consequences for the stated objectives of cohesion policies. The discussion groups demonstrated that with the removal of discourses of suspicion the common ground of Britain's urban multiculture was a sufficient basis for sympathetic exchanges. The people participating drew lessons from the comparison of the two eras in a way policymakers have not.

Acknowledgement

The research on which this article was based was funded by the Economic and Social Science Research Council – ESRC Reference: RES-062-23-106.

Notes on contributors

Mary J. Hickman is professor of Irish Studies and Sociology at London Metropolitan University and director of the Institute for the Study of European Transformations. She has been visiting professor at New York University, Columbia University, Victoria University, Melbourne and University College Dublin. Her publications include *Migration and Social Cohesion in the UK* (Palgrave, 2012, with N. Mai and H. Crowley).

Lyn Thomas is professor of Cultural Studies and deputy director of the Institute for the Study of European Transformations at London Metropolitan University, where she has taught French, film and media since 1989. Her writings include *Annie Ernaux, an introduction to the writer and her audience* (Berg, 1999) and *Fans, Feminisms and 'Quality' Media* (Routledge, 2002). She has edited a collection on *Religion, Consumerism and Sustainability: Paradise Lost?* (Palgrave, 2010) and co-edited *The Theory and Politics of Consuming Differently* with Kate Soper and Martin Ryle (Palgrave, 2008). She was a member of the *Feminist Review* Editorial Collective from 1998 to 2011.

Dr Henri C. Nickels currently works at the European Union Agency for Fundamental Rights (FRA), Vienna, Austria, where he is a programme manager of research – Social Science. There, he works on issues related to racism, xenophobia, anti-Semitism, Islamophobia and related intolerances. Prior to that, Dr Nickels was a research fellow at the Institute for the Study of European Transformations at London Metropolitan University, UK, and a research officer at the University of Surrey, Guildford, UK.

Sara Silvestri holds a PhD and MPhil from Cambridge University (UK) and a 'laurea' from La Sapienza University (Italy). She is currently senior lecturer at City University London, where she teaches courses on Religion and Politics, the EU and Islamist movements. She is also a research associate at Cambridge University and has directed the Muslims in Europe programme for the European Policy Centre in Brussels. Her research and publications focus on Islamic organisations and Muslim–government relations, counterterrorism, migration, Europe's Muslim women and faith-based lobbies in the EU.

References

Alexander, C., 2007. Cohesive identities: the distance between meaning and understanding. *In*: M. Wetherell, M. Lafèche, and R. Berkeley, eds. *Identity, ethnic diversity and community cohesion*. London: Sage, 115–125.

Bari, M.A., 2011. No section of British society should be treated with suspicion. *OpenDemocracy* [online]. Available from: http://www.opendemocracy.net [Accessed 26 June 2011].

Berman, P., 2003. *Terror and liberalism*. New York: WW Norton.

Blair, Tony, 2005. IRA are not al-Qaeda says Blair. *BBC News*. 26 July [online]. Available from: news.bbc.co.uk/1/hi/uk_politics/4718223.stm [Accessed 29 November 2010].

Blok, A., 1998. The narcissism of minor differences. *European Journal of Social Theory*, 1 (1), 33–56.

Blunket, D., 2004. *New challenges for race equality and community cohesion in the 21st century: a speech by the Rt. Hon. David Blunkett MP, Home Secretary, to the Institute of Public Policy Research*. London: Home Office Communications Directorate.

Burman, J., 2010. Suspects in the city. *Cultural Studies*, 24 (2), 200–213.

Cameron, D., 2011. PM's speech at Munich Security Conference [online]. 5 February. Available from: http://www.number10.gov.uk/news/speeches-and-transcripts/2011/02/pms-speech-at-munich-security-conference-60293 [Accessed 10 March 2011].

Cantle, T., 2001. *Community cohesion: a report of the independent review team. Chaired by Ted Cantle*. London: Home Office.

Cantle, T., 2008. *Community cohesion: a new framework for race and diversity*. London: Palgrave Macmillan.

Clarke, J. and Newman, J., 1997. *The managerial state*. London: Sage.

Clutterbuck, L., 2006. Countering Irish Republican terrorism in Britain: its origin as a police function. *Terrorism and Political Violence*, 18 (1), 95–118.

Commission on Integration and Cohesion, 2007. *Our shared future*. London: Department of Communities and Local Government.

Delanty, G., 2003. *Community*. London: Routledge.

Gilroy, P., 2005. Multiculture, double consciousness and the war on terror. *Patterns of Prejudice*, 39 (4), 431–443.

Greer, S., 2008. Human rights and the struggle against terrorism in the United Kingdom. *European Human Rights Law Review*, 2, 163–181.

Greer, S., 2010. Anti-terrorist laws and the United Kingdom's 'suspect Muslim community'. A reply to Pantazis and Pemberton. *British Journal of Criminology*, 50, 1171–1190.

Hall, S., 2002. Political belonging in a world of multiple identities. *In*: S. Vertovec and R. Cohen, eds. *Conceiving cosmopolitanism. Theory, context, and practice*. Oxford University Press, 25–31.

Hardt, M. and Negri, A., 2000. *Empire*. Cambridge, MA: Harvard University Press.

Hickman, M.J., Crowley, H., and Mai, N., 2008. *Immigration and social cohesion in the UK: the rhythms and realities of everyday life* [online]. York: Joseph Rowntree Foundation. Available from: http://www.jrf.org.uk/sites/files/jrf/2230-deprivation-cohesion-immigration.pdf [Accessed 24 August 2010].

Hickman, M.J. and Walter, B., 1997. *Discrimination and the Irish community in Britain*. London: Commission for Racial Equality.

Hillyard, P., 1993. *Suspect community: peoples experience of the prevention of terrorism acts in Britain*. London: Pluto Press in association with Liberty.

Hollander, N.C. and Gutwill, S., 2006. Despair and hope in a culture of denial. *In*: L. Layton, N.C. Hollander, and S. Gutwill, eds. *Psychoanalysis, class and politics: encounters in the clinical setting*. London: Routledge, 81–91.

Home Office, 2011. *Prevent strategy* [online]. Available from: http://www.homeoffice.gov.uk/publications/counter-terrorism/prevent/prevent-strategy/prevent-strategy-review?view=Binary

Jackson, R., 2008. Counter-terrorism and communities: an interview with Robert Lambert. *Critical Studies on Terrorism*, 1 (2), 293–308.

Layton, L., 2008. What divides the subject? Psychoanalytic reflections on subjectivity, subjection and resistance. *Subjectivity*, 22, 60–72.

Lewis, P., 2010. Police surveillance of Muslims set up with 'no regard for law'. *The Guardian* [online], 30 September. Available from: www.guardian.co.uk/uk/2010/sep/30/police-surveillance-muslims-no-regard-law [Accessed 1 October 2010].

Lianos, M. and Douglas, M., 2000. Dangerization and the end of deviance. *British Journal of Criminology*, 40, 261–278.

Local Government Association, 2002. *Guidance on social cohesion*. London: Department of Communities and Local Government.

Maguire, A., 1994. *Why me? One woman's fight for justice and dignity*. London: HarperCollins.

Maguire, P., 2009. *My father's watch. The story of a child prisoner in 70s Britain*. London: Harper Perennial.

Malik, K., 2005. Multiculturalism has fanned the flames of Islamic extremism. *The Times* [online], 16 July. Available from: http://www.timesonline.co.uk/tol/comment/columnists/guest_contributors/article544443.ece [Accessed 17 July 2005].

McGhee, D., 2005. *Intolerant Britain? Hate, citizenship and difference*. Milton Keynes: Open University Press.

McGovern, M., 2010. 'The IRA are not al-Qaeda': 'new terrorism' discourse and Irish republicanism. *In*: K. Hayward and C. O'Donnell, eds. *Political discourse and conflict resolution: debating peace in Northern Ireland*. London: Routledge, 192–208.

Michael, L. 2008. Securing civic relations in the multicultural city. *CSD Proceedings*, 164–186.

Mythen, G. and Walklate, S., 2006. Criminology and terrorism. Which thesis? Risk society or governmentality? *British Journal of Criminology*, 46 (3), 379–398.

Nickels, H., *et al.*, forthcoming-a. Constructing 'suspect' communities: Irish and Muslim communities in the British press, 1974–2007. *European Journal of Communication Studies*, 27 (2).

Nickels, H., *et al.*, forthcoming-b. De/constructing 'suspect communities': a critical discourse analysis of British newspaper coverage of Irish communities and Muslim communities, 1974–2007. *Journalism Studies* [online], 13 (3). Available from: http://www.tandfonline.com/doi/abs/10.1080/1461670X.2011.616412 [Accessed 7 October 2011].

Pantazis, C. and Pemberton, S., 2009. From the 'old' to the 'new' suspect community: examining the impacts of recent UK counter-terrorist legislation. *British Journal of Criminology*, 49 (5), 646–666.

Runnymede Commission on British Muslims and Islamophobia, 1997. *Islamophobia. A challenge for us all*. London: The Runnymede Trust.

Schlesinger, P., 1991. *Media, state, nation: political violence and collective identities*. London: Sage.

Sharma, S. and Sharma, A., 2003. White paranoia: orientalism in the age of empire. *Fashion Theory*, 7 (3/4), 301–318.

Silvestri, S. and Charti, M., 2007. *Report on London and Birmingham focus groups for research project Muslims in Europe after 9/11*. Rome: Etnobarometro. Unpublished.

Spalek, B. and Imtoual, A., 2007. Muslim communities and counter-terrorism responses: 'hard' approaches to community engagement in the UK and Australia. *Journal of Muslim Minority Affairs*, 27 (2), 185–202.

Spalek, B. and Lambert, R., 2008. Muslim communities, counter-terrorism and counter-radicalisation: a critically reflective approach to engagement. *International Journal of Law, Crime and Justice*, 36 (4), 257–270.

Uniting Britain Trust, 2004. *Islamophobia: issues, challenges and action*. Stoke on Trent: Trentham Books.

Wetherell, M., 2008. Speaking to power: Tony Blair, complex multicultures and fragile white English identities. *Critical Social Policy*, 28 (3), 299–319.

Wilkinson, P., 2006. *Terrorism versus democracy*. London: Routledge.

'Events dear boy, events': terrorism and security from the perspective of politics

Andrew W. Neal

Politics and International Relations, University of Edinburgh, Edinburgh, UK

> This article asks what it would mean to consider terrorism and security from the perspective of politics. It argues that security politics – defined as the activity of politicians when connected in some way to security – has been largely excluded from existing scholarly approaches to terrorism and security. In contrast to the assumptions about existential threat and sovereign/executive power characteristic of existing approaches, the article argues that if we consider security in terms of what is at stake for politicians, then it can no longer be considered as separate from 'normal' politics. From the perspective of politics, security events are just like other politically salient events.

Introduction

In the 10 years of scholarship on terrorism and security since 9/11, there has been a heavy focus from some quarters on the nature of threats and a heavy focus from others on the critique of sovereign power and security governance. Following the nomenclature of this journal, we might call these two strands 'traditional' security scholarship and 'critical' security scholarship, although such categories are always fuzzy and contestable. This article argues that there is something missing from the attentions of both, and that is security politics. By politics, I mean the activity of professional politicians (Weber 1994, Palonen 2006), rather than simply governments or political leaders, and by security politics, I mean when this activity relates to security in some way, whether objectively, discursively or by some other connection. My argument is that despite their differences, traditional security scholarship and critical security scholarship perform the same classic security trope: that security is an existential realm of sovereign or executive prerogative. The assumption is that if we want to understand security, we need to analyse how political leaders and the executive branch of government conceive, identify and tackle security threats. This trope leads to the analytical exclusion of security politics.

    This matters because there is a great deal of activity by politicians relating to terrorism and security that does not fall under the umbrella of sovereign or executive power. For example, security policies have been contested in national parliaments; members of legislatures have set up inquiries and committees (for example, on extraordinary rendition (Intelligence and Security Committee 2007) or fast-track legislation (House of Lords Select

Committee on the Constitution 2009)); and politicians have published reports (such as the 9/11 commission report (National Commission on Terrorist Attacks upon the United States *et al.* 2004)), scrutinised military and intelligence service budgets and fought elections at least in part on national security tickets. This activity, understood as *security politics*, involves backbench politicians, opposition parties and political leaders and ministers in their capacity as politicians rather than as executive office holders.

In the aftermath of 9/11 and other spectacular acts of political violence since, terrorism and security scholarship has been understandably drawn to focus on executive and governmental responses, some of which have been equally spectacular. Such responses to perceived security emergencies do appear to adhere to the classic sovereign security trope in the short term, with executive prerogative asserted, critical deliberation sidelined and concerns about liberties and rights pushed aside (Medical Foundation for the Care of the Victims of Torture *et al.* 2001, Chang 2002, Goldberg *et al.* 2002, Bamford 2004, Liberty 2004, Scheuerman 2006, Hewitt 2008). But the passing of 10 years since 9/11 has seen this short-term logic fade and more diverse forms of politics return. Ten years has allowed a broader range of political activities relating to security to play out, and the classic sovereign security trope does not do them analytical justice.

The classic trope assumes, implicitly or explicitly, that security transcends 'normal' politics because of its existential importance. The trope ultimately derives from Hobbes and finds repeated expression to the present day. In Hobbes there can be no industry, arts or anything of civilised value without security, and therefore the security provided by the sovereign must be the first freedom in any modern state (Hobbes 1996, p. 89). Versions of this trope are reproduced in Locke, Montesquieu, Hume, Smith, Bentham, Mill and Schmitt (for overviews, see Hussein 2003, pp. 16–22, Neocleous 2008, pp. 11–38). It is Carl Schmitt who constructs the starkest argument for a necessary link between sovereign security prerogative and existential threat on the basis of the inevitability of 'the exception': 'a case of extreme peril, a danger to the existence of the state, or the like ... It is precisely the exception that makes relevant the subject of sovereignty, that is, the whole question of sovereignty' (Schmitt 1985, p. 6). The idea of 'the exception' has been subject to intense legal and political debate and is beyond the scope of this article (Fitzpatrick 2003, Huysmans 2004, 2008, Agamben 2005, Johns 2005, Prozorov 2005, Tierney 2005, Gross and Ní Aoláin 2006, Neal 2006, 2008a, 2008b, 2010, Doty 2007), but what concerns us here is the sovereign security prerogative as expressed repeatedly in modern Western political thought and practice. The classic trope assumes that the existential realm of security is of such importance that normal politics and law should give way to sovereign or executive power in order to deal with security threats.

The analytical and political effect of this trope is the reification of sovereign or executive power as the fundamental security actor, excluding a wider analysis of *security politics*. It also has the effect of separating the realm of security from 'normal' politics. The trope can be performed in a variety of ways, but the effect is the same. It can be performed philosophically, as in the work of Agamben (1998, 2005). It can be performed discursively or sociologically in the vein of securitisation studies (Wæver 1995, Buzan *et al.* 1998, Balzacq 2011). Or it can be reproduced through its critique in the name of human security or emancipation (Booth 1991, Fierke 2007, pp. 186–205). The performance of the trope creates an analytical blind spot regarding security politics and an incomplete picture of the workings of security. It diverts attention from the multiple ways in which professional politicians mobilise and organise around security issues, the ways they contest rather than make policy, the diversity of political discourse beyond executive pronouncements and the shear breath of professional political activity that does not simply defer to executive security prerogative.

Most significantly, the existential logic of the classic sovereign security trope conceals the quite different political logics that may be at work in the activity of professional politicians. The point is not to question whether security threats are really existential or not, although this can certainly be a feature of political security debates. This would be to play into an old debate on objective/subjective security introduced by Wolfers (1952): a condition of objective security or insecurity being impossible to measure except perhaps in hindsight and subjective security being a psychological condition measured only by its deviation from 'reality' (Buzan and Hansen 2009, pp. 32–33; see, for example, Mueller 2005). The point is that existential survival of the state, nation or any other publicly articulated referent object is not necessarily the primary stake for professional politicians involved in the activity of security politics.

This article therefore asks what it would mean to rethink security from the perspective of *politics*, rather than through the critique of sovereign, executive or governmental power. What happens to our understanding of security if we refuse its separation from 'normal' politics? What happens if instead of beginning with the problem of existential threat (its identification, declaration, contestation and apprehension), we consider security politics in terms of the stakes involved for politicians? This move potentially undermines the reification of sovereign power performed by terrorism and security studies, critical or otherwise. The article will argue that understanding security from the perspective of politics means that what is at stake is not existential survival but *political* survival. This has very different implications for security analysis.

The first part of the article makes some further qualifications about the meaning of *security politics* and considers its exclusion from scholarship in more depth. The second part critiques securitisation theory as a sophisticated example of this exclusion. And the final part proposes an alternative theoretical framing for understanding security from the perspective of politics.

Security politics and its exclusion

A few qualifications are necessary first. By 'security politics' I do not mean the wider critique of what is *political* about security. Security practices, security policies and security discourses are all political in the sense that they implicate power relations and can be critiqued and politicised as such. The potential scope of what is political about the problem of security is ever expanding thanks to a broad range of critical scholarship, from feminist approaches that unpack the gendered power relations of security practices (Hansen 2000, Richter-Montpetit 2007) to analyses of proliferating techniques of security governance such as risk management, insurance, bordering and surveillance (Vaughan-Williams 2007, Amoore and de Goede 2008, Salter 2008a, Basaran 2010, Lobo-Guerrero 2011). Jef Huysmans argues that such contest over the political meaning of security calls into question not only the identification of security threats but also the nature and limits of political community itself. For example, contest over the relationship between executive security prerogative and judicial application of human rights laws brings into question the proper relationship between the different branches of government (Huysmans 2006, pp. 11–12). The question of 'the political' is therefore an expansive one, expressed succinctly by the political scientist Colin Hay as follows: 'the political should be defined in such a way as to encompass the entire sphere of the social . . . All events, process and practices which occur within the social sphere have the potential to be political' (2002, p. 3).

In contrast to this expansive notion of 'the political', in this article I mean security politics in a narrow sense: the activity of politics as practised by politicians. I mean the kind of political activity examined by Max Weber in 'The Profession and Vocation of Politics', which considered the modern conditions under which the political activity of professional politicians takes place (Weber 1994). It is not my intention to privilege this notion of politics over any other, but rather to draw attention to its neglect in terrorism and security scholarship. The classic security trope does not capture the diverse ways in which politicians are called to engage with terrorism and security. Existing assumptions do not capture the full extent of the activity of security politics.

My grounds for problematising security politics stem from my ongoing empirical research on counterterrorist lawmaking in the British parliament (see Neal 2012a). This focuses on the arguments, practices and tactics of the full range of parliamentarians at different times, not only in the wake of perceived security emergencies but also when there is no perceived emergency and when such perceptions are fading into the political background. My core claim, based on an analysis of these unexpectedly diverse parliamentary discourses and activities, is that a whole sweep of political actors, namely politicians, have been excluded from the analysis of security because of an overwhelming focus on the executive branch of government, broadly understood. This analytical neglect of politicians not only is true of traditional strategic studies and international relations (IR) approaches in their state centrism and focus on executive decision makers (e.g. Waltz 1979, Vasquez 1993, p. 105) but is also true of much of critical terrorism and security studies in its critique of sovereign power, its deconstruction of government security policies and its empirical mapping of techniques of government. All these areas of analysis can be filed under the broad category of executive power, even when that power is devolved to bureaucracies, technical operatives or arms-length agencies (see Bigo 2002, Butler 2004, Amoore 2009). Politicians have been marginally included as 'domestic factors' in some approaches, for example, in foreign policy analysis (Hudson 2007, pp. 125–142). Politicians could also be considered through securitisation theory as a kind of 'audience' for executive security discourses (to which we will return), but almost no terrorism or security analysis has placed politicians and the activity and practice of *security politics* at its centre. To foreground security politics would mean considering not simply the leaders, ministers and governments whose statements and policies are often the focus of security analysis, but rather the whole range of politicians who are members of political institutions, such as legislatures in sovereign states and others such as those of the EU. There are strong empirical grounds to argue that security does not simply involve the decisions of sovereigns or expansive techniques of government, but mobilises and engages politicians in diverse ways.

The analytical neglect of security politics is largely due to the structure and evolution of academic disciplines. Terrorism and security studies developed as an extension of the discipline of IR and as such excludes the political activities of politicians, other than statesmen, leaders and key ministers, leaving this to the discipline of political science. But at the same time, political science has been happy to leave the analysis of security to security studies and IR, and when it has considered questions of security it has simply performed the classic sovereign security trope. The outcome is that a proper consideration of *security politics* has been excluded from both disciplines. But furthermore, beyond academic scholarship, politicians themselves defer heavily to the executive in the aftermath of spectacular acts of political violence, marginalising their own political activity and any reflexive consideration of the relationship between politics and security. *Security politics* is therefore subject to a triple exclusion: first, by terrorism and security studies as a sub-discipline of IR; second, by the discipline of political science; and third, by politicians themselves in their at times uncritical reinforcement of sovereign or executive security prerogative. Let us unpack the three aspects of this exclusion a little more.

The identity of any academic discipline is constituted by what it includes and excludes. Buzan and Hansen argue that the boundaries of what they tellingly call '*international* security studies' (ISS) [emphasis added] have changed over time and have never been clearly defined. Sometimes its exclusions have been successfully challenged. As they argue:

> ISS . . . does not have clearly defined borders. Instead it has 'frontier zones' where its debates blend into adjacent subjects, ranging from IR theory to IPE, to foreign policy analysis and Political Theory. (Buzan and Hansen 2009, p. 18)

In writing a history of ISS, Buzan and Hansen admit that they necessarily reproduce the history of its exclusions (2010, p. 661). However, it is notable that 'politics' is not included in the boundary subjects they list, suggesting that it has not even been registered by the discipline as excluded. This is not to suggest that security studies and its frontier zones are not political or consider no political questions, but rather that the activity of security politics as practised by politicians is missing.

Political science as a scholarly discipline, or more narrowly the academic study of the activity of politics, remains rather insulated from security studies, and vice versa. There has been little communication between them. Few security scholars will have engaged with the works of Philip Norton or Bernard Crick, who represent disciplinary staples in the study of politics, particularly of British parliamentary politics. When the discipline of 'politics' does engage with questions of security, it largely reproduces the classic sovereign security trope. For example, Bernard Crick, in the British classic 'In Defence of Politics', argues that in a 'state of emergency' open, free and consultative politics must be brushed aside in favour of 'the [sovereign] capacity to act without compromise or normal consultation' (Crick 1982, p. 27).

Beyond scholarly disciplines, my empirical research on counterterrorist lawmaking shows that politicians themselves perform and reproduce the classic security trope when they adhere to the constitutional convention of legislative consensus and deference to the executive at times of perceived emergency (Neal 2012a, 2012b). Politicians defer to, and therefore recognise and legitimise, the security prerogative of the sovereign. This means that at times of perceived emergency, there is a lack of open reflection by politicians on their own engagement in the activity and practice of security politics. From a different scholarly perspective, there is quantitative evidence that a post-attack 'rally round the flag effect' is a common phenomenon in Western democracies (Chowanietz 2011). However, this emergency political reaction does not encompass the whole of security politics, as the playing out of time beyond the aftermath of the 'emergency' reveals. When there is no perceived emergency, or when it is fading into the background, security politics becomes more critical, deliberative and reflexive.

The fundamental question implied by this exclusion is whether security politics is different or separate from 'normal' politics. Both the disciplines of politics and security studies/IR have perpetuated the separation of security from politics by reproducing the classic sovereign security trope. Security becomes a matter for the executive, not for politicians in general. For security studies/IR, the politics of politicians is of marginal concern compared with executive practices and the decisions of statesmen. For the discipline of politics, security begins where politics stops. This separation of security from the activity of politics is true of even the most sophisticated critical approaches to security, one of which we will look at now.

The separation of security from politics and the example of securitisation theory

Securitisation theory has been a growth area in security studies for the past two decades and has probably come closest to considering the role of politicians in the problem and practice of security. Yet at its core it is built on a separation of security from politics: the act of securitisation is conceived as the discursive movement of issues from the 'normal' sphere of politics to the 'exceptional' sphere of security by security elites (Buzan *et al.* 1998, p. 23). Securitisation is defined by urgency, crisis and exceptionality and thus set apart from mere politics (Buzan *et al.* 1998, p. 23).

The theory has formed the basis of a successful research programme for studying how issues and events get constructed and framed as security threats. Securitisation-based approaches analyse the statements of elites in terms of three things: first, security discourse/language (the grammar of security); second, institutional, historical and empirical context; and third, the 'audience' of securitising moves. This frame of analysis can be mapped quite neatly onto the field of politics as practised by politicians, but it is insufficient for understanding the empirical variety of political activity connected to security issues. The notion of discursive action that the theory is built upon is merely a sophisticated version of the classic sovereign security trope. The following criticisms all relate to the construction of the theory around sovereign security prerogative and its role in moving issues from the sphere of 'normal politics' to a rarefied realm of existential security, thus reproducing their separation.

First, as I and others have argued elsewhere, securitisation theory is elite led, and this in itself reproduces the classic sovereign security trope (Williams 2003, Neal 2010). The elite-led assumption is based, perhaps quite reasonably, on the empirical claim that it is usually the state or state elites who securitise (Wæver 1995, p. 51). However, this move is not simply an innocent reflection of the way security works, but a reproduction of a particular understanding of security that separates it from politics. It is true that securitisation theory does not consider speech acts to occur in a vacuum of pure decisionist freedom, but in a historical, discursive, institutional and material context. The theory conceptualises this as the 'felicity conditions' which affect the chances of success of a securitising speech act (Wæver 2000, pp. 252–253). These conditions can include the social capital of speakers, the institutionalisation of security responses, commensurability with existing discourses (such as racial fears and prejudices) and the presence of objective material conditions such as troops massing on the border or images of physical destruction. Nevertheless, the elite-led understanding of securitisation, even if contextualised, does not fully encompass the activity of politics and the diverse ways that it can be connected to security.

Second, securitisation and security politics are not synonymous. Securitisation is the discursive construction of security threats. This does happen of course, but it is one political phenomenon among many possible in security politics. Even if we accept the premise that all security problems are ultimately constructed, the problem is that this is too narrow an analytical lens for the study of political activity relating to security. Studying the activity of security politics does not require a formal definition of security, but rather a willingness to be analytically led by empirical political connections to security issues of all kinds, whether objective, subjective or discursive.

It is easy to think of examples of political activity that reference security but do not neatly fit the securitisation model. For example, parliamentary discussion of new evidence about the complicity in torture by the British security services is not a case of securitisation because it does not primarily involve the construction of a security threat. Individual speakers in such a debate may indeed attempt to construct 'the security threat' in a certain way, but framing analysis around this and its contestation will not analytically capture the full scope and diversity of such political activity.¹ A parliamentary report hearing over a failed IT contract to build an 'E-borders' system is not a case of securitisation because the participants will be focused on ministerial decisions and allocation of budgets and contractual terms, even if, again, such a debate may feature specific attempts to characterise security threats (Home Affairs Committee 2011). Making the scrapping of ID cards a manifesto commitment is not a case of securitisation, or even for that matter desecuritisation, because although the debate about ID cards did involve discussion of their use to counter security threats (as well as a whole menu of other uses), this alone did not encompass the entirety of ID cards as a political issue (Huysmans and Buonfino 2008, The Conservative Party 2010).

Third, politicians cannot be reduced to the 'audience' of elite securitising moves. To reduce politicians to 'audience' would be to assume that politicians are mostly reactive in their political activity, responding to the securitising moves of leaders or ministers. Although this purely reactive modality does appear to exist during periods of political consensus following spectacular acts of political violence, it is certainly not always the case, as I have suggested above. More sociological developments of securitisation theory have tackled the 'audience' problem by stressing the iterative possibilities of security discourse, whereby security claims can be modified in the discursive interplay between groups (Stritzel 2007, p. 371, Salter 2008b, p. 321).

These sociological variants of securitisation theory have done much to reduce its elite-led basis and thus offer a potential way out of its reproduction of the classic sovereign security trope. For example, Thierry Balzacq offers a sophisticated rethinking of the theory, arguing that analysis of securitisation should focus on the degree of congruence between statements, discursive/institutional contexts and material events themselves (2011, pp. 6–14). Balzacq loosens many of the quite restrictive formal conditions of the original Copenhagen School conception of the theory. For example, in their 1998 *Security: a new framework for analysis*, Buzan et al. (1998) are quite explicit that securitisation means an 'issue is presented as an existential threat, requiring emergency measures and justifying actions outside the normal bounds of political procedure' (p. 23). Balzacq offers a lengthy redefinition of securitisation that I will not reproduce in full here. In place of speech acts it stresses a wide array of 'contextually mobilized ... heuristic artefacts' such as metaphors, images, emotions and intuitions; in place of 'existential threat' it stresses 'critical vulnerability'; and in place of 'emergency measures' it stresses a 'customized policy ... undertaken immediately' (Balzacq 2011, p. 3). Balzacq's reformulation is promising and takes securitisation theory quite far from its original conception, making it easier to fit the label 'securitization' to a wider variety of security-implicated situations. Even in this guise, however, the approach does not foreground the question of security politics, but rather includes it, along with potentially everything else, in the ever-expanding variables of 'context'. Moreover, it maintains the separation between the realm of security, even as expanded through broadened criteria, and the realm of 'normal' politics.

Even with a reduced emphasis on elite prerogative and existential threat, all forms of securitisation theory assume that security has a specific logic that makes it, at the very least, a special and distinct form of political activity. It takes security discourses, broadly conceived, at face value and treats them as signs of the logic of securitisation. This 'specialness' of security suggests that securitisation theory remains an extension of the disciplinary logic that constitutes security studies and IR as separate from political science. In this sense, securitisation remains an expression of the classic sovereign security trope. The defining, constitutive, organising stake in this logic is the construction of an existential threat (or critical vulnerability) to a referent object such as the state, society or environment and its connection to certain privileged actors and means of redress. And although the innovation of securitisation theory is that 'existential threat' may be a discursive construction rather than an objective condition, it still assumes that the construction of existential threat is the central stake and that the prime mover is some form of nominalist security prerogative under certain conditions. However, if we were to understand terrorism and security from the perspective of the activity of politics, rather than on the basis of this classic sovereign security trope, the logic and stakes would look rather different.

Security from the perspective of politics

Although politicians may indeed perceive or construct security threats as an existential threat to some referent object or other, this is not necessarily their primary motivation and not necessarily what is at stake for them politically. We should not take their claims at face value for there may be a different political logic at work. From the perspective of professional politics, we might consider that the biggest 'existential threat' for politicians is not to a publicly cited referent object, but to the electoral life of a government or their own political careers. This is quite different.

Securitisation analysis, which focuses on the public articulation of security discourses and their reception and acceptance by particular audiences, cannot easily incorporate this logic. Politicians could not in all seriousness publicly invoke the political life of a government or their own political career as the referent object of securitisation. Although sociologically we can say that politicians often invoke and modulate discourses of existential threat, foregrounding this distracts from what is at stake in *security politics*, and indeed in politics generally. This hidden stake in security politics, existing behind publicly articulated discourses of security threat, makes security politics a 'double game', as conceptualised by Pierre Bourdieu. Bourdieu argues that apparent concern for the interests of the politically represented public often 'conceals the relation of competition between the representatives' (Bourdieu 1992, p. 183). For politicians, terrorism and security may well be urgent problems to be solved, constructed or not, but the conventions of cross-party consensus and deference to the executive involved may conceal partisan political strategies and forms of opportunism. Political parties are, after all, struggling to win elections and secure control of government, but perhaps dare not speak this openly on the sensitive issue of terrorism.

My argument is that the fear and threat that drive politicians and governments may not be existential but political. The survival at stake for politicians is not existential survival but political survival. This is because security events and the way they are handled or mishandled, regardless of whether constructed or not, can make or break a government. In fact this is true of all events. Rethinking security as a problem of politically important events, rather than in terms of sovereign or elite prerogative over existential threats, puts quite a different complexion on how we understand *security politics*.

In order to consider terrorism and security from the perspective of politics and to reflect what is at stake for politicians, we need a shift of ontology. What we need is a Machiavellian ontology, not a Hobbesian/Schmittian one as assumed by the classic sovereign security trope. This is a theoretical distinction I have previously made elsewhere (Neal 2010, p. 73), but one I would like to extend here. The key distinction is that in the statist ontology of Hobbes and Schmitt, the survival of the state, and thus the survival of the people within the state, is what is at stake. In Machiavelli the reign of the Prince is at stake, which is not the same thing. The reign of the Prince is akin to the reign of a government, not the survival of a state, people or indeed other referent object.

Under a Hobbesian/Schmittian ontology the state is sovereign. The state is not just politically sovereign, but ontologically sovereign. There are no higher forces at work than the state, other than the necessities for state survival that the ontology implies. Although states can, with some difficulty, be destroyed, the ideal form of the state for Hobbes and Schmitt is a state in sovereign command of its fate. In this sense, the sovereign state is a mortal God. It decides what is a threat, decides what needs to be done about it and does it. In contrast, Machiavelli's Prince is not a mortal God. He remains subordinate to the superior forces of *fortuna* or fate (Machiavelli 1999, p. 84). The Prince may build defences against the vicissitudes of *fortuna* and learn historical lessons of how to perpetuate his reign, but *fortuna* will always win in the end. The Prince cannot master contingency forever and he cannot always be in command of the meaning of events. A Machiavellian ontology is the one we should apply to security politics.

The point is that the eventual failure of the Prince's reign is part of the rules of the game. This is very different to the existential security trope in which 'failure is not an option'. It is not that the Prince can fail and the state (or securitising elites) cannot, but that the stakes and rules of the game are different. Governments will fall as a matter of course. But in stable liberal democracies at least, this is not an existential catastrophe. Governments accept this as part of the rules of the game, as must the Prince. Politicians, including those out of power, know the rules, must play by them if they want to be successful and consider the game worth playing (Bourdieu 1992, p. 180). In the meantime governments must build their political defences and try to hold on to power. Governments always try to plan and control their programme in government, to stick to their policies, to not tilt. But they cannot anticipate what *fortuna* may throw at them, and this is not a problem of existential threat, but of unforeseen, politically significant events. As Harold Macmillan is reported to have said (possibly apocryphally), the things prime ministers fear the most, the things most likely to blow a government off course, are *events dear boy, events*. This captures the political stakes of security politics, and indeed all politics, rather well.

In a book on the discipline of politics, the political scientist Jean Blondel opens with a remarkably Machiavellian account of the role of events in politics. His argument is that in politics, enormous changes can occur because of knife-edge results, unforeseen events and accidents and scandals that take on a life of their own. For example, governments can fall on votes of no confidence by a margin of one because an MP happens to be ill and absent. This is what happened to Prime Minister James Callaghan in March 1979 (Blondel 1981, p. 1). Similarly, winner-takes-all elections that are too close to call can unprecedentedly swing on the decisions of Supreme Court judges, as with Bush and Gore in 2000. Governments can misinterpret and misjudge their ability to handle unforeseen events, as with the fall of the Spanish Aznar government in the wake of the Madrid bombings. Luck and an unknown number of unforeseen circumstances outside of individual or party control can make or break political careers, and Blondel suggests this is more so in politics than in any other walk of life. The unexpected death or resignation of a colleague can open up a space for a new leader or minister; a scandal blowing up out of nowhere can discredit an opponent; and bad weather affecting voter turnout can affect the result of an election (Blondel 1981, p. 6).

> Politics is peculiar . . . in that straightforward 'accidents' uncannily erupt on the political scene. Accidents are those non-political or tenuously political events which come to have a sharp political impact. A natural calamity, such as an earthquake or landslide, the illness or the death of a leader may produce major ripples. Human error, a rail or ship disaster, for instance, may surge on the political scene. Thus the 'normal' course of affairs may be upset because an event, which leaders could not predict or avoid – or could avoid only at considerable financial cost – largely because it had no political significance, creates a new situation which upsets calculations and modifies the equilibrium of forces. (Blondel 1981, p. 7)

Now, this is not to say that the meaning of political events is objectively contained in the events themselves – precisely the contrary. There is no inherent political meaning in a sudden death or a rail disaster. The problem is not simply that events are unforeseen, but their political significance is unpredictable. The question is whether or not governments and politicians can steer a safe path through events; whether they can remain in command of the situation and make the most of a good crisis; or whether, like Callaghan, they come to appear 'no longer able to dominate events' (Blondel 1981, p. 4).

Neither is this to say that events are random. Events have causes, but those causes may remain unknown, unseen and multiple. And as Blondel argues, with the passing of time, events can be seen in perspective and perhaps as part of an inevitable trend (Blondel 1981, pp. 7–8). Callaghan would have fallen sooner or later. And the impact of events may not be as great as initially thought: 'It is rare for the whole political system, or even governmental policies to be markedly altered in view of an "accident"' (Blondel 1981, p. 7). But trends lead to outcomes, and while trends can be examined, mapped and modelled, 'the process in which *a trend is converted into an outcome*' is more mysterious: 'it is *one* outcome *or* another which occurs in politics, not a trend ... by its very nature, the analysis of trends cannot lead to a precise prediction' (Blondel 1981, p. 13) [his italics].

This understanding of events does not fit the trope offered to us by terrorism and security studies. Unlike traditional strategic studies with its emphasis on states and the use of military force, there is no cold hard meaning contained in any particular event (Buzan and Hansen 2009, p. 83). But unlike in securitisation theory, actors do not construct the meaning of events either, try as they might. The events that take on the most dramatic political significance seem to come from nowhere to exceed the predictive, preparatory and prophylactic capabilities of politicians. And even when events seem part of an analysable trend, the outcomes of those trends are fundamentally uncertain and can flip on the tiniest of margins. Certainly, governments' successful or unsuccessful attempts to 'spin' the meaning of events may have a large bearing on whether they are able to appear to remain in command, but under this alternative ontology the meaning and construction of events is not dominated by political elites. It is not their prerogative. Rather, events appear to take on a life of their own.

Adopting a Machiavellian political ontology based on the priority of events and the inevitable but non-catastrophic fall of governments gives an interesting complexion to the question of security politics. From this perspective, there is no difference between security events and other events. The question is not which unforeseen, contingent events will prove to be exceptional, existential security threats (the Schmittian formulation), but rather which events will be politically significant. This is equally unknown and contingent, but it is defined not by existential threat, but by its impact on the life of a government or the career of a politician. From the perspective of political survival, there is no difference between a terrorist attack, an economic crisis or a political scandal. Of course, there may be different ways of dealing with them politically and governmentally, but the *political* stakes are the same.

If there is no political distinction between security events and other events, then this dissolves the problematic separation of politics and security discussed earlier. Security is not defined by its separation from normal politics, as in the Copenhagen School mould. If we rethink the stakes as political and not existential, then this challenges the primacy of the classic sovereign security trope. From the perspective of politics and what is at stake for politicians, security politics is no different to politics in general. A Machiavellian ontology reflects this different tradition regarding the role of events in politics.

Conclusions

On the basis of the argument presented here, one should be prompted to stop and think hard before adopting the naturalised disciplinary assumptions that seem to accompany existing analyses of terrorism and security. This article is thus intended as a way of rethinking the exclusions of scholarly approaches to terrorism and security. While this scholarship is broad and diverse, it seems to suffer from certain preoccupations to the exclusion of others; at stake is either the nature of threats or the nature of the sovereign, executive or governmental power that defines and handles threats. This trope suffers from four problems: first, it risks taking security discourses at face value when there might be other logics at work; second, it does not encompass the empirical breadth of politics as it relates to security; third, it risks reifying a certain understanding of political power at the expense of a more plural understanding of politics; and fourth, it risks allowing a particular object – which I have called the classic sovereign security trope – to define the discipline itself. These points raise a further question: to what extent do terrorism and security studies require security to be 'special' in order to justify their own importance?

We can consider this problem by turning to Michel Foucault. In *The Archaeology of Knowledge*, Foucault rejects the idea that discourses are constituted by a common object (Foucault 2002, pp. 35–36). This means, for example, that just because there is a large discourse about madness, this does not mean that madness is a single unified thing. Rather, madness is understood so differently from the perspective of different times and positions in the discourse on madness that it makes no sense to consider it as an objective thing (Foucault 2006). This is why he later said that his method consisted in saying

> Let's suppose that madness does not exist. If we suppose that it does not exist, then what can history make of these different events and practices which are apparently organised around something that is supposed to be madness? (Foucault 2008, pp. 20–21)

To translate this to the problem of security, we can ask whether terrorism and security studies are constituted by the assumption of a common object: the classic sovereign security trope. However, this article has shown that from a different perspective – that of politics as an activity – this object looks different to the extent that it is not the same thing. If we rethink security in terms of *politically salient events* as suggested here, security loses its specialness as an object. This is a way of asking 'what if security does not exist?' Thus, in answer to my initial question, this is what it would mean to rethink security from the perspective of politics.

Acknowledgements

I am grateful for comments on the article by Philippe Bonditti, Victoria Loughlan, Richard Jackson, my colleagues in the IR Research Group at the University of Edinburgh and the two anonymous reviewers for CST.

Note

1. Hansard HC vol 505, cols 914–926 (10 February 2010), David Miliband.

Notes on contributor

Andrew W. Neal is a lecturer in Politics and International Relations at the University of Edinburgh. He is the author of *Exceptionalism and the Politics of Counter-Terrorism: Liberty, Security and the War on Terror* (Routledge 2010) and co-editor (with Michael Dillon) of *Foucault on Politics, Security and War* (Palgrave 2008).

References

Agamben, G., 1998. *Homo sacer: sovereign power and bare life*. Translated by D. Heller-Roazen. Stanford, CA: Stanford University Press.
Agamben, G., 2005. *State of exception*. Translated by K. Attell. Chicago, IL: University of Chicago Press.
Amoore, L., 2009. On forgetting the war on terror. *In*: A.C. Stephens and N. Vaughan-Williams, eds. *Terrorism and the politics of response*. Abingdon: Routledge, 130–143.
Amoore, L. and de Goede, M., 2008. *Risk and the war on terror*. London: Routledge.
Balzacq, T., 2011. *Securitization theory: how security problems emerge and dissolve, PRIO new security studies*. Abingdon: Routledge.
Bamford, B., 2004. The United Kingdom's 'war against terrorism'. *Terrorism and Political Violence*, 16 (4), 737–756.
Basaran, T., 2010. *Security, law and borders*. London: Routledge.
Bigo, D., 2002. Security and immigration, toward a critique of the governmentality of unease. *Alternatives: Global, Local, Political*, 27 (1), 63–92.
Blondel, J., 1981. *The discipline of politics*. London: Butterworths.
Booth, K., 1991. Security and emancipation. *Review of International Studies*, 17 (4), 313–326.
Bourdieu, P., 1992. Political representation: elements for a theory of the political field. *In*: J.B. Thompson, ed. *Language and symbolic power*. Cambridge: Polity, 171–202.
Butler, J., 2004. *Precarious life: the powers of mourning and violence*. London: Verso.
Buzan, B. and Hansen, L., 2009. *The evolution of international security studies*. Cambridge: Cambridge University Press.
Buzan, B. and Hansen, L., 2010. Beyond the evolution of international security studies? *Security Dialogue*, 41 (6), 659–667.
Buzan, B., Wæver, O., and Wilde, J.D., 1998. *Security: a new framework for analysis*. Boulder, CO: Lynne Rienner.
Chang, N., 2002. *The silencing of political dissent*. London: Turnaround.
Chowanietz, C., 2011. Rallying around the flag or railing against the government? Political parties' reactions to terrorist acts. *Party Politics*, 17 (5), 673–698.
The Conservative Party, 2010. *Invitation to join the Government of Britain: the conservative manifesto 2010*. London: Conservative Research Department.
Crick, B., 1982. *In defence of politics*. 2nd Pelican ed. Harmondsworth: Penguin.
Doty, R.L., 2007. States of exception on the Mexico-US border: security, 'decisions,' and civilian border patrols. *International Political Sociology*, 1 (2), 113–137.
Fierke, K.M., 2007. *Critical approaches to international security*. London: Polity.
Fitzpatrick, J., 2003. Speaking law to power: the war against terrorism and human rights. *European Journal of International Law*, 14 (2), 241–264.
Foucault, M., 2002. *The archaeology of knowledge*. Trans. A.M.S. Smith. London: Routledge.
Foucault, M., 2006. *History of madness*. Trans. J. Murphy and J. Khlafa. Abingdon: Routledge.
Foucault, M., 2008. *The birth of biopolitics: lectures at the college de France, 1978–1979*. Ed. A. Davidson and trans. G. Burchell. Basingstoke: Palgrave Macmillan.
Goldberg, D., Goldberg, V., and Greenwald, R., 2002. *It's a free country: personal freedom in America after September 11*. New York: RDV Books.
Gross, O. and Ní Aoláin, F., 2006. *Law in times of crisis: emergency powers in theory and practice*. Cambridge: Cambridge University Press.
Hansen, L., 2000. The Little Mermaid's silent security dilemma and the absence of gender in the Copenhagen School. *Millennium-Journal of International Studies*, 29 (2), 285–306.
Hay, C., 2002. *Political analysis: a critical introduction*. Basingstoke: Palgrave.
Hewitt, S., 2008. *The British war on terror: terrorism and counter-terrorism on the home front since 9/11*. London: Continuum.
Hobbes, T., 1996. *Leviathan*. Ed. R. Tuck. Cambridge: Cambridge University Press.
Home Affairs Committee, 2011. *Oral evidence taken before the Home Affairs Committee: UK border agency enforcement*, 5 April [online]. Available from: http://www.publications.parliament.uk/pa/cm201011/cmselect/cmhaff/uc929-i/uc92901.htm [Accessed 16 December 2011].
House of Lords Select Committee on the Constitution, 2009. *Fast-track legislation: constitutional implications and safeguards*. London: The Stationery Office Limited.

Hudson, V.M., 2007. *Foreign policy analysis: classic and contemporary theory*. Lanham, MD: Rowman & Littlefield.
Hussein, N., 2003. *The jurisprudence of emergency*. East Lansing: The University of Michigan Press.
Huysmans, J., 2004. Minding exceptions. Politics of insecurity and liberal democracy. *Contemporary Political Theory*, 3 (3), 321–341.
Huysmans, J., 2006. *The politics of insecurity: fear, migration and asylum in the EU*. London: Routledge.
Huysmans, J., 2008. The jargon of exception – on Schmitt, Agamben and the absence of political society. *International Political Sociology*, 2, 165–183.
Huysmans, J. and Buonfino, A., 2008. Politics of exception and unease: immigration, asylum and terrorism in parliamentary debates in the UK. *Political Studies*, 56 (4), 766–788.
Intelligence and Security Committee, 2007. *Rendition*. London: The Stationery Office.
Johns, F., 2005. Guantanamo Bay and the annihilation of the exception. *European Journal of International Law*, 16 (4), 613–635.
Liberty, 2004. *The impact of anti terrorism powers on the British Muslim population*. London: Liberty.
Lobo-Guerrero, L., 2011. *Insuring security: biopolitics, security and risk*. Abingdon: Routledge.
Machiavelli, N., 1999. *The prince*. Translated by G.A. Bull. London: Penguin.
Medical Foundation for the Care of the Victims of Torture, The Law Society, Immigration Law Practitioners Association, Refugee Legal Centre, and Liberty, 2001. Joint Statement – Anti-Terrorism, Crime and Security Bill.
Mueller, J., 2005. Simplicity and spook: terrorism and the dynamics of threat exaggeration. *International Studies Perspectives*, 6 (2), 208–234.
National Commission on Terrorist Attacks upon the United States, Kean, T.H., and Hamilton, L., 2004. *The 9/11 commission report: final report of the national commission on terrorist attacks upon the United States*. Washington, DC: Government Printing Office.
Neal, A.W., 2006. Foucault in Guantanamo: towards an archaeology of the exception. *Security Dialogue*, 37 (1), 31–46.
Neal, A.W., 2008a. Exceptionalism: theoretical and empirical complexities. *International Political Sociology*, 2 (1), 87–89.
Neal, A.W., 2008b. Foucault and Butler on discourses of war, law and exceptionalism. *In*: M. Dillon and A.W. Neal, eds. *Foucault on politics, security and war*. Basingstoke: Palgrave Macmillan, pp. 43–64.
Neal, A.W., 2010. *Exceptionalism and the politics of counter-terrorism: liberty, security and the war on terror*. Abingdon: Routledge.
Neal, A.W., 2012a. Normalization and legislative exceptionalism: counterterrorist lawmaking and the changing times of security emergencies. *International Political Sociology*, 6 (3).
Neal, A.W., 2012b. Terrorism, lawmaking and democratic politics: legislators as security actors. *Terrorism and Political Violence*, 24 (3).
Neocleous, M., 2008. *Critique of security*. Edinburgh: Edinburgh University Press.
Palonen, K., 2006. Two concepts of politics: conceptual history and present controversies. *Distinktion: Scandinavian Journal of Social Theory*, 7 (1), 11–25.
Prozorov, S., 2005. X/Xs: toward a general theory of the exception. *Alternatives: Global, Local, Political*, 30, 81–112.
Richter-Montpetit, M., 2007. Empire, desire and violence: a queer transnational feminist reading of the prisoner 'abuse' in Abu Ghraib and the question of 'gender equality'. *International Feminist Journal of Politics*, 9, 38–59.
Salter, M.B., 2008a. Imagining numbers: risk, quantification, and aviation security. *Security Dialogue*, 39 (2–3), 243–266.
Salter, M.B., 2008b. Securitization and desecuritization: a dramaturgical analysis of the Canadian air transport security authority. *Journal of International Relations and Development*, 11 (4), 321–349.
Scheuerman, W.E., 2006. Survey article: emergency powers and the rule of law after 9/11. *Journal of Political Philosophy*, 14 (1), 61–84.
Schmitt, C., 1985. *Political theology: four chapters on the concept of sovereignty*. Translated by G. Schwab. London: MIT Press.
Stritzel, H., 2007. Towards a theory of securitization: Copenhagen and beyond. *European Journal of International Relations*, 13 (3), 357–383.

Tierney, S., 2005. Determining the state of exception: what role for parliament and the courts? *The Modern Law Review*, 68 (4), 668–673.

Vasquez, J.A., 1993. *The war puzzle*. Cambridge: Cambridge University Press.

Vaughan-Williams, N., 2007. The shooting of Jean Charles De Menezes: new border politics? *Alternatives: Global, Local, Political*, 32 (2), 177–195.

Wæver, O., 1995. Securitization and desecuritization. *In*: R.D. Lipschutz, ed. *On security*. New York: Columbia University Press, 46–86.

Wæver, O., 2000. The EU as a security actor: reflections from a pessimistic constructivist on post-sovereign security orders. *In*: M.C. Williams and M. Kelstrup, eds. *International relations theory and the politics of European integration: power, security, and community*. London: Routledge, 250–294.

Waltz, K.N., 1979. *Theory of international politics*. London: McGraw-Hill.

Weber, M., 1994. The profession and vocation of politics. *In*: P. Lassman and R. Speirs, eds. *Weber: political writings*. Cambridge: Cambridge University Press, 309–369.

Williams, M.C., 2003. Words, images, enemies: securitization and international politics. *International Studies Quarterly*, 47, 511–531.

Wolfers, A., 1952. '"National security" as an ambiguous symbol'. *Political Science Quarterly*, 67 (4), 481–502.

Terrorism and violence: another violence is possible?

Helen Dexter

Department of Politics and International Relations, University of Leicester, Leicester, UK

> This article sets out to explore whether the category of 'terrorism' improves or impedes our intellectual understanding of violence. By addressing key concepts at the heart of common definitions of terrorism, the article asks these questions: What does the category of 'terrorism' mean for that violence that is, by definition, left beyond the scope of terrorism studies? What assumptions about violence *per se* are exposed by definitions of terrorism? It is argued, first, that definitions of terrorism that place the targeting of civilians as the central defining feature of the term rest on the assumption of distinct ethical categories of human beings, categories that this article argues do not reflect the human condition in war. Second, it is argued that definitions of terrorism that have 'intent' as the central defining feature restate and reinforce the principle of the doctrine of double effect. Third, those definitions that label terrorism as a communicative form of violence – violence intended to send a message – expose and perpetuate a lack of understanding of what violence is and does. Finally, the treatment of terrorism as a distinctly 'bad' form of violence suggests that another category of violence exists – one that does not function as terrorism does: 'good' violence. The category of terrorism sustains the notion that political violence is controllable and can be made fit for purpose. In conclusion, the article argues that the concept of terrorism serves to sustain the taken-for-granted notion that violence works – that another violence, one that does not function as terrorism does – is possible.

It is now commonplace to start academic investigations into terrorism by first acknowledging that terrorism as a concept is both ambiguous and contentious. Yet, few if any authors follow up on this definitional confusion by asking the next logical question. 'No one', Smith argued in a paper addressing the intellectual development of low-intensity warfare and guerrilla war, 'has pushed these doubts to the logical conclusion: that if the object one is trying to categorise defies categorisation, then does it actually exist?' (Smith 2003, p. 22). This article does not seek to define terrorism. Nor does it simply state that 'terrorism' does not exist as an objective ontological category of violence (although this may be deduced from the article's conclusions). Rather, this article springs from a simple question: does the concept of 'terrorism' improve or impede our intellectual understanding of violence? In order to explore this, the article asks a number of sub-questions. Taking my

---

This article was presented as a paper at the conference 'A Decade of Terrorism and Counter-Terrorism since 9/11: Taking Stock and New Directions in Research and Policy' held at the University of Strathclyde, Glasgow, 8–11 September 2011. It develops arguments made in Dexter (2011).

cue from Smith's assessment that labels such as guerrilla warfare and low-intensity conflict are 'fundamentally flawed academic abstractions' (Smith 2003, p. 37) and do not exist as distinct forms of warfare, I ask the same questions of 'terrorism'. Does non-terroristic violence function any differently than terrorist violence? This article also asks what the consequences of treating terrorism as a coherent object of analysis are. Does the compartmentalisation of violence as terrorist and non-terrorist in academic discourse have productive effects? Essentially, *what does the category of 'terrorism' mean for that violence which by definition is left beyond the scope of terrorism studies?* What assumptions about violence *per se* are exposed by definitions of terrorism?

With terrorism studies now one of the fastest growing academic disciplines and particularly with the recent 'critical turn' in approaching the study of terrorism (one that begins by questioning the political convenience and definitional complexities of the concept), it appears that there is still some reluctance to answer this question. More than this, it is implied by some that to ask the question in the first place is somehow illegitimate. In the inaugural edition of the journal, *Critical Studies on Terrorism*, Burke qualified his argument about the ethical ends of terrorism studies with the following introductory statement:

> My aim is not to engage with postmodern sophistry or cleverness, or to so discredit the concept of terrorism that it disappears as a coherent object of analysis . . . [terrorism] constitutes a problem of great moral, political and sociological importance. (2008, p. 39)

Likewise in a piece that makes the case for the development of 'critical terrorism studies', Gunning asserts that 'a critically constituted field cannot afford either morally or pragmatically to abandon the term "terrorism"' (Gunning 2007a, p. 384).

The term terrorism is nowadays used to refer to a wide array of actions, many of which are not acts of *physical* violence, such as computer hacking. Acts classed as 'terrorism offenses' are even more numerous, for example, fundraising, conspiracy or the possession of certain substances. This article is concerned primarily with definitions of terrorism that refer to the act or threat of physical violence. The term violence, however, brings with it problems of its own. 'Violence' is by no means any more of a stable ontological phenomenon than 'terrorism'. Whilst 'violence' is as contested a term as terrorism, it is argued here that thinking in terms of violence at least serves to broaden the scope of our conversations, whereas 'terrorism' serves to restrict them and may better bring to the surface those political, cultural or moral particularities that are obscured by the ever reoccurring 'definitional debate' in terrorism studies. The problems associated with the definitions of terrorism identified in this article are not unique to terrorism. They are quite simply a problem of language. It is not suggested here that broadening our analysis from 'terrorism' to 'political violence' solves these problems. In fact, this article concludes that theorising violence may prove an impossible task. It is this *impossibility* that defining some violence as terrorism continues to mask.

The article considers four key features/themes common to the definition of terrorism: that violence is targeted against civilians, non-combatants or innocents; that violence *intentionally* targets civilians or *intentionally* terrorises; that terrorism is a communicative form of violence; and finally that terrorism is an exceptional form of violence. The article draws a number of conclusions. The first part of the article explores the productive effects of terrorism as a concept. Here it is argued, first, that definitions of terrorism that place the targeting of civilians as the central defining feature of the term rest on the assumption of distinct ethical categories of human beings. Terrorism, as a category of violence, assumes that the ethical waters are clear rather than murky (Dauphinée 2007, p. 33), and the uncritical academic use of the term that treats terrorism as a 'coherent object' simply reinforces and reifies these ethical categories. As will be demonstrated, these categories of human beings themselves have *productive* effects. Second, definitions of terrorism that have 'intent' as the central defining feature (violence *intended* to kill civilians, violence *intended* to coerce and violence *intended* to cause terror) restate and reinforce the principle of the doctrine of double effect. The category of terrorism then could be seen as a restatement and reinforcement of Just War doctrine. Third, definitions such as Stohl's that label terrorism as a communicative form of violence – violence intended to send a message – expose and perpetuate a lack of understanding of what violence is and does (Stohl 2008, pp. 5–16). Likewise, the treatment of terrorism as a distinctly 'bad' form of violence suggests that another category of violence exists – one that does not function as terrorism does: 'good violence'. The category of terrorism sustains the notion that political violence is controllable and can be made fit for purpose. This stems from the continuing failure to understand that any strategic effect produced by violence comes, as Burke argues, not from its physical impact but from its normative force (Burke 2008, p. 40).

Any critical approach to terrorism then cannot exist in isolation from a critical approach to political violence. If this other category of 'good violence' does *not* exist, if we *cannot* show that non-terroristic violence functions differently to terrorism, then we have to ask the question – what exactly are we distinguishing terrorism from? Why does this category persist? This article would not be the first to suggest that the concept of terrorism produces a moral hierarchy of violence. The most accurate definition of terrorism is, according to Brian Whitaker writing in *The Guardian*, 'violence committed by those we disapprove of' (Whitaker 2001). Likewise, Gearty suggests that 'To call an act of violence a terrorist act is not so much to describe it as condemn it, subjugating all questions of context and circumstance to the reality of its immorality' (Gearty 1997, p. 11). It is suggested here that perhaps one answer to the question 'why does the category of terrorism persist' is that the term 'terrorism' provides academics with a research 'comfort zone'. The categorisation of terrorism as something *distinct*, as an exception or anomaly in political violence, allows for the strategic and moral critique of *some* violence without engaging in the moral and strategic critique of violence *per se*. This allows for the possibility that *our* violence is different. By condemning *some* violence, the category of terrorism also serves to legitimise violence by suggesting that an alternative violence is possible, violence that only targets the guilty, that only produces what is intended, that does not communicate a message (of fear) and that serves a progressive purpose.

Defining terrorism

The politics involved with constructing a definition of terrorism have been well rehearsed and do not need to be repeated here. It is now oft-repeated that Alex Schmid recognised over 100 different definitions of terrorism in 1984 (Schmid 1984, pp. 119–158). The definitional debate asks: Is terrorism defined by its actions or by the actor? Is terrorism a tactic or an ideology? Is it a form of warfare or insurgency? Is it a form of resistance or coercion? Is terrorism an atrocity, a war crime or simply a crime (Burke 2008, p. 38)? In the inaugural edition of the journal, *Critical Studies on Terrorism*, Burke suggests that although an agreed definition of terrorism has yet to be reached, there is at least 'broad agreement that there is a phenomenon called terrorism' (Burke 2008, p. 39).

Those concerned with the development of 'terrorism' as a category and of terrorism studies would do well to look at other concepts that have previously been heralded as a new threat or challenge and were at one time considered the central or most pressing concern for security analysts. 'Guerrilla warfare', 'counter-insurgency' and 'low-intensity conflict' are prime examples. These 'new' categories of violence that entered the military and political lexicon in the 1950s, 1960s and 1970s respectfully were thought, like terrorism today, to require new knowledge and new approaches that set them aside from the 'convention'. Following the trajectory of these concepts within the academe can help shed light on why terrorism studies as a discipline exists. That terrorism has been considered a distinct category of violence something *other* than the study of conventional warfare has, according to Smith, more to do with the academic discipline of Cold War strategic studies than with the distinctiveness or prevalence of the violence itself (Smith 2003).

One of the mistakes made by counter-insurgency theorists in the 1960s was to try to connect a diverse set of conflicts by way of their tactical similarities. According to Smith:

> Rather than treat the practitioners of armed force, and the conflicts in which they are a part, as uniquely individual objects of study, they are instead drawn together under the rubric of low-intensity conflict and thereby disconnected from their historical and political settings by the attempt to make theoretical generalisations primarily on the grounds of their *modus operandi*. (2003, p. 23)

Perhaps exposing its intellectual heritage, terrorism studies constructs its object of analysis in the same way with the same consequences. For terrorism as a concept to refer to a coherent object of analysis then – for the term to have a unifying function – vastly different episodes of violence have to be merged into a single narrative. To talk of 'terrorism' as a singular threat or 'counter-terrorism' as general theory necessitates the de-contextualising and de-politicising of violence. According to Burnett and Whyte:

> When violent resistance is abstracted from its formative conditions in its crude form, only then can the terrorist threat be known and created in a form that enables the Palestinian intifada, the Chechnyan resistance, and the various armed groups in Iraq to be understood as part of the same threat to order. (2005, p. 14)

Likewise, Gunning comments that '[t]here is little that the Unabomber, anti-abortionists, US officers training Nicaraguan Contras and Hamas have in common beyond their use of a similar tactic' (Gunning 2007b, p. 239). In terms of grouping together a particular set of instances of violence the category of terrorism offers little coherence.

Terrorism, violence and categories of human beings

One unifying theme amongst the many definitions of terrorism is that terroristic violence is directed against civilians, non-combatant or the innocent. Coady, for instance, argues that terrorism is 'the organised use of violence to attack non-combatants or innocents (in a special sense) or their property for political purposes' (Coady 2004, p. 772). For Laqueur, terrorism can be defined as 'the illegitimate use of force to achieve a political objective by targeting innocent people' (Laqueur 1987, p. 72). A definition of terrorism proposed by the US State Department in 1984 suggests: 'The term "terrorism" means premeditated politically motivated violence perpetuated against non-combatant targets by sub-national groups or clandestine agents, usually intended to influence an audience' (Wilkinson 2006, p. 3). Burke's definition of terrorism is one arrived at whilst consciously taking a *critical* approach to the topic. Burke defines terrorism as: 'A form of political violence directed against civilians with a coercive intent that rests on the production of a state of fear or terror' (Burke 2008, p. 39). Burke recognises that this definition is similar to the definition of terrorism offered by the UN in the 2004 *Report of the High Level Panel on Threats, Challenges and Change*. This report categorises terrorism as follows:

> [Acts] intended to cause death or serious bodily harm to civilians or non-combatants, when the purpose of such act, by its nature or context, is to intimidate a population, or compel a Government of an international organization to do or abstain from doing any act. (United Nations 2004)

Whilst the agents of violence may differ in these definitions of terrorism, what unite them are the targets of violence, namely civilian, non-combatants or the innocent.

Terrorism as a category of violence can only be understood in relation to warfare more broadly. Many definitions of terrorism distinguish terrorism from 'conventional warfare'. For White:

> Terrorism occurs outside the 'rules' of warfare and criminal activity. Terrorism uses violence or threatened violence against innocent people to achieve a social or political goal. Terrorism is a method of fighting somewhat greater than civil disobedience and somewhat less than guerrilla warfare. (2006, p. 7)

Definitions of terrorism based on actions rather than agents (those that allow for states to be considered terrorist agents) do not necessarily make this distinction, and 'terrorists' themselves often view their violence as part of war (Dexter 2011, pp. 148–153). Either way, terrorism is defined in relation to war – either as an illegitimate act that may take place as part of a war (or not) or as an act that is distinguished from an act of war by the nature of its illegitimacy. Terrorism as a category of violence, then, depends on and reproduces the category of 'war'. At the heart of this category of violence and the rules to which White refers is the distinguishing of combatants from non-combatants.

By categorising a certain violent act as terrorism, we are also by (most) definition(s) categorising those killed as innocents. This, of course, may not have been how the perpetrators of the violence themselves categorised the intended targets. Those who define terrorism as the targeting of innocent civilians must then consider whether 'other' violence can be as easily categorised as violence that targets only the guilty – those deserving of violence. If we are to maintain the category of terrorism, we must also ask these questions: Who possesses the right to judge innocence? Whose lives may be legitimately ended?

Zehfuss has written that what makes the institution of war particularly problematic is that it legitimises the one act that outside of 'war' is prohibited, namely, killing. In order to make the practice of war (more) thinkable, a hierarchy of killing has been constructed, one that is founded on two principles – distinction and intentionality:

> It is on the whole considered acceptable to kill enemy combatants, both intentionally and accidentally, unless they are *hors de combat*. Civilians in contrast, must not be killed intentionally, though incidental or accidental killings may be justified. (Zehfuss forthcoming)

Whilst the prohibition on deliberately killing civilians is central to ethical thinking about war, Zehfuss demonstrates that this principle is more often asserted as obvious or intuitive than it is *shown*. Zehfuss argues that whilst the idea of non-combatant immunity is intuitive, '[. . .] the question of *why* non-combatants should be entitled to special protection is actually difficult to answer' (Zehfuss forthcoming).

Like the dominant ethical, legal and strategic doctrines relating to warfare, defining terrorism as a distinct category of violence rests on the notion that the 'civilian' is a fixed, unproblematic moral identity. Our ethical, legal and strategic discourses on warfare are based around a set of binaries: war/peace, friend/enemy, combatant/non-combatant, innocence/guilt and just/unjust. War is understood, explained and enabled through this series of binaries. Our narratives depend on them. Yet when faced with the experience of war, those binaries are challenged. Are human beings so easily categorised? In *The Ethics of Researching War*, Dauphinée argues that when faced with conflict we have a responsibility both to the perpetrator and to the victim of violence. This is because the labels 'perpetrator' and 'victim' are both inadequate and ultimately unsustainable – humans defy categorisation:

> This is not to deny the abject position of the murdered as murdered, nor to deny the responsibility of the murderer by attenuating the reader to extenuating circumstances or to the fact that the murderer may also be a victim of another sort in another situation. The point is to suggest that the complexity of these relationships exposes the ethical water as fundamentally murky, and that there is a difficulty in assigning an ethical position to the belligerent violence of the resistance leader who nevertheless remains marginalized, disenfranchised, and victimized. (Dauphinée 2007, p. 33)

This is not to suggest that there are no innocents in war, but rather that the fixed identity of 'civilian' and 'combatant' is not adequate for understanding the complexities of the human experience. As Dauphinée has eloquently stated: 'We are always more and less and other than what we think and do and are' (Dauphinée 2007, p. 129). If we understand identity to be neither fixed nor stable but rather produced through discourse and in relation to others, then the categories on which war and terrorism are founded start to crumble.

Whether one adopts a post-structural ethos or not, the practice of violence undermines any ethical certainties that may be arrived at in abstract. Whether non-combatant or civilian status is arrived at via moral innocence or from 'doing no harm', neither is without problematic exception in practice. Who, for instance, is to be considered the more 'guilty' in war – the reluctant conscript (traditionally identified as a combatant and therefore a legitimate target) or the war-mongering politician who may have orchestrated the war and be responsible for perpetuating it but who is traditionally considered a non-combatant and therefore an illegitimate target? Who is more likely to cause harm – the army civil engineer whose role is reconstruction and development or the civilian 'pilot' of a CIA drone remotely dropping bombs? Who is then the more legitimate target?

It is worth pausing to consider the productive effects of the category of terrorism, its reification of fixed moral identities and of 'war' as an institution that can and does distinguish between them. The war on terror hinges on the notion of the civilian and the ability of the United States and her allies to determine who those civilians are. The war on terror should be considered within a post-Cold War context that has seen what Lawler, Shaw and others recognise as the return of the good war (Shaw 2001, Lawler 2002, Dexter 2007). More than just a developing norm of humanitarian intervention, the post-Cold War years saw 'humanitarian intervention' become synonymous with legitimate warfare. As the next step in this development, the war on terror has been presented as more than a legitimate war of necessity: it is a war of *moral obligation* fought not to eliminate a security threat but to counter an 'evil' (Jackson 2005).

What enabled the return of the good war was the revolution in military affairs (RMA) as heralded by the United States. The RMA was a response to the public outcry against the brutality and messiness of the Vietnam War. For war to be a legitimate policy of state in the eyes of the domestic population, it had to be seen as clean, precise and restrained. It was not just the deaths of American servicemen that outraged the US public during the Vietnam

War but also the involvement of US forces in the massacres of the like seen in My Lai. War had to be able to distinguish between 'civilians' and 'combatants' and put limits on the violence used (Dexter 2007). The principle of distinction is now central to the narrative that accompanies the war on terror and it is this ability to distinguish between targets that legitimises Western violence as legal and civilised in contrast to the barbaric violence it seeks to eliminate (see Borger 2001, Holland 2007, Montopoli 2010). This sentiment was summed up by president Obama in 2010 when he told a press conference: 'We distinguish between civilians and combatants – something by the way that our enemies do not do – and that puts us more at risk, and it makes it more difficult. But that's a burden that we're willing to bear' (Obama cited in Montopoli 2010).

The war on terror and, in particular, the opening of Guantanamo Bay did spark a debate about how to classify human beings in war. The war on terror as a 'new war' encountered 'new warriors' who did not wear uniform or play by the established rules of the game. The United States began to question under what circumstances a person is considered under international law as a legitimate combatant. The term 'unlawful combatant' made its way into political, legal and public debate. While the qualifications of the combatant have been opened up for scrutiny, the same cannot be said for the 'civilian'.

An instance of conflict clearly produces the category of the 'civilian' or 'non-combatant'. However, the 'civilian' as a category is not merely produced through warfare; it also has productive effects. Kinsella asks why during the war on terror the Bush administration had gone to great lengths to demonstrate that it respected and upheld the laws protecting civilians in conflict, yet so forthrightly discarded the laws designed to protect prisoners of war. What her subsequent analysis suggests is that: '[I]nsofar as the war on terror can be claimed as a war in defence of civilisation it must be constituted as a war in defence of civilians' (Kinsella 2005, p. 163). In the logic of the war in terror then, the category of the 'combatant' can be acknowledged as socially constructed and open to question; the 'civilian', on the other hand, remains a fixed ethical identity. The ethical murky waters that Dauphinée refers to have no place in the war on terror, it appears. Although the actions of the United States and her allies have (depending on your view) either abandoned the long-established distinction between the treatment of combatants and non-combatants or exposed the long-standing inadequacy of those categories, the rhetorical distinction has been crucial in enabling the war itself. The United States and her allies protect the innocent and punish the guilty. This is the mark of the civilised:

> It is here that observance of the distinction between combatants and civilians is invoked to order the difference between civilised and barbaric states. This observance equally cites a hierarchy of lawful, moral violence and unlawful, immoral violence. (Kinsella 2005, p. 182)

Terrorism, violence and intentionality

In the definitions of terrorism above (and many more besides), the civilians themselves that are the targets of violence may not be the people the terrorists want to coerce. Instead, this may be (for example) the civilian's government, an armed faction associated with these civilians or the nation as a whole. Nevertheless, 'the *specific* or *primary* targets will be civilians' (Burke 2008, p. 39; my emphasis). 'Civilians' or non-combatants have always been victims of warfare. What defines terrorism then is not just that it describes violence in which civilians are killed, but rather violence that specifically sets out to kill civilians. Setting aside the problems associated with categorising human beings as civilians or innocents, this part of the definition of terrorism also raises questions. Does violence not specifically or primarily directed at civilians function any differently to that which is? Should violence that is *not* 'specifically or primarily' targeted at civilians and yet still causes civilian deaths fall into a different category of violence?

Categorising something on the basis of intention rather than action is a moral practice. If the act of terrorism is defined by an actor's intentions rather than just actions, does terrorism as a category of violence rest on the doctrine of double effect? The doctrine of double effect suggests that morally deplored acts (such as the deaths of civilians) are legitimate if they are the unintended side effects of a morally desired act (the death of combatants or destruction of other military targets). The morally deplored side effects must be proportional to the end desired and independent from it. In *Just and Unjust Wars*, Walzer sets out the doctrine of double effect thus:

(1) The act is good in itself or at least indifferent, which means, for our purposes, that it is a legitimate act of war.
(2) The direct effect is morally acceptable – the destruction of military supplies, for example, or the killing of enemy soldiers.
(3) The intention of the actor is good, that is, he aims only at the acceptable effect; the evil effect is not one of his ends, nor is it a means to his ends.
(4) The good effect is sufficiently good to compensate for allowing the evil effect; it must be justifiable under Sidgwick's[1] proportionality rule (Walzer 2000, p. 153).

What is particularly contentious about the doctrine of double effect is that the death of civilians (for example) in order to hit military targets may be *entirely predictable* and *unavoidable* and yet remains legitimate if it is not *intended*. Walzer himself is doubtful of the doctrine's restraining effects. He states:

> But we have to worry, I think, about all those unintended but foreseeable deaths, for their number can be large; and subject only to the proportionality rule – a weak constraint – double effect provides a blanket justification. The principle for that reason invites an angry or cynical response: what difference does it make whether civilian deaths are a direct or indirect effect of my actions? It can hardly matter to the dead civilians, and if I know in advance that I am likely to kill so many innocent people and go ahead anyway, how can I be blameless? (2000, p. 153)

This is not enough for him to reject it, however. In the final analysis, Walzer argues that soldiers cannot merely not intend the deaths of civilians; they must make a positive commitment not to kill civilians, even if this means additional risk for the soldier (Walzer 2000, p. 156). There is a limit to this risk, however, and there is no absolute prohibition on killing civilians in war. 'War necessarily places civilians in danger; that is another aspect of its hellishness. We can only ask soldiers to minimise the dangers they impose' (Walzer 2000, p. 156). Terrorism then is considered distinct from other forms of violence that may unintentionally but predictably and unavoidably have the same effect.

Where does terrorism (and terrorism studies) then fit within the frameworks that dominate our ethical considerations about warfare? Just War theory overlaps considerably with liberal-legal frameworks for war. Intent, as Dauphinée notes, is also problematically central to the laws of war:

> In identifying the criminal, the focus of law is concerned with what can be known about intention and does not consider effect as such. To adjudicate on the basis of *effect* is to lodge an equivalence between civilian and military deaths and between the tactics used to kill and injure in war. It is to suggest that 'accidents' or the successful targeting of 'legitimate' populations

(i.e. military personnel) is not effectively different from any other sort of death in war, for human death is still death. (2008, p. 62)

How does terrorism relate to Just War principles? Do definitions of terrorism imply that the civilian deaths caused by terrorism are an end in themselves rather than a means to an end? This of course is not merely implied but strongly argued by those who recognise the ideology of 'new terrorism' where it is claimed that a high civilian death rate is an aim in itself, not a means to an achievable end (Laqueur 1999, Lesser *et al.* 1999, Aubrey 2004). In an earlier work, Burke (2004) has convincingly argued for the 'utter ethical inadequacy' of Just War theory. After analysing the moralising language of the war on terror founded on moral binaries such as 'justice and injustice, humanity and inhumanity, civilisation and barbarity', Burke concluded that: 'Just War theory has colonised the space of moral discourse in relation to war and strategy' (Burke 2004, p. 337). This is significant because '. . . moral rules about war's justification, process and restraint may function not so much as limitations on war as tools for its liberation' (Burke 2004, p. 330). It seems strange then that whilst rejecting Just War theory, Burke (2008) would avoid discrediting the category of terrorism.

Just War theory like international law is not merely a set of principles for passing judgement on violence. Just War theory produces categories of violence. Without the principle of distinction, proportionality and the doctrine of double effect, terrorism as a distinct category of violence would make little sense. Conversely, the category of terrorism contributes to the reification of those fixed ethical identities that enable the Just War tradition and legal-liberal frameworks which in turn enable the institution of war. Without the principle of intention, all deaths become equivalent and the institution of war itself comes under question. By reinforcing the centrality of intention in determining legitimate killing from illegitimate killing, any definition of terrorism prevents this more fundamental critique. Categorising violence in this way is incompatible with cosmopolitanism, for human death is *not*, according to these categories, *still human death*.

Terrorism, violence and communication

For Michael Stohl, what sets terrorism aside from 'simple violence' is that rather than simply being a destructive force, terrorism is a process of political communication. For Stohl, what defines terrorism is that it is communicatively constituted violence. It is violence conducted in order to send a message. Stohl defines terrorism thus: 'Terrorism is the purposeful act or the threat of the act of violence to create fear and/or compliant behaviour in a victim and/or audience of the act or threat' (Stohl 2011).

Does the communicative nature of terrorism distinguish it from other forms of violence? State terrorism would by this definition be the use of violence by a state against one group of people in order to send a message to another. What then would serve as a counter-example to state terrorism? What would class as the 'simple violence' Stohl refers to, violence which is intended only to destroy? I find it difficult to find an example of violence committed by the state, or by any other actor, that *does not* send a message. Every act of violence communicates a message, whether it is intended or not. The bombing of a bridge might be planned as a purely destructive act, a way of stopping supply lines. It also sends a message of strength, capabilities, resolve and resources. If that bridge has cultural and historical significance, however, the destructive act may communicate a message not intended or foreseen by the actor(s) responsible.

The execution of a prisoner for murder is carried out as punishment. But it also sends a message. Whilst the state might hope that this message serves as a warning or deterrent against future crime, statistics suggest that this message does not have the desired effect (Amnesty International USA 2011). Other messages may also be sent by capital punishment such as that violence serves as a form of justice or that violent retribution is an appropriate response to a wrongdoing. Even violence that is not witnessed, such as enforced disappearances, communicate a message. Whilst a NATO bombing campaign or US-led invasion might wish to communicate a message of humanitarianism or support for liberal freedoms, the effect of the bombs dropped may communicate a very different message to those on the ground. Whilst economic sanctions may be designed to send a signal to political elites, a message is also sent to the parents of children who die as a result of the sanctions.

Stohl himself acknowledges that every act of violent political communication has numerous audiences. These may include but are not limited to those the actor opposes, those the actor acts on behalf of, the actor's own supporters and a wider audience not connected but still witness to the act. Each audience will receive a different message. The specific circumstances of those who witness or hear of the violent act will determine how they interpret it. The growing number of mediums through which an act is communicated only serves to complicate things further. This is the case for all political communication. A politician may want to communicate with a domestic audience; however, she will, whether she intends to or not, also communicate with an international audience who may respond to her message very differently than the intended audience.

Terrorism, and violence more generally, is a particularly poor form of communication. This is because, as Burke has commented (2008), whilst the perpetrators of violence may have some, albeit limited control over the physical destruction produced through the act, the perpetrators of violence cannot control the normative impact of violence:

> The perpetrators of violence do not control how their acts and results are interpreted, narrated and circulated and how they shape subjectivities and systems of consent. Even if widespread fear and anxiety are provoked, they do not result in a linear or controllable system of effects. (2008, p. 40)

How violence is interpreted is beyond the control of those who carry it out. Whilst those who experience violence, witness it or are simply aware of it may infer meaning from the act, the circumstances of violence mean that the original motive (if there was indeed a single coherent motive) is lost.

In his article 'Why terrorism does not work', Abrahms (2006) draws on correspondence inference theory in order to explain why terrorism is such a poor form of communication. Correspondence inference theory claims that individuals infer the motives of an actor from an actor's behaviour. Take, for instance, if I were to get up during a conference presentation and open a window. The room becomes cooler. From this, the correspondence inference would be that I was too hot and wanted to cool down. Translating this into acts of violence, if an act of violence resulted in loss of life, fear, disruption to daily life, political turmoil and the curtailment of civil liberties, it might be inferred from this that the perpetrator of the act wanted to destabilise the society (Abrahms 2006).

Violent acts, particularly those which undermine ontological security, cry out for narration, for a moral framework of understanding. The ontological shock caused to many Americans by the events of 11 September 2001 was quickly filled by the Bush administration's explanation that al-Qaeda attacked the United States because '[t]hey hate our freedoms: our freedom of religion, our freedom of speech, our freedom to vote and assemble and disagree with each other' (Bush 2001). Whether the Bush administration genuinely believed that this is what had motivated the attacks, the effects of the attacks combined with the authorities' chosen narrative provided a compelling explanation for frightened Americans. The effects of 9/11 were enough to legitimise Bush's claims. Few if any journalists directly referred to communications from Bin Laden to seek explanations. Bin Laden's communications in fact made little reference to American culture, freedom or rights. Bin Laden himself denied that this was ever a motivating factor in the attacks (Lawrence and Howarth 2005). Regardless of 'genuine' intentions, be they radical, moderate or noble, the effects of violence cannot be predicted. Whilst meaning is inferred from the immediate effects of a violent act, how this act will be interpreted depends on the subject positions of those that witness it. Not only should this fact guide future counterterrorism campaigns, it should guide all uses of armed force or coercion, be they air strikes, humanitarian interventions or economic sanctions.

If all violence is both a form of destruction *and* a form of communication and if *all* violence is a particularly poor way of successfully communicating a message, then what is it that distinguishes terrorism from other forms of (political) violence? For Stohl, what distinguishes terrorism is *intent*. Terrorism is the use of violence with the specific *intent* to communicate a message to others. Again then, we have to ask what the significance of intent is, particularly in a circumstance where it appears that there is not only *no choice* but to communicate a message with an act of violence, but that that message also cannot be controlled.

Violence and exceptionalism

The implicit, if not explicit, definition of terrorism is that it is an exceptionally *bad* form of violence. It is either bad because it is perpetrated by illegitimate non-state actors, bad because it kills civilians, bad because it deliberately intends to kill civilians or because it is violence that intends to terrorise in order to coerce. According to Just War and liberal-legal frameworks, terrorism is normatively reprehensible. If terrorism warrants study in its own right because it is such a problematic form of violence, this by definition suggests that another form of violence exists – one that functions differently to terrorism.

Terrorism is not alone in functioning in this way. The category of the war crime is a useful comparison. The criminalisation (or de-legitimisation) of one action serves to reinforce the legitimacy of another. As Gordon terms it, implicit in the stigmatising of a limited number of financial deals as 'exceptionally rotten' is the assertion that most economic transactions are fair and decent (Gordon 1983). Translated into the paradigm of war, the process of highlighting some of the trappings of war fighting as illegal – as war crimes – has a number of functions. As well as suggesting that war is an institution governed by enforceable rules, the category of war crime performs an important enabling function. By singling out certain acts as illegal, too brutal or inhumane for the 'civilised' prosecution of warfare, it offers all other conducts a façade of legitimacy and humanism. The legal killing of another person, the use of legal chemical weapons, the legal detention of persons are acts that are somehow shielded from criticism. Violence, if it stays within the boundaries of law, appears to justify what Sarat and Kearns describe as a 'presumption of warrantability' (Sarat and Kearns 1995, p. 222). Rather than limiting war, Dauphinée argues that the increasing recourse to an ever-expanding humanitarian law in fact serves to reinforce the social institution of warfare, rather than limit it. One of the effects of demarcating *some* violence as a war crime is to normalise violence in war more generally:

> By training our gaze on only the very specific acts of violence that the trial illuminates, analyses that seek to critique war itself as the permissive condition within which war crimes become possible in the first place are made more difficult. In effecting the excision of the war criminal from the realm of legitimate war-making agents, the war crimes trial actually assists in the tacit dismissal of most death and injury in the context of war as acceptable, and indeed, necessary. (Dauphinée 2008, p. 51)

Like the war crime then, the exceptionalism associated with terrorism suggests that there is something extraordinary about terroristic violence – that it belongs outside the norm of warfare or legitimate violence. 'Terrorism' shares the same normative space as 'atrocity'. The label serves the purpose of marking a certain event as a one-off, the acts of a few bad apples or the accumulation of a series of unfortunate and unforeseeable events. When one digs deeper, 'atrocities' such as those acts designated as war crimes are not exceptional – the events at Abu Ghraib provide a stark example (see Brown 2005). If not intended, they, like the collateral damage legitimised by the doctrine of double effect, are utterly predictable and perhaps unavoidable. They are instances where brutality breaks through and exposes the façade of norm. The label of 'accident' or 'atrocity' is a response designed to demarcate these acts as exceptional or unique – to divorce them from the structures that produced them (Owens 2003). Demarcating terrorism as 'bad' violence obscures the fact that the effects of violence not categorised as terrorism differ little if at all from that which is defined as terrorism.

Violence

On the face of it then, 'terrorism' produces a moral hierarchy of violence demarcating 'good' violence from 'bad'. This is not unique to terrorism. Fraser and Hutchings trace the relationship between politics and violence in political thought and philosophy. They identify that some, such as Machiavelli, Hobbes or Weber, view political power as the power to coerce. In this state-centric view, the state and violence are 'inextricably intertwined'. Marx, Sorel, Fanon and Sartre approach the relationship between politics and violence from the perspective of the oppressed, distinguishing revolutionary, emancipatory violence from oppressive violence. The liberal tradition of political thought of Lock, Rawls and Nozick *et al.* suggests instead that in theory at least, politics can be divorced from violence, as individuals can rationally agree to be governed by consent. What unites these positions on the relationship between politics and violence, however, is that '[a]ll of these projects rely, to some extent, on distinguishing between justifiable and unjustifiable, legitimate and illegitimate, good and bad forms of violence' (Fraser and Hutchings 2008, pp. 90–93). There is, then, a very long tradition of the moral categorising of violence.

More than demarcating good violence from bad, the concept of terrorism sustains the taken-for-granted assumption that violence works by avoiding a critique of violence *per se*. Arendt is one voice, however, who, by questioning the instrumentality of violence *per se*, has challenged the way in which political thought has traditionally tied violence to politics (Arendt 1969, Fraser and Hutchings 2008). Arendt takes a rare critical approach to violence that questions its place in political life and rejects its 'normality'. By distinguishing power from violence, Arendt problematises violence and argues that it does not work in anything beyond short-term effects (Arendt 1969, Young 2002). In *On Violence*, Hannah Arendt writes that being so central to history and politics, violence is taken for granted and neglected as an object of study:

> No one engaged in thought about history and politics can remain unaware of the enormous role violence has always played in human affairs, and it is at first glance rather surprising that

violence has been singled out so seldom for special consideration. (In the last edition of the Encyclopaedia of the Social Sciences 'violence' does not even rate an entry.) (1969, p. 8)

Violence, like terrorism, is very much a contested term. For Arendt, violence is mistakenly equated with power. This is due as much to a misunderstanding about the nature of power as it is a misunderstanding about the nature of violence. Power is not, according to Arendt, the relationship between command and obedience. The ability to coerce another into fulfilling your will is not a matter of power but rather strength. Strength can be held individually and increased through the use of violence. However, by Arendt's definition, the more violent a government, the less powerful it is. For Arendt, power

> ... corresponds to the human ability to act but to act in concert. Power is never the property of an individual; it belongs to a group and remains in existence only so long as the group keeps together. When we say of someone that he is 'in power' what we actually refer to is him being empowered by a certain number of people to act in their name. (1969, p. 44)

Arendt acknowledges that power may not always be benign. Power may at times serve the same function as violence. However, they should not be mistaken as being the same. Violence, Arendt writes, can only extinguish power, never create it:

> Violence can always destroy power. From the barrel of a gun grows the most effective command resulting in the most instant and perfect obedience. What can never grow out of it is power ... Violence appears where power is in jeopardy, but left to its own course it ends in power's disappearance. (1969, pp. 53–56)

Power then is not the ability to command obedience or to coerce but rather stems from *consent*. From power stems authority – the ability to command obedience without having to coerce; and for this, authority must be respected by those who choose to obey.

Violence in Arendt's analysis is characterised by its instrumentality – it relies on instruments: 'Violence is by nature instrumental; like all means it always stands in need of guidance and justification through the end it pursues. And what needs justification by something else cannot be the essence of anything' (Arendt 1969, p. 51). Arendt's analysis of violence (separating it conceptually from power, force and authority) makes two important points (Arendt 1969, Young 2002). First, violence is rarely if ever irrational, as violence in public life requires instruments; it is a calculated act rather than senseless. Second, and significantly for this article, violence as a form of action is entirely unpredictable.

Arendt sets out her theory of action more fully in *The Human Condition* (1958). Here, action is contrasted with labour and work. Action, according to Arendt, is relational. It is subject to interpretation both by the agent of action and by others who respond to it. Because it relies on the interpretation of others, its results cannot be known in advance. In the words of Slaughter, 'the performer cannot predict its consequences because he or she cannot predict how others will respond' (Young 2002).

For Arendt then, the problem with using violence instrumentally is that violence is always in danger of overwhelming the end for which it is used:

> Moreover, the danger of violence, even if it moves consciously within a nonextremist framework of short-term goals, will always be that the means overwhelm the end. If goals are not achieved rapidly, the result will be not merely defeat but the introduction of the practice of violence into the whole body politic. Action is irreversible, and a return to the *status quo* in case of defeat is always unlikely. The practice of violence, like all action, changes the world, but the most probable change is to a more violent world. (1969, p. 80)

According to Arendt's critique of violence, beyond very limited short-term effects, violence is unpredictable. In this assessment, the restrained, precise, progressive violence that the concept of terrorism suggests is possible, the violence that terrorism is defined in relation to, does not exist.

Those who wish for a more peaceful world would do well to explore the nature, function and logic of *violence* before demarcating some violence as exceptional. Prior to the question of 'what is terrorism?' must surely be the question 'what is violence?' Before terrorism can be categorised as a specific function of violence, we must first investigate the function of violence itself as a phenomenon. If Arendt is correct in her analysis, then understanding the nature and consequences of violence itself should prove a significant force for 'anti-terrorism' or the non-use of force for political ends.

For Fraser and Hutchings, whilst Arendt might raise questions about the utility of an instrumental approach to violence, she herself conceptualises violence as a tool, something that an individual can pick up or put down as necessary. This crucially misses the embedded nature of violence, the extent to which violence involves *being* as much as *doing*:

> ... [T]his account individualises responsibility for violence and ignores the ways in which individuals are invested in the repertoires of violence prior to any decisions being taken about the use of violence in this or that instance. The repertoires of violence are at work in the meaning of manhood, womanhood and citizenship, and they are at work in the economic, social and political institutions of all known societies. (Fraser and Hutchings 2008, p. 105)

What Arendt's analysis misses then is the *productive* nature of violence and the relationship between violence and self, violence and the production of the subject.

This article argues that asking questions of terrorism means asking questions of violence. But asking questions of terrorism also involves asking questions of ourselves. Why is it that certain acts of violence demand so much of our scholarly attention whilst others are neglected? Why do certain acts of violence offend our ethical sensibilities whilst others are considered routine? Asad writes:

> I want to ask: Why do people in the West react to verbal and visual representations of suicide bombing with professions of horror? Unimaginable cruelties perpetrated in secret or openly by dictatorships and democracies, criminals and prison systems, racially oriented immigration policies and ethnic cleansing, torture and imperial wars are all evident in the world today. What leads liberal moralists to react to suicide bombings with such horror? Why are there so many articles, books, TV documentaries, and films on the topic? Why are people – myself included – so fascinated and disturbed by it? (2007, p. 65)

The scholarly attention paid to terrorism and its treatment as a coherent object of analysis also suggests that cultures of violence (both academic and societal) need to be investigated. In asking questions about terrorism, must we also ask question about our attitudes to killing, dying and death?

Conclusion

The question for terrorism studies, both 'critical' and 'traditional', is then: What does the concept of terrorism, as a distinct category of violence, mean for that violence that falls outside of its definition? Does it suggest that violence that fails to meet the criteria of terrorism can and does distinguish between civilians and combatants? (Does it suggest that the identity of civilians is not problematic or that those who define terrorism also have the right and the ability to name the innocent?) Does violence not categorised as terrorism kill only those who are legitimately killable? (Does the concept of terrorism presuppose that some human beings *are legitimately killable*?) Can violence that falls beyond that which is labelled as terrorism be used in a way that *does not* produce terror and fear? (Does a definition of terrorism rest on the assumption that terror and fear are externally produced and controllable?) Can political violence be used in a way that *is not* coercive? (Can we ever predict and control the effects of violence?)

These are not questions of terrorism. These are questions about the function and logic of violence *per se*. Before compartmentalising violence into fixed and morally guarded categories, should we not first theorise violence itself? This may prove to be an impossible task. Yet the acknowledgement of this impossibility itself critically destabilises the ground that traditional moral legal and strategic frameworks stand on. Arendt's claims about the unpredictability of violence undermine the definitional distinction between terrorism and violence *per se*. To understand the dogged persistence of this category, however, we need to explore the 'repertoires of violence' that sustain and reproduce it. In acknowledging the shortcomings of Arendt's understanding of violence, Fraser and Hutchings offer this thought to those who wish to challenge the strategic rationality of violence:

> If one is to unravel the idea that violence works, then one must unravel the extraordinary and complex ideational and material infrastructure needed to sustain a world in which the fact that violence works is self-evident. (2008, p. 105)

This article suggests that the category of terrorism is part of the ideational infrastructure to which Fraser and Hutchings refer.

Acknowledgements

I am grateful to Maja Zehfuss and Ronan O'Callaghan for their comments on an earlier draft of this article. I am also grateful to the two anonymous reviewers for their close reading of the article and constructive feedback. All remaining mistakes are my own.

Note

1. Walzer here refers to English philosopher Henry Sidgwick who argued against excessive harm in warfare; see Walzer (2000, pp. 129–133).

Notes on contributor

Helen Dexter is a teaching fellow in International Relations at the University of Leicester. Her current research takes an interdisciplinary approach towards a critical understanding of political violence. Two strands of research make up this general research theme. One strand of her research agenda addresses the nature and logic of violence by analysing dominant categories of war and conflict. The second strand explores the structuring discourses that produce violence. In particular, this strand of research investigates the relationship between moral and legal discourses and contemporary warfare.

References

Abrahms, M., 2006. Why terrorism does not work. *International Security*, 31 (2), 42–78.
Amnesty International USA, 2011. *The death penalty and deterrence* [online]. Available from: http://www.amnestyusa.org/our-work/issues/death-penalty/us-death-penalty-facts/the-death-penalty-and-deterrence [Accessed 30 September 2011].
Arendt, H., 1958. *The human condition*. Chicago: Chicago University Press.
Arendt, H., 1969. *On violence*. New York: Harcourt Brace and Company.

Asad, T., 2007. *On suicide bombing*. New York: Columbia University Press.
Aubrey, S.M., 2004. *The new dimension of international terrorism*. Zurich: VDF.
Borger, J., 2001. Rumsfeld blames regime for civilian deaths. *The Guardian* [online], 16 October. Available from: http://www.guardian.co.uk/world/2001/oct/16/afghanistan.terrorism8 [Accessed 7 December 2011].
Brown, M., 2005. 'Setting the conditions' for Abu Ghraib: the prison nation abroad. *American Quarterly*, 57 (3), 973–997.
Burke, A., 2004. Just war or ethical peace: moral discourses of strategic violence. *International Affairs*, 80 (2), 329–353.
Burke, A., 2008. The end of terrorism studies. *Critical Studies on Terrorism*, 1 (1), 39.
Burnett, J. and Whyte, D., 2005. Embedded expertise and the media. *Journal for Crime, Conflict and the Media*, 1 (4), 10–18.
Bush, G.W., 2001. Address to the joint session of congress and the nation, 20 September 2001. Available from: http://articles.cnn.com/2001-09-20/us/gen.bush.transcript_1_joint-session-national-anthem-citizens?_s=PM:US [Accessed 6 February 2012].
Coady, C.A., 2004. Terrorism, morality and supreme emergency. *Ethics*, 114 (4), 772–789.
Dauphinée, E., 2007. *The ethics of researching war*. Manchester: Manchester University Press.
Dauphinée, E., 2008. War crimes and the ruin of the law. *Millennium: A Journal of International Studies*, 37 (1), 49–67.
Dexter, H., 2007. New war, good war and the war on terror: explaining, excusing and creating Western neo-interventionism. *Development and Change*, 38 (6), 1055–1071.
Dexter, H., 2011. Terrorism. *In*: K.E. Haug and O.J. Maaø, eds. *Conceptualising modern war*. London: Hurst and Company.
Fraser, E. and Hutchings, K., 2008. On politics and violence: Arendt contra Fanon. *Contemporary Political Theory*, 7, 90–108.
Gearty, C., 1997. *The future of terrorism: predictions*. London: Phoenix.
Gordon, R.W., 1983. Critical legal histories. *Stanford Law Review*, 36 (1/2), 57–125.
Gunning, J., 2007a. A case for critical terrorism studies? *Government and Opposition*, 42 (3), 384.
Gunning, J., 2007b. Babies and bathwaters: reflecting on the pitfalls of critical terrorism studies. *European Political Science*, 6 (3), 236–243.
Holland, S., 2007. US blames Taliban for Afghan casualties. *Reuters* US edition [online]. Available from: http://www.reuters.com/article/2007/05/20/us-nato-bush-idUSN2026925620070520 [Accessed 7 December 2011].
Jackson, R., 2005. *Writing the war on terrorism: language, politics and counterterrorism*. Manchester: Manchester University Press.
Kinsella, H., 2005. Discourses of difference: civilians, combatants and compliance with the laws of war. *Review of International Studies*, 31, 163–185.
Laqueur, W., 1987. *The age of terrorism*. Boston, MA: Little, Brown.
Laqueur, W., 1999. *The new terrorism: fanaticism and the arms of mass destruction*. Oxford: Oxford University Press.
Lawler, P., 2002. The good war after September 11. *Government and Opposition*, 37 (2), 151–172.
Lawrence, B. and Howarth, J., eds., 2005. *Messages to the world: the statements of Osama Bin Laden*. London: Verso.
Lesser, I.O., et al., 1999. *Countering the new terrorism*. Santa Monica, CA: Rand.
Montopoli, B., 2010. Obama: I am accountable for Afghan civilian causalities. *Political Hotsheet, CBS News* [online]. Available from: http://www.cbsnews.com/8301-503544_162-20004790-503544.html [Accessed 7 December 2011].
Owens, P., 2003. Accidents don't just happen: the liberal politics of high-technology 'humanitarian' war. *Millennium: Journal of International Studies*, 32, 595–616.
Sarat, A. and Kearns, T.R., 1995. Making peace with violence: Robert Cover on law and legal theory. *In*: A. Sarat and T.R. Kearns, eds. *Law's violence*. East Lansing, MI: Michigan University Press.
Schmid, A., 1984. *Political terrorism: a research guide to concepts, theories, databases and literature*. Amsterdam: Elsevier Science Ltd.
Shaw, M., 2001. *The return of the good war* [online]. Available from: http://www.theglobalsite.ac.uk/press/104shaw.htm [Accessed 30 September 2011].
Smith, M.L.R., 2003. Guerrillas in the mist: reassessing strategy and low intensity warfare. *Review of International Studies*, 29, 22.

Stohl, M., 2008. Old myths, new fantasies and the enduring reality of terrorism. *Critical Studies in Terrorism*, 1 (1), 5–16.

Stohl, M., 2011. Don't confuse me with the facts: knowledge claims and terrorism. Paper presented at the conference *A decade of terrorism and counter terrorism*, 10 September 2011. Glasgow: University of Strathclyde.

United Nations, 2004. A more secure world: our shared responsibility. *Report of the high-level panel on threats, challenges and change.* New York: United Nations.

Walzer, M., 2000. *Just and unjust war: a moral argument with historical illustrations*. New York: Basic Books.

Whitaker, B., 2001. The definition of terrorism. *The Guardian*, Monday, 7 May. Available from: http://www.guardian.co.uk/world/2001/may/07/terrorism [Accessed 6 February 2012].

White, J.R., 2006. *Terrorism and homeland security*. Belmont, CA: Cengage Learning.

Wilkinson, P., 2006. *Terrorism versus liberal democracy: the liberal state response*. New York: Routledge.

Young, I.M., 2002. Power, violence, and legitimacy: a reading of Hannah Arendt in an age of police brutality and humanitarian intervention. *In*: M. Minow, ed. *Breaking the cycles of violence: memory, law and repair*. Princeton, NJ: Princeton University Press.

Zehfuss, M., forthcoming. Killing civilians: thinking the practice of war. *British Journal of Politics and International Relations*.

Index

Abdul Rahman, Omar 52, 65–6
Abdulkahar, Mohammed 82
Abrahms, M. 130
Abu Ghraib 64, 132
Adams, John Quincy 65
Afghanistan 38, 39, 43, 55; CIA provision of Stinger missiles to rebels 56
Africa 42
Agamben, G. 52, 60, 108
Ahmad, M. 53, 54
Alexander, C. 92, 103
Alston, Philip 54
Amoore, L. 79, 80, 109, 110
Anderson, B. 71
anthropology 11, 15, 17–18, 21, 52, 57–8; dual sovereignty 60, 62
Anwar, Aamer 2
Araj, B. 14
Arendt, H. 132–4, 135
art 16, 22
Asad, T. 134
assassinations 35, 57
Atif Siddique, Mohammed 2
Aubrey, S.M. 129
Australia 35
Azar, Edward 15
Aznar, José María 115

Balzacq, T. 108, 113
Bamford, B. 108
banking counter staff 79
Banksy 16
Bari, M.A. 100, 103
Basaran, T. 109
Baumann, B. 16
Bendle, M. 23
Bentham, J. 108
Bergen, P. 14, 43
Berlinski, David 64
Berman, P. 90
Bettison, N. 78
Bigo, D. 110

Bin Laden, Osama 14, 42, 45–6, 52, 55–6, 66, 131
biological terrorism 62
Blair, Tony 74, 90
Blakeley, R. 19
Blok, A. 91
Blondel, J. 115, 116
Blunket, D. 92
Bongar, B. 37
Booth, K. 108
Borger, J. 127
Boulding, Kenneth 15
Bourdieu, P. 23–4, 114, 115
Brecher, R. 22
Briggs, R. 77
Brown, M. 132
Burke, A. 122, 123, 124–5, 127, 129, 130
Burman, J. 97
Burnett, J. 17, 124
Burton, J. 11, 15
Bush, George W. 41–2, 47, 58, 61, 64, 115, 127, 130–1
Butler, J. 65, 70, 79, 110
Buzan, B. 108, 109, 111, 112, 113, 116

Callaghan, James 115, 116
Callinicos, A. 13
Cameron, D. 102
Canada 35, 97
Cantle, T. 92
capital punishment 130
Capote, Truman 58, 64
Carr, R. 43
Carter, Jimmy 62
Caryl, C. 53, 54, 56
Chang, N. 108
Cheney, Dick 61, 62, 64
Chentouf, Houria 74
Chowanietz, C. 111
Chrishanthakumar, Aranachalam 74
civilians and combatants 124–9
Clarke, J. 91
Clutterbuck, L. 91

INDEX

Coady, C.A. 124
Coaffee, J. 71
Cody, E. 20
Cold War 63, 124
Cole, D. 20
'collective intellectual' project, CTS as 23–5
combatants and civilians 124–9
communicatively constituted violence, terrorism as 34–6, 42, 123, 129–31; claims of responsibility 40–1; lethality 36–9
community *see* suspect communities
conflict resolution 15, 21
correspondence inference theory 130
counter-insurgency 124
counterterrorism 47; prevention in UK counterterrorism policy *see separate entry*; as self-fulfilling prophecy *see* self-fulfilling prophecy; subjugated knowledge 14, 15, 17, 19, 20, 21, 22, 23, 24
Crelinsten, R. 14
Crenshaw, Martha 14–15, 33–4, 36
Crick, B. 111
criminology 15, 21, 33, 70, 92–3
Cuban missile crisis 63
cultural racism 91
Curle, Adam 15

Dalacoura, K. 11
Dauphinée, E. 123, 126, 127, 128–9, 131–2
De Avila, Gesio 81
De Goede, M. 71, 79, 80
De Menezes, Jean Charles 70, 80–1, 82, 85
Dean, M. 72
definitions of terrorism 34–5; violence and *see* violence and terrorism
Delanty, G. 92
Della Porta, D. 11
deportation/ exclusion orders 72–3, 83
Dershowitz, A. 18
Dexter, H. 22, 125, 126, 127
disappearances, enforced 130
divination 58
Dixit, P. 23
Dodds, K. 16
Doty, R. 71, 108
drone attacks 53–5, 56, 60, 62, 65, 66, 67, 126
Dugan, Laura 40

economic sanctions 130
Eisenhower, Dwight D. 63
Eland, I. 14
empirical testing 31–4; new terrorism thesis *see separate entry*
enforced disappearances 130
English, R. 11, 14
ethnography 18, 58, 64
Evans-Pritchard, E. 58, 60

exclusion orders 72–3, 83
extrajudicial killing 51, 54; *see also* drone attacks
extraordinary rendition 107

falsifiability, principle of *see* new terrorism thesis
Fanon, F. 132
fantasy in US counterterrorism, force of 51–3, 65–7; drone attacks 53–5, 56, 60, 62, 65, 66, 67; from the one percent thinking to poker thinking 62–4; ignoring that we know: impasses in knowledge 54–6; perversion of temporality 56–60; secret knowledge and state of exception 60–2
Farrall, L. 45
fast-track legislation 107–8
Feldman, A. 11
feminism 15, 21, 109
Fierke, K.M. 108
films 16, 22
financial middle managers 79
Fitzpatrick, J. 108
Flemming, P. 37–8
forensic psychology 33
Fortin, A. 22
Foucault, M. 12, 13, 15, 19, 20, 22, 23, 117
Franks, J. 12
Fraser, E. 132, 134, 135
Free, Gary 40
Friedman, T. 43

Galtung, Johan 15
Gates, Bill 64
Gearty, C. 123
Gerges, F. 42
Gilmore Commission (1999) 13
Gilroy, P. 91
Githens-Mazer, J. 71, 75
Giuliani, Rudolph 20
Goddin, R. 22
Goldberg, D. 108
Gordon, A. 12
Gordon, R.W. 131
Gore, Al 115
governmentality, extending processes of 19
Grabosky, P. 35, 40
Greer, S. 90, 93
grievances driving terrorism 14, 15, 16, 21, 90–1, 130–1
Gross, O. 108
Guantanamo Bay 51, 60, 64, 65, 127
guerilla warfare 124
Gunning, J. 22, 122, 124
Gurr, T. 14–15, 32

Hall, S. 71, 103

INDEX

Hansen, L. 76, 109
Hardt, M. 91
Hastings, T. 11
Hay, C. 109
Heath-Kelly, C. 23, 71, 75
Hellmich, H. 14, 19, 20
Henningsen, G. 66
Herring, E. 23
Hewitt, S. 73, 75, 83, 84, 108
Hickman, M.J. 72, 76, 82, 91, 99, 100
Hillyard, P. 21, 76, 91, 92, 93, 95
Hiro, D. 13
historical studies: Irish nationalism 16
Hobbes, T. 108, 114–15, 132
Hoffman, B. 36, 38
Holland, S. 127
Hollander, N.C. 102
Horgan, J. 52
Howe, Geoffrey 81
Hudson, V.M. 110
Hulsse, R. 23
human rights 21, 101, 109
humanitarian law 131–2
Hume, D. 108
Hurd, Douglas 74
Hussein, N. 108
Hussein, Saddam 52, 61, 62
Huysmans, J. 108, 109, 113

Ignatieff, M. 65
Ilardi, G. 18
immigration officials 79, 80, 97
international law 54, 60, 127; humanitarian law 131–2
international relations (IR) 31–2, 110, 111, 113
internment 72, 73, 83, 84
Iraq 38, 39, 52, 55, 56, 57, 58, 59, 61
Irish Republican Army (IRA) 70, 72, 74, 75, 76, 81, 83, 90–1
Irish suspect communities 70, 75–7, 78, 84; petty sovereigns and false positives 70, 78–9, 81–3, 84; social cohesion and suspect communities *see separate entry*
Israel 19, 23, 42; direct dialogue 14

Jabri, V. 22
Jackson, R. 12, 18, 19, 21, 23, 103, 126
Jarvis, L. 12, 19, 22, 23
Jenkins, B.M. 13, 37, 38
Johns, F. 108
Johnson, C. 60
Johnston, D. 42, 43
Johnston, H. 11
Jones, D.M. 3, 18, 23
Jorgensen, M. 16, 19
Joseph, J. 23

just war 59, 62, 123, 128–9, 131

Kahler, M. 44, 45
Kennedy, J.F. 57, 63
Kennison, P. 80, 81
Kerry, John 65
Khadra, J. 16
Khaled, L. 16
Kilcullen, D. 55–6, 57–8, 60, 65
Kinsella, H. 127
Kitson, F. 75
knowledge: 'mind the gap' *see* prevention in UK counterterrorism policy
knowledge claims: testing through principle of falsifiability *see* new terrorism thesis
knowledge subjugation in terrorism studies 11–13; codes of legitimation for speakers 17, 18; conclusion: from Foucault to Bourdieu 22–5; CTS and de-subjugation of knowledge 21–2; endogenous knowledge 13–15; epistemic community 17; exogenous knowledge 15–16; Foucault and 13–16; processes and mechanisms 16–19; ritual of moral condemnation 18–19; unknown knowns and hegemonic discourse 19–21
knowledge in terrorism studies, crisis of *see* fantasy in US counterterrorism, force of
Kundnani, A. 71, 75, 84

Lambert, R. 1–2, 3–4, 20, 71, 77
Laplanche, J. 66
Laqueur, W. 13, 36, 124, 129
Lawler, P. 126
Lawrence, B. 16, 131
Layton, L. 102
Leach, E. 61
Lebanon 38
Lederach, John Paul 15
Lederer, Katy 64
Leitenberg, Milton 62
Lenoir, R. 24
Lesser, I.O. 129
Lewis, P. 98
Lianos, M. 102
Lindlaw, S. 53
Lobo-Guerrero, L. 109
Locke, J. 108, 132
low-intensity conflict 124
Lum, C. 33, 34
Lutz, J. 23

McAllister, B. 44
McCants, W. 42
McClintock, M. 13
MacFarquhar, N. 66
McGhee, D. 91
McGovern, M. 91

INDEX

Machiavelli, N. 114–15, 132
McManus, J. 63, 64
Macmillan, Harold 115
Maguire, A. 92
Maguire, P. 92
Maguire Seven 82–3, 92
Mahmood, C. 21, 22
Malik, K. 90
Marciano, F. 16
Marx, K. 132
Massumi, B. 81–2
media 35–6, 44, 59, 65; broadcasting ban 72, 73; suspect communities 76, 91, 93, 102, 103
memoirs 16
Menezes, Jean Charles de 70, 80–1, 82, 85
Merari, A. 32–3
Merton, R. 56, 58
Meyer, J. 43, 44
Michael, L. 103
Mickolus, E.F. 38
Mill, J.S. 108
Miller, D. 2, 3–4, 12, 17
Miller, J. 43
Milliken, J. 16, 17, 19, 22
Mills, T. 4
Mitchell, Chris 15
Moloney, E. 74
Montaigne 66
Montesquieu 108
Montopoli, B. 127
moral condemnation, ritual of 18–19
Morris, Nancy 40
Mueller, J. 13, 38, 62, 109
Mujaheddin-e Khalq (MEK) 20
Mukasey, Michael 20
multiculturalism 91–2
mus (Basque card game) 63
Muslim suspect communities 70, 76–8, 84; petty sovereigns and false positives 70, 78–83, 84; social cohesion and suspect communities *see separate entry*
Mythen, G. 99

Neal, A.W. 108, 110, 111, 112, 114
Needham, R. 75–6
Neill, W. 76, 77
Neocleous, M. 108
networks 74; nature of the network of terror 41–6
Neuman, J. von 63
Neumann, P. 14
new terrorism thesis 31–2, 47; American public's sense of security 46–7; definition of terrorism 34–5; increasing lethality claim 36–9, 129; network of terror 41–6; problem 32–4; responsibility, claims of 40–1; subjugated knowledge 14, 16, 19; terrorism as communicatively constituted violence 34–6, 42; *see also* violence and terrorism
New York Times 61, 65, 66
Nicholson, M. 31–2
Nickels, H. 93, 103
Nietzsche, F. 71
non-combatants and combatants 124–9
Northern Ireland 19, 72, 90–1, 104; broadcasting ban 72, 73; direct dialogue 14; exclusion orders 72–3, 83; governing 'suspect' sea 'they' swim in 75–7, 78; internment 72, 73, 83, 84; petty sovereigns and false positives 70, 78–9, 81–3, 84; proscribing organisations 72, 73; Provisional Irish Republican Army (PIRA) 70, 72, 74, 75, 76, 81, 83, 90–1; PTAs 71–4, 84; Ulster Defence Association (UDA) 72, 73; urban regeneration 76–7; *see also* Irish suspect communities
Norton, P. 111
novels 16, 22
Nozick, R. 132

Obama, Barack 42, 47, 65, 127
old and new terrorism *see* new terrorism thesis
Omand, D. 71, 72, 78–9, 81
organisations and terrorism 41–6
Oslender, U. 24
Oslo terrorist attacks (July 2011) 20–1
Owens, P. 132

Pakistan: drone attacks 53–5, 56, 60, 62, 65, 66, 67, 126
Palonen, K. 107
Pantazis, C. 76, 77, 92, 93
Pape, R. 14, 20
Pappe, I. 11
participant action research 18
'pattern of life' analysis 54
peace and conflict studies: subjugated knowledge 11, 12–13, 15, 16–18, 21, 22, 23
Phillips, M. 23
pilotless drone attacks 53–5, 56, 60, 62, 65, 66, 67
policing: stop and search 3, 76, 77, 81, 83, 97; suspect communities 97–8
political science 111, 113
politics, security 107–9, 117; exclusion of 109–11; security from perspective of politics 114–16; separation of security from politics and example of securitisation theory 112–14
Porter, G. 45
Powell, Colin 61

INDEX

prevention in UK counterterrorism policy 69–70, 84–5, 104; contemporary salience of gap 83–4; CONTEST 71, 72, 75, 76, 77, 78–80, 83–4; deportation/exclusion orders 72–3, 83; dual constitution of communities 76–8, 83; encouragement of terrorism 74–5; genealogical research 71; 'glorification' of terrorism 74; Kratos 80–1; networks 74; petty sovereigns and false positives 70, 78–83, 84; PTA as criminal justice model 71–5, 92; radicalisation discourse 75, 79, 83–4; suspect communities 70, 75–8, 83, 84; vulnerability 75, 78, 84

Provisional Irish Republican Army (PIRA) 70, 72, 74, 75, 76, 81, 83, 90–1

Prozorov, S. 108

Pugliese, J. 80, 81

Purvis, T. 16

Al-Qaeda 42–6, 55–6, 74, 91, 130–1; drone attacks 55; subjugated knowledge 14, 20; suspect communities 98

racism, cultural 91

Ramsbotham, O. 11, 12, 15

RAND Corporation 17

Ranstorp, M. 12

Raphael, S. 12, 22

Rawls, J. 132

Reid, E. 12, 17, 18

religion 14, 19, 20, 22, 34, 36, 90; communities 92; internment 83; *see also* Muslim suspect communities

rendition, extraordinary 107

Rice, Condoleeza 13

Richards, A. 75

Richmond, O. 11, 12, 17

Richter-Montpetit, M. 109

Ricks, T. 61

Ridge, Tom 20

rogue states 13

Saad, L. 46

Sabir, Rizwaan 3

Salter, M.B. 109, 113

sanctions 130

Sarat, A. 131

Sartre, J.-P. 132

Saudi Arabia 42

Saul, B. 74

Schelling, T. 35, 36

Scheuerman, W.E. 108

Schlesinger, P. 91

Schmid, A. 11, 18, 23, 32, 33–4, 123

Schmitt, C. 108, 114–15

Schneider, Bill 64

security politics 107–9, 117; exclusion of 109–11; security from perspective of politics 114–16; separation of security from politics and example of securitisation theory 112–14

security threat of terrorism 13–14, 20, 21

Sederberg, P. 11

Sedgwick, M. 42

self-fulfilling prophecy, counterterrorism as 19, 51–3, 65–7; anticipatory regimes 71; divination 58; drone attacks 53–5, 56, 60, 62, 65, 66, 67; dual sovereignty 60, 62; from the one percent thinking to poker thinking 62–4; ignoring that we know: impasses in knowledge 54–6; perversion of temporality 56–60; secret knowledge and state of exception 60–2; taboo 52, 53, 54, 57, 58, 62; witchcraft 57, 58–9, 62, 64, 66–7

Shahzad, Faisal 55

Shane, S. 58

Sharma, S. 91

Shaw, M. 126

Silberstein, S. 19

Silke, A. 12, 19, 33

Silvestri, S. 99

Sinn Fein 72, 73

Sluka, J. 53, 55, 65

Smith, A. 108

Smith, M.L.R. 3, 121–2, 124

Soans, R. 16

social cohesion and suspect communities 89–90, 101–4; community cohesion and notion of 'suspect communities' 91–3; everyday encounters and experiences 94–7; impacts of constructing communities as 'suspect' 98–9; policing as part of everyday experiences 97–8; research methods 93–4; similarities and differences between the two eras 99–101; two eras of political violence: basis for comparison 90–1

social media 36

sociology 11, 15, 17, 70; critical 24

Sorel, G. 132

South Africa 19; direct dialogue 14

sovereignty 108; dual 60, 62; Pakistan 54

Spalek, B. 99, 103

Spencer, A. 23

Stampnitzky, L. 12, 13, 15, 18, 19

state terrorism 13, 19, 20, 32, 35, 129–30

Stohl, M. 14–15, 34, 42, 123, 129, 130, 131

Stone, D. 17

stop and search 3, 76, 77, 81, 83, 97

Stritzel, H. 113

Stump, J. 23

subjugated knowledge 11–13; codes of legitimation for speakers 17, 18; conclusion: from Foucault to Bourdieu 22–5; CTS and de-subjugation of knowledge 21–2; endogenous knowledge 13–15;

epistemic community 17; exogenous knowledge 15–16; Foucault, terrorism studies and 13–16; processes and mechanisms 16–19; ritual of moral condemnation 18–19; unknown knowns and hegemonic discourse 19–21
suicide terrorism 20, 80
Suskind, R. 62
suspect communities 70, 75–8, 83; petty sovereigns and false positives 70, 78–83, 84; social cohesion and *see separate entry*
Swartz, D. 24

taboo 18–19, 52, 53, 54, 57, 58, 62
Tagma, H. 79
Tawil, C. 45
Taylor, J.R. 44, 45
Taylor, P. 16
Thatcher, Margaret 72, 74
Thomas, P. 78
Thornton, T. 13
Tierney, S. 108
Tilly, C. 11
Toros, H. 22, 23
torture 51, 64, 65, 112–13
Townsend, Frances 20
Trevor-Roper, H.R. 62
Tucker, D. 34

Uganda 35
Ulster Defence Association (UDA) 72, 73
United Kingdom 35; Northern Ireland *see separate entry*; prevention in UK counterterrorism policy *see separate entry*; security politics 107–8, 110, 111, 112–13; social cohesion and suspect communities *see separate entry*
United Nations 125
United States 23, 41–2, 51–2, 58, 102, 124; 9/11 Commission Report 52, 108; Abu Ghraib 64, 132; civilians and combatants 126–7; criminal code 35; grievances driving anti-American terrorism 14, 20; Guantanamo Bay 51, 60, 64, 65, 127; nature of the network of terror 41–6; public's sense of security 46–7; self-fulfilling prophecy, counterterrorism as *see separate entry*; subjugated knowledge 13–14, 17, 20;

suicide terrorism 20; US VISIT programme 79; Vietnam War 126–7

Vasquez, J.A. 110
Vaughan-Williams, N. 71, 80, 81, 109
Vico, Giambattista 65
Vietnam War 126–7
violence and terrorism 121–3, 134–5; categories of human beings and 124–7; communication and 129–31; defining terrorism 123–4; intentionality and 127–9; violence 132–4; violence and exceptionalism 131–2
von Neuman, J. 63

Wæver, O. 108, 112
Waltz, K.N. 110
Walzer, M. 128
war 19, 125–7; doctrine of double effect 128, 129; just 59, 62, 123, 128–9, 131
war crime 131–2
weapons of mass destruction (WMD) 13–14, 52, 59, 60, 61, 62
Weber, M. 107, 110, 132
Weiner, T. 62
Wetherell, M. 92
Wheeler, E. 63
Whitaker, B. 123
White, H. 66
White, J.R. 125
Wilkinson, P. 90, 124
Williams, M.C. 112
Winch, P. 58–9
witchcraft 57, 58–9, 62, 64, 66–7
Wolfers, A. 109
Wright, L. 42

Yallop, D. 16
Yemen 42
Young, I.M. 132, 133

al-Zarqawi, Abu Musab 45
Zartman, I.W. 11
al-Zawahiri, Ayman 66
Zehfuss, M. 125
Zulaika, J. 6, 11, 12, 15, 18, 19, 20, 52, 54, 57, 58

www.routledge.com/ 9780415500548

Related titles from Routledge

Mothers, Infants and Young Children of September 11, 2001

A Primary Prevention Project

Edited by Beatrice Beebe, Phyllis Cohen, K. Mark Sossin and Sara Markese

The group of papers presented in this volume represents ten years of involvement of a group of eight core therapists, working originally with approximately forty families who suffered the loss of husbands and fathers on September 11, 2001. The project focuses on the families of women who were pregnant and widowed in the disaster, or of women who were widowed with an infant born in the previous year.

In 2011, marking the 10th anniversary of the World Trade Center tragedy, the Project continues to provide services without cost for these mothers who lost their husbands, for their infants who are now approximately ten years old, and for the siblings of these children.

This book was originally published as a special issue of the *Journal of Infant, Child and Adolescent Psychotherapy.*

February 2012: 246 x 174: 272pp
Hb: 978-0-415-50054-8
Pb: 978-0-415-50779-0
Hb: £80 / $125 Pb: £24.99 / $39.95

For more information and to order a copy visit
www.routledge.com/9780415500548

Available from all good bookshops

www.routledge.com/9780415639613

Related titles from Routledge

Intersections of Crime and Terror

Edited by James J. F. Forest

During the last ten years an increasing number of government and media reports, scholarly books and journal articles, and other publications have focused our attention on the expanded range of interactions between international organized crime and terrorist networks. A majority of these interactions have been in the form of temporary organizational alliances (or customer-supplier relationships) surrounding a specific type of transaction or resource exchange, like document fraud or smuggling humans, drugs or weapons across a particular border. The environment in which terrorists and criminals operate is also a central theme of this literature.

These research trends suggest the salience of this book which addresses how organized criminal and terrorist networks collaborate, share knowledge and learn from each other in ways that expand their operational capabilities. The book contains broad conceptual pieces, historical analyses, and case studies that highlight different facets of the intersection between crime and terrorism. These chapters collectively help us to identify and appreciate a variety of dynamics at the individual, organizational, and contextual levels. These dynamics, in turn, inform a deeper understanding of the security threat posed by terrorists and criminal networks and how to respond more effectively.

This book was published as a special issue of *Terrorism and Political Violence*.

December 2012: 246 x 174: 208pp
Hb: 978-0-415-63961-3
£85 / $145

For more information and to order a copy visit
www.routledge.com/ISBN 9780415639613

Available from all good bookshops

www.routledge.com/9780789019189

Related titles from Routledge

Trauma Practice in the Wake of September 11, 2001

Edited by Steven N. Gold and Jan Faust

This essential book responds to the traumatic impact of the terrorist attacks on America and their implications for trauma practice.

Trauma Practice in the Wake of September 11, 2001 is your key to state-of-the-art information on the psychology of terrorism, the traumatic impact of terrorism on those directly affected and on the general population, and ways to help children, adolescents, and adults cope with the aftermath of the attacks. It also shows how to deal with "compassion fatigue," the potentially debilitating impact that working with traumatized individuals can have on practitioners when responding on-site to a catastrophic incident such as the attack on the World Trade Center.

October 2002: 184pp
Hardback: 978-0-7890-1918-9 | **£25** | **$40**
Paperback: 978-0-7890-1919-6 | **£18.50** | **$29.95**

For more information and to order a copy visit
www.routledge.com/9780789019189

Available from all good bookshops